MAGI

AN AMAZON TOP 10 B ... **FOR MEMOIR**

"*Magic Is Dead* is itself a magic trick: unexpected, mesmerizing, smoothly executed, and—above all—fun. With verve and wit, Ian Frisch infiltrates a mysterious world with a vibrant cast of characters (I'm looking at you, Laura London), and explores the powerful nature of secrets—and why it's sometimes best to keep them."

—Karen Abbott, *New York Times* bestselling
author of *Liar, Temptress, Soldier, Spy*

"A fascinating read—and I'm from this world. It had me hooked."

—Dynamo

"A fascinating book."   —Kai Ryssdal, host of *Marketplace*

"Funny, illuminating, and personal. Not really about card tricks or stage illusions, it's about adjusting the lens through which you view magic and, consequently, the world."   —*The Brooklyn Rail*

"A seriously engaging, often intimate look at a world few of us have access to, and an insightful study of the history of an art form."

—CrimeReads

"A meeting with Shaquille O'Neal where they discuss the loss of their fathers . . . may be the most magical thing he writes."

—*Post-Gazette* (Pittsburgh)

"Frisch's enthusiastic deep dive into the world of magic is infectious enough that it just might send readers to the stores for their own magic sets."   —*Publishers Weekly*

MAGIC IS DEAD

MAGIC
IS DEAD

MY JOURNEY INTO THE WORLD'S MOST
SECRETIVE SOCIETY OF MAGICIANS

IAN FRISCH

DEY ST.
An Imprint of WILLIAM MORROW

DEY ST.

The chapter "By Any Means Necessary" includes material originally published in *Deviations: Madisonist Edition* by Daniel Madison. Reprinted with permission.

HarperCollins books may be purchased for educational, business, or sales promotional use. For information, please email the Special Markets Department at SPsales@harpercollins.com.

A hardcover edition of this book was published in 2019 by Dey Street, an imprint of William Morrow.

FIRST DEY STREET PAPERBACK EDITION PUBLISHED 2019.

Designed by Michelle Crowe
Chapter opener art by Daniel Madison, Neema Atri, and S. W. Erdnase

---

The Library of Congress has catalogued a previous edition as follows:
Names: Frisch, Ian, 1989–author.
Title: Magic is dead : my journey into the world's most secretive society of magicians / Ian Frisch.
Description: First edition. | New York, NY : Dey Street, [2018]
Identifiers: LCCN 2018048007| ISBN 9780062839282 (hardcover) | ISBN 9780062839305 (ebk.) | ISBN 9780062896643 (audio) | ISBN 9780062896650 (audio)
Subjects: LCSH: Magic tricks. | Magicians. | 52 (Society) | Magicians--Societies, etc. | Secret societies. | Frisch, Ian, 1989-
Classification: LCC GV1547 .F75 2018 | DDC 793.8—dc23 LC record available at https://lccn.loc.gov/2018048007

ISBN 978-0-06-283929-9 (pbk.)

19 20 21 22 23   RS/LSC   10 9 8 7 6 5 4 3 2 1

For Mom. May you always catch on the river.

♠ ♥ ♦ ♣

Deceiving others . . . That is what the world calls a great romance.

—OSCAR WILDE

CONTENTS

PART II:
EVERY ONCE IN A WHILE, THE LION
HAS TO SHOW THE JACKAL WHO HE IS

AUTHOR'S NOTE

This is a work of nonfiction. I have, however, allowed myself certain storytelling liberties, including, for the sake of structure and clarity, compositing certain conversations and adjusting the chronology of a few events. Although I found these measures necessary to create a clear and complete body of work, I have not embellished the content of my experiences, or the experiences of other characters.

Prologue

THIS IS ME NOW

Time was running out. Everything was falling apart.

An army of slot machines dinged and whirled like a lazy, out-of-sync marching band. Corset-clad waitresses, faces layered in makeup, waited at the bar to pick up a fresh round of drinks. Off in the distance, tourists hitched up their belts, tossed fistfuls of chips onto horseshoe-shaped blackjack tables, and puffed on cheap brown cigars. I was almost jealous of them: the thrill of the big bet, the whizz and click of the roulette wheel, the *ffffph* of the card next dealt. But I wasn't here to gamble.

I slumped low in my chair, nearly defeated, stewing in the stale air of the casino bar, crumpled cigarette butts piled in the ashtray in front of me. Orphaned playing cards—aces and threes and jacks, hearts and clubs and diamonds, dropped and discarded after a long week—littered the carpet at my feet, taunting me. It was our last day in Las Vegas and my big reveal was crumbling. I needed to improvise, to do something—*anything*—to pull off my scheme. I had been setting it up for weeks. I couldn't let myself fail.

I was surrounded by magicians. They stood all around me—

some of whom, over the past year, had become my best friends. There was Jeremy Griffith, the card junkie from Los Angeles; Xavior Spade, the no-bullshit sleight-of-hand master from New York City; and Chris Ramsay, the bearded and tatted-up YouTube pioneer—the guy who had gotten me into this mess in the first place. It had been a year since I first fell into the underground world of magic and became friends with its key players. Everything had been building up to this point. I couldn't let it all come tumbling down.

It was now or never.

We were in Las Vegas for Magic Live, the largest magic convention in the United States. Each August, thousands of professional and amateur magicians flock to the Orleans, a depressing casino a mile south of the main strip and a few years past its prime. Bits and pieces of the themed décor, or at least the lifestyle associated with the slouchy wetness of New Orleans and the Gulf states, peppered its game room floor, and all the magicians invariably gathered at the Mardi Gras Bar for drinks and talk. This little Bourbon Street–themed lounge had more or less been our home since we showed up a few days earlier. I figured that I had plenty of time to pull off my plan. I thought I was all set.

I had been keeping my secret for months, and it was nearly killing me. But I had devised a scheme and I was determined to stick to it.

"Ramsay," I called out. He was chatting with Xavior. "Come over here. I want to show you something that I've been working on."

He walked over, and I pulled a new deck of cards from my backpack. My heart raced and my hands shook as I fumbled with the box's cellophane wrapper, my fingers effectively turning to useless nubs.

Ramsay chuckled sarcastically. "Let me know when you get that figured out, bud," he said, turning to walk away.

"You open it, then," I said. He took the deck from me, tore off the wrapper, and sliced through its adhesive seal with his middle finger—the symbol for the four of spades tattooed on its side, near the deepest knuckle. He handed the deck back to me and I took the cards out of the box.

Ramsay hiked up the sagging waist of his jeans, swiveled his baseball cap backward, stroked his beard, and waited for me to begin. My heart lodged itself in my throat. I wasn't sure words could get past the dense pulse.

"Just point to a card," I said, stretching the cards out like a ribbon as I drew my hands apart. Ramsay pointed to one near the middle.

"That one?" I asked.

He nodded.

"Let's have a look." I squared up the stack and turned it over, revealing Ramsay's selection.

"The two of clubs," I said. "Good choice. Now, let's take your card"—I pulled it from the deck, held it in my right hand, and placed the rest of the deck on a table next to us—"and just . . ."

I ripped off the card's top-right corner, a foot away from Ramsay's face.

". . . watch," I said, slowly opening my right hand, which held the torn piece. I went from pinky to index, slowly lifting each finger one by one. But when my hand was completely open, there was nothing there. The piece had disappeared.

"Check your back pocket," I said after a pause.

"*No!*" Ramsay shouted. He smiled, reached into his pocket, and pulled out the ripped corner. "Ah, man," he said, laughing.

"Check it," I told him. "Make sure it fits—that it's from the same card." He brought the two pieces together. The torn edges lined up perfectly.

"That was really good, man," he said. "You got me. I'm impressed."

"But here's the thing," I said, holding out my hand. "Let me see the piece." He placed it into my hand, faceup, the two and the club symbol, the card's index, visible to us. "This is a special card." I paused and looked up at him. His brow crinkled, unsure of what I was getting at.

"Because this is *me* now," I said. "I'm the Two of Clubs. I'm in."

WELCOME TO THE UNDERGROUND

I love magicians because they are honest men.
—ELBERT HUBBARD

The strongest magic does not lie. It invites the audience to lie to themselves.
—DANIEL MADISON

1

A WAY OF LIFE

I was homeless.

I wasn't living on the street or under a bridge, but I had $188 in my bank account and couldn't pay the rent for my apartment in Brooklyn. I was running out of options. My old friend Nick worked on the second floor of an office building in Portsmouth, New Hampshire, and told me that the room across the hall from him had been vacant for a while. It didn't seem like anyone was going to rent it, he said, so if I kept a low profile, I could crash for the summer. We called it an adventure, but technically—and legally—I was squatting. It was June 2015, I had just turned twenty-eight years old, and I had started freelancing full-time as a journalist earlier that year. And I was dead broke. I accepted his offer, found a subletter for my room in Brooklyn, packed my bags, and headed north.

The space turned out better than I had expected. It had a big window that faced the town's north bay, a sturdy desk, and a little bathroom (with a shower!) just down the hall. Plus, Nick, whom I've known since childhood, was there, trying to get his video production company off the ground. I kept my expenses minimal. I bought an air mattress at Walmart, nabbed a three-piece wicker furniture set for twenty-five dollars at a nearby thrift store, ate cheap turkey sandwiches for lunch and dinner, and did my laundry at Nick's apartment. With all the basics squared away, I kept my output high. I scoured for compelling story ideas and voraciously pitched them. The great thing about being a freelance journalist is that personal circumstances—squatting in an office building, for example—are irrelevant to an editor. All they care about is your idea and how it could blossom into a captivating article. So I unloaded my pitches into editors' inboxes with abandon. I had nothing to lose. I was a young writer with only a handful of clips to my name, but I knew I could convince magazines that my ideas were better than anyone else's and that I was talented enough to execute them. They didn't have to know that I was in dire straits.

I landed a few great stories from my illegal apartment, including a profile of Shaquille O'Neal for *Vice*, for which I tagged along while he performed at an electronic music festival in Georgia; another feature for *Vice* about a basketball team in Nebraska composed exclusively of Sudanese refugees; and one for *Wired* detailing the technology behind a highway interchange in Dubai. I wrote them all in that nondescript office building, secretly scraping by, subsiding on deli-meat sandwiches and off-brand yogurt, hiding in plain sight.

One day, just after lunch, I was sprawled out on the lawn outside of the office building, reading, when my phone rang. It was my mother.

"Mom—what's up?" I said.

"Hey, honey. How are you? What are you up to?"

"I'm good," I said, clapping my book closed. "Just taking a break—reading a bit, enjoying the sun. It's beautiful up here."

"Haven't gotten caught yet, have you?" she asked, followed by a light chuckle. I had told her about my circumstances—broke, squatting, struggling. She was sympathetic and said she would've offered me money if she had any. Money hadn't been the same since my father died fifteen years ago and, plus, I didn't want to burden her. I could take care of myself. I could deal with a little adventure. She, after all, managed to take care of me after my dad died, and I was scrappy like her. My father was the breadwinner, and we had to get creative after he passed away. There was life insurance money, sure, but they had just built their dream home in the woods of central Massachusetts, just under two hours from where I was in New Hampshire, accompanied by a hefty mortgage. She didn't have a job, so she started playing poker—for groceries, gas money, to keep the phone bill paid and the lights on. We ended up losing the big dream house after the housing crash, but she found another place to live—and kept playing cards. Which, I could tell by the lilt in her voice, was why she was calling me.

"I was thinking I would come visit you this weekend," she said.

"You're going to come all the way here, just to see my homeless-guy setup?" I asked suspiciously.

She laughed. "Well . . ."

"Mom, c'mon, what do you have planned? Are you coming up here for a poker game?"

"There's a great tournament twenty minutes away! I thought I could come see you, and then we could play."

"Well, Mom, hate to break it to you, but I'm broke. The office building. Squatting. Can't pay my rent. Remember?"

"Don't worry about it, honey. I'll bankroll you. It's only a hundred dollars per person. Nothing huge. I just want to see you. If you send me the address to where you're staying, I can be there on Saturday—by 11 A.M.? The tournament starts at one."

"Well, if you're paying, I'm in. Did you win recently? Where is this extra money coming from?"

"I played a cash game last week—sat down with two hundred dollars and walked away with a thousand."

"Holy shit. A good night's work."

"It's all those macho dudes, thinking they can push me around," she said. "There was this one guy—a real piece of work. He just wouldn't fold against me, Ian. He looks at me and sees someone who is weak; he sees this little old woman and thinks, *There's no way she can beat me*. So, I trapped him. I just let him keep betting, and I stuck with him until the end. You should've seen his face when I turned my cards over. I took almost four hundred dollars on that one pot."

"Damn! Works every time," I said.

She chuckled. "Of course. You have to be able to know how to play the game—any game—to your advantage." I laughed along with her and glanced up to my room on the second floor of the office building. It didn't feel like I was cheating. The crime was victimless given that I had no clue who owned the place. I didn't feel bad, and neither did my mother; deception has been in our blood for a long time.

My mother is stout, barely five feet tall, with white hair and a piercingly innocent smile. She is largely taken for granted at the poker table and, to some extent, the same has been true in every aspect of her life. She grew up the eldest of eight children in Fitchburg, Massachusetts—a small city next door to where I grew up—where her outgoing and mischievous personality won her popularity as a teenager. Her catlike eyes and petite figure meant she earned numerous yearbook superlatives during senior year of high school, but she spent much of her free time in local bars, drinking beer and playing pool. After graduation, she drove across the United States in an RV, lived in Portland, Oregon, for a year, returned home, saved some money by working nights at a nursing home, and ventured off again down the East Coast with her friend Joyce, hoping to eventually make it to Texas. "I was looking for an adventure," she told me once. "Being home, I felt stuck. It was a dead end, so I left, hoping I'd find something better." But they ran out of money in Fort Myers, Florida, and had to live in a tent at a campground for a while, where they cleaned up trash for money. They hung around in local bars, and my mother hustled men at pool.

They eventually made their way to New Orleans and then Houston, where my mother worked nights at Joe and Gary's, a beaten-down beer-and-wine shack on the side of the road. She made a circle of friends and played a lot of pool, but also began throwing down money in backroom poker games. She had played a lot of poker in high school when she wasn't hustling pool at the bar, and quickly found herself a natural at the table. She began to play cards constantly in Houston, mainly with friends and friends of friends, and gained a reputation for winning. "The challenge was being able to figure out other people," she told me. "It was like solving a puzzle." And then, one day, while at work, my father, who had moved to Houston from Ohio, walked through the door, sat down at the bar, ordered a beer, and, well, the rest is history.

Eventually, my parents moved back to Massachusetts. I was born, and they needed a more normal, stable life. But we were always a family with a few decks of cards lying around—a piece of my mother before she became my mother. We'd play games of five-card draw with play money, or deal to an invisible series of players to see what hands would come out. She'd teach me about strategy and tells. I first learned to shuffle a deck of cards when I was six years old. There are dozens of photographs of me as a child holding a deck during our annual camping trips, dealing cards under the glow of our lantern. My mother even taught me how to cheat at poker. She showed me how to shuffle the cards in such a way as to keep an ace on top of the deck, or how, if you bend the cards enough while you're shuffling, you can peek at them, or denote their specific order.

Aside from knowing how to cheat at poker, my childhood was standard-issue American middle-class. My father was a blue-collar entrepreneur, a tile man by trade, and we lived frugally during the early years of him being his own boss. We lived in a small, one-story ranch near the center of my hometown while my parents saved money and built their dream house on its outskirts. We all went camping and swimming in the summer, watched football in the fall, went to the movies, hosted cookouts. I started playing sports early, and my father coached my football team. Despite my small stature, I played quarterback and linebacker. I was actually pretty good. Our team always made the playoffs, and my father would give rousing speeches to us before games, vigorously clapping his hands and shouting to get us riled up. When we'd win, I'd drive home with him in his truck, and he'd lovingly grab my shoulder and tell me how well I played. Our life was as simple as a small-town existence could get.

Until it wasn't.

After my father died, everything changed. He was the rock who kept our family grounded. My mother worked with him on his business, and his ambition to build a stable, successful family kept all of us on track. When he met my mother, she was a freewheeling twentysomething—the pool-hustling and cardsharping walkabout. She was on the search for purpose in her young life, and she found a way forward with my father. Together they formed an equilibrium. But after he was gone, she was lost. So, with the pressure of being a single mother mounting, she went back to something on which she knew she could rely: poker.

Deception at the card table became her primary coping mechanism. It was the closest thing she had to an escape. Sadly, it sometimes wasn't enough to erase the loss she carried around in her chest. She still came home every night to an empty bed—to an empty heart. I, too, got lost. A father is supposed to show his son how to become a man, and I've had to navigate my adolescence and young adulthood alone. And, I'll admit, squatting in that office building, although adventurous, didn't make me feel like I was living up to the expectations my father had set out for me—and what I set out for myself.

But, over the years, poker became a way for my mother and me to bond; amid the Texas hold 'em boom of the mid-aughts, I myself began to play competitively. We'd play a lot: pickup games, legitimate tournaments, whatever we could find. We'd try to help each other get better. She'd stand outside during breaks, a cigarette perched between her fingers, and pick at a cuticle with the long, sharpened tip of her thumbnail, thinking about the lies she told wrong and how she could hone her deceptions once she returned to the table. I'd stand outside with her during those moments and think, *That's my mother.* And I'd admire her for being so true with herself, with what she hoped to get out of this game, of deceiving those sitting across from her at the card table. Poker became our time together—just a mother and son becoming a couple of liars for the weekend.

She'd always want to play, all throughout my twenties. So I was excited to sit down at a game up in New Hampshire, if not to win some money then just to be with her for a day. I waited for her outside the office building, eating lunch at a picnic table on the lawn, and watched the neighbor's dog chase a family of geese. She pulled up in her junky little Toyota Camry and stepped out. I walked over and gave her a hug. She smiled. We had time before the tournament started, so I took her through the back entrance into the office building. We climbed the stairs, cut right, and walked over to my room.

"I changed the locks," I told her, taking out my keys, "just in case someone from the building comes. That'll at least buy me some time to figure something out." I opened the door. "But it's not bad, right?"

"Holy shit, Ian!" she exclaimed, laughing. "This is actually really nice! Hell, I'd live here!"

"Yeah, I mean, the air mattress deflates during the night," I said, pushing my hand into the squishy plastic bed, "but it's not that bad. That's where I work," I continued, pointing to my desk, which sat in front of the window facing the bay. "It's actually been really nice up here. And there's central air-conditioning."

"Well, I'm glad you're working things out," she said, touching my arm and smiling. "I knew you would."

We walked back down to the car and drove to the poker room. Poker is legal in New Hampshire, so the space felt like a real casino. A manager checked your ID, signed you up for the tournament, gave you a seat assignment, and exchanged your cash for chips. Dealers wore uniforms, and the tables were laced in felt, ringed in padded leather, and dotted with cupholders. Waitresses scuttled about, taking drink orders, and the sound of tossed chips and shuffling decks filled the room. The tournament was in the back, and forty players had signed up. By chance, my mother and I were assigned to the same table. We took our seats and waited for the game to begin.

The first hour was fairly slow. Nothing big came my way, and my mother played only one hand (she folded before having to match another player's bet). Over the next hour, I played a series of hands, but got beat and lost most of my chips. My mother played slow, letting the other players (all middle-aged men) conclude that she was just a table tourist. And then, on one hand, she raised. A guy at the other end of the table, potbellied with a five o'clock shadow and a grimy T-shirt, shot her a look, curled his lip, and threw in his chips. They continued back and forth the entire hand—she'd bet into him, he'd call her bet, and the next card was dealt. On the last round of betting, he went over the top with a huge raise—all in, everything he had. She peeked at her cards, glanced over at me, and matched his raise. The dealer called for them to turn over their cards. She'd had a straight the entire time, crushing his two pair. Her lips peeled back, revealing a sly grin. She wrapped her arms around the sea of chips and pulled them to her chest. The guy grunted, got up, stuffed a cigarette into his mouth, and walked toward the exit.

I got busted out shortly thereafter, and my mother played for a few more hours. She got beat a few times and, eventually, got knocked out. She grabbed her purse, shrugged her shoulders, and we walked out into the parking lot. We got back into the car, stewed in our defeat for a couple of minutes, and drove toward the center of town, back to the office building. It was a sunny day, clear and bright, and a warm breeze blew in through the windows. My mother sparked a cigarette.

"How are the stories going, honey?" she asked, taking a drag.

"Going really well, actually," I said. "I just finished the Shaq piece, so that should be published soon."

"I'm really excited to read that one. You were such a big fan of his when you were a kid. Do you remember when Dad took you to get his autograph?" She smiled.

"Yeah, it was such a trip to be around him. But I just found something else that I'm thinking about."

"Another sports story?"

"No. It's kind of weird, but I've been talking with this guy—he's a magician."

"A magician?" she said, laughing.

"I know, pretty random, but he doesn't *look* like a magician. His name is Chris Ramsay. I found him on Instagram—he's got sixty thousand followers. He has this super slick style—beard, tattoos, backward hat, this whole cool, streetwear vibe. It's hard to explain, but he also has a YouTube channel with a bunch of performances, and he's insanely good."

"So, what are you going to do? You think it'll turn into something?"

"I don't know, but he's part of this entirely new generation of magicians. No one knows much about these guys in the mainstream media. Could be a cool story—get me out of this rut, you know?" We pulled into the parking lot of the office building. She stopped and threw the car into park.

"You've never been someone to turn down an adventure," she said. "You get that from me."

"Yeah, he mentioned something about a magic convention in England in the next couple of months. He said I should go with him."

She looked at me. "Well, you're going to go, right?"

2

BLACKPOOL PROBLEMS

The alley was narrow and dark. A sharp wind cut down its center. Chris Ramsay thrust his hands into the front pockets of his jeans and, trudging through the darkness, his leather boots licked the pavement. A sturdy six foot three, he wore a full beard under ice-blue eyes, and tattoos spilled onto his wrists from beneath the sleeves of his crew-neck sweatshirt. I pulled my jacket's zipper to my chin and walked behind him toward our rendezvous point.

We stopped in front of a bar. "Dude," he said, pointing to the sign above the door, its letters hung in the wash of a dingy yellow light. *The Liars' Club.* He smiled. "This must be the place." We entered and walked down the stairs.

Although Canadian (who can easily pass as an American), Ramsay was born in Herbolzheim, Germany, a small town in the southwestern nook of the country, a stone's throw away from France. His father was in the military, and they moved around a lot: Germany to Ontario, then back to Germany, back to Ontario, Germany again, New Brunswick, Quebec City, Montreal. He attended more than a dozen schools throughout his childhood, always the new kid, the perpetual outcast. The language barrier didn't help, either. Although he spoke German, French, and English, his accents were always off. He was bullied a lot but did his best to win over kids in class. He had a leg up on them: he knew a few cool magic tricks.

Ramsay first fell in love with magic when his grandfather showed him a simple vanishing-coin trick. Captivated, he began to perform basic effects to classmates at school. He'd gather kids around his desk and pull out a napkin and a penny. He'd place the penny on top of the napkin, fold it up like an envelope, and hold it in his hands. Then he'd grab two corners of the napkin and quickly unfurl the paper. The penny had disappeared.

The penny was coated in soap, which acts like an adhesive, and when he unflapped the napkin, the penny merely stuck to its backside, unseen by the spectator. "I'd go to school with napkins and pennies and chunks of soap in my pocket," Ramsay told me, laughing. Although a dumb trick, the psychological effect it had on him was profound. "Seeing your peers be impressed by you for the first time created an incredible sense of confidence that I never felt before, especially as a kid coming into new schools all the time," he told me. At that age, however, magic was just something Ramsay did to fit in. He didn't think it could become a job or have a prominent role in his future. To him, it was a means of survival amid a tumultuous, jackknifed upbringing.

After high school, Ramsay moved to Quebec City, 160 miles northeast of Montreal, and began selling drugs—all types of drugs, as long as he and his crew were making money. It was a bad crowd and a dangerous lifestyle, but it paid the bills. Looking back on it now, Ramsay thinks his life of crime as a young adult was an extension of the compulsive shoplifting he did as a child. The thrill of stealing or switching price tags on expensive items also mirrored the euphoria he felt while performing magic. But, by age twenty-one, three years into the drug-dealing game, he had had enough. "One night, I called my mom at three in the morning and said, 'I can't do this anymore.'" She drove the three hours from Montreal to Quebec City and brought him home.

Starting from scratch, Ramsay got a job tending bar in downtown Montreal. That's when he started getting serious about magic. "You are dealing with a place that has low light and loud music. I had power, too, being behind the bar. I had all the key ingredients to help cultivate my magic," he told me. "It was a great way to get extra tips, too."

Jay, a regular at the bar, would come in every Friday night and put down a wager: If Chris could fool him three times, he would give him a $50 tip—a lot of cash, considering that $100 was the normal bounty for a shift. Every week, the same thing: $50 for three tricks. But Ramsay quickly began to run out of material. So, over the next few years, he devoured as much instructional content as he could and honed his skills.

After getting sick of the bar scene, he eventually landed a job at a regional tile and marble company and was soon promoted to one of their wholesaler's public relations teams because of his charismatic personality. He always did a little magic when meeting with clients, who in turn hired him to gig at their private events. But his dream was always to become a respected member of the magic industry—inventing new effects and routines, consulting for other magicians, pushing magic forward as an art form—and hopefully becoming a community centerpiece.

We had talked a lot about his upbringing and love for magic, and his rise to fame in the time since, but he said I needed to see the scene myself. "We've got a lot of ground to cover," he told me one day in late summer, while I was still living in the office building in New Hampshire, just before my mother visited me. "I think it'd be a good idea if you came to Blackpool, England, with me in February. You need to meet Madison and Laura."

With the added encouragement from my mother, I booked a flight. It was my chance at something big. What did I have to lose?

Laura London and Daniel Madison waited for us in the back of the bar, huddled around a small table, nursing a round of drinks. A petite woman in her thirties, Laura beamed a large smile framed by scarlet lips. Her hair—an asymmetrical crimson bob—veiled sneaky, compact eyes. She wore a formfitting black dress, leather-fronted, with velour sleeves dotted in a midnight-purple leopard print, equal parts elegant and over-the-top panache.

Madison was decked out in all black, and the wide-cut collar of his T-shirt revealed tattoos running underneath his collarbones. They carried over onto his arms and down to his hands, with the faces of his knuckles and the sides of his fingers also scrawled in ink. His black hair was messy, and his thick eyebrows pinched down toward his nose. He held a deck of playing cards and, just before greeting Ramsay, put them into his back pocket.

"It's been too long, my friend," Madison said, resting his hand on Ramsay's shoulder. Then he turned to me and said, "Ian, hey. It's great to meet you. We've heard a lot about you." He reached out and shook my hand.

"It's great to be here," I replied, kind of awkwardly. It took me off guard that Ramsay had been speaking to them about me. I was just a curious writer. What could've prompted them to talk among themselves and agree to meet with me? Laura stood behind him, a smile creeping across her cheek under her jagged bangs. We ordered a round of whiskey, clinked glasses, and drank up.

This meeting was, in fact, a secret.

Just after I showed up in Blackpool, Ramsay informed me, to my great excitement, that Daniel Madison and Laura London had agreed to meet with me. "They're down in Manchester," he said. "We can't tell anyone that we are going to go see them, but we should leave soon." Despite being two of the most well-known magicians in England, Madison and Laura keep much of their daily lives concealed from the public, including when they are out having drinks or meeting old friends. It seemed strange to me— why not just come to Blackpool and hang out?—but Ramsay explained that their social reservations were part of their "brand," whatever that meant. So, we made the hourlong drive south, and after arriving in the city center, we turned down a tiny side street, texted Madison to make sure we were in the right spot, and made our way to the bar.

After getting our drinks, Madison and Ramsay each took out a deck of cards and began doing sleight-of-hand maneuvers: a series of complicated and visually stunning shuffles, hiding cards in their hands by palming them, secretly maneuvering cards from one spot in the deck to another. They only got to see each other a few times a year and were clearly excited to show each other some new moves. I watched as the cards fluttered between their finger- tips, moving effortlessly around one another, flourishing, nearly escaping their grip. It was not only an incredible display of dex- terity, as if each finger had a mind of its own, but of dedication. I later learned that it takes *years* to handle a deck of cards with such grace.

Within the array of tattoos blanketing all of their hands, I could make out that each had a tattoo in the same place, a card sym- bol on the insides of their middle fingers—the Four of Spades for Ramsay, the Nine of Clubs for Madison. Laura had the King of Diamonds.

After another round of drinks, we all went outside to smoke, and Laura pulled a deck of cards from her purse. The backs were cherry colored, similar to her hair, and I started to sense that this was all part of her shtick, her brand.

"Pick a card," she told me, fanning the deck. I pulled out the ten of spades. She handed me a marker and told me to sign it.

"There's no other card like this card because it has your name on it, right?"

I nodded.

"If I take the ten and I place it in the middle, would you be amazed if I made it jump from there"—she touched the card, its edge protruding from the deck—"to there?" she asked, moving her finger to the top of the deck.

I nodded again. She pushed the card fully into the middle, shook the pack, picked up the top card, and turned it over. It wasn't my card. She laughed. "I can't do that. I wish I could! But maybe you can help me."

She turned the top card back over. "Just click your fingers for me."

I snapped my fingers. She turned over the top card. It was the ten of spades, complete with my signature. "Oh, wow. You're good," she said. She then took my card and placed it back into the middle and had me push the card in until it was flush with the rest of the deck. She asked that I snap my fingers again. *Snap.*

She turned over the top card. There it was: the ten of spades.

"Ah, come on!" I exclaimed.

"Now," she said, "I am a sleight-of-hand artist. And because of that I am able to control this card." She spun my ten of spades on the tip of her middle finger like a basketball. "I'll give you an example. If I flick through the cards, I can count very quickly. So, if I do this"—she dragged her thumb along the corner of the deck and stopped halfway through—"this is the twenty-sixth card, which makes your card"—she slid it into the deck—"in twenty-seventh position. Now I know exactly where your card is. I can control it and place it wherever I like."

She cut the deck twice, shuffled it, and cut it again. "And the reason I can shuffle these like this is because your card is no longer inside the deck." She fanned the cards out, faceup, in front of me. The ten of spades was gone. "So, if your card's not here, where is it?"

Laura took a step to her right and looked down at the pavement. Three feet behind her, tucked within a shadow that ran alongside the alley's brick wall, lay the deck's box. She crouched down and picked it up, a grin creeping from behind her jagged bangs—that same sly smirk from when I first walked into the bar. She stood and gave the box a shake. Something inside knocked around.

She handed it to me. I opened it and pulled out a card that had been folded twice. I flattened it out. In my hand rested the ten of spades, with my name, in black ink, on its face. I froze, the card still faceup in my hand. I was at a loss for words. *What just happened?*

Laura broke the silence, whispering, with that grin still spread across her face, "That's yours to keep." I slid the card into my front pocket. We stood out in the cold for a little longer before parting ways. "We'll be in touch," Madison said.

With that, Ramsay and I headed back to Blackpool. We sat in silence for most of the way, tired from a day of traveling, my mind still spinning from Laura's routine. The conflict that arises after seeing such a mind-blowing magic trick sat in my gut like a rock. On one hand, I wanted to know the method—to understand how I had been so thoroughly deceived. But, on the other hand, I loved the feeling of being tricked by someone so supremely talented. It's a strangely delicious pill to swallow: I enjoyed being the fool. It was almost liberating.

As I dropped Ramsay off and watched him saunter toward the entrance of his hotel, I couldn't help but feel that I had fallen in with a gang of thieves or a touring rock band—not a group of magicians. And these weren't like any magicians I had seen before. They seemed to be plotting something, in cahoots—the tattoos on their fingers, each of a different playing card, must've had something to do with it. Ramsay climbed the stairs to his hotel, turned back, and flashed a tiny smile before going inside.

Blackpool hangs off England's northwestern coast. A once-bustling seaside tourist destination, it has, over the years, fallen into despair: a bad-dream Las Vegas with multilevel casinos and flickering arcades next to boarded-up ice cream stands, abandoned fish-and-chip shops, and decrepit motels coated in grime and seagull shit. For the last sixty years, however, the town has been the home of the Blackpool Magic Convention. It's the largest magic convention in the world, with nearly four thousand attendees, including young guns like Chris Ramsay, who flock to the town every year to meet with industry friends, get roaring drunk, and see what's new in the world of magic. Aside from introducing me to Madison and Laura, that's why Ramsay invited me to England.

The thing about magic conventions is that most of the dealers sell junky, stereotypical effects and props, which invariably attract cringeworthy customers. Magicians milled about the convention, many of whom embodied the modern clichés associated with the profession: oversized black polyester button-up shirts with tribal graphics on the sleeves, wide-legged cargo shorts with tchotchkes and chains hanging from the belt loops, ugly haircuts and hideous necklaces. I don't think I have ever seen so many fedoras in one room in my entire life.

On the first day of the convention, Ramsay and I checked out the hundreds of dealer tables and watched sellers hawk their wares to impressionable young hobbyist and middle-aged magicians. Most were the props you'd see at a little kid's birthday party: fake money, appearing canes, sponge balls, thumb tips, top hats, bedazzled blazers, box illusions, cups and balls, levitation stools, charged dice, magic tongues, dynamic coins, and trick candy. Ramsay shook his head, visibly frustrated at the stereotypes that many magicians continued to embrace. "This is the shit that we're trying to avoid," he said. "There's a lot of bad magic out there."

As we walked through the convention hall, Ramsay stopped here and there to greet acquaintances and pose for photographs with fans. I trailed behind him, making sure to get out of the frame when a kid begged for a selfie. Everywhere we went, people's heads craned toward us. *Wow*, I thought. *This dude really is famous.*

We soon ran into magicians more in line with Ramsay's vibe. We came across Damien O'Brien, a short and flashy Brit with torn jeans and a fitted cap, as well as Dee Christopher, a "paranormalist" from outside London—"Death, the supernatural, I love that shit," he told me—with dark eyeliner and long hair, clad in a knee-length black overcoat. Damien and Dee had both appeared on BBC Three's *Killer Magic*, a British competition show, which aired in 2015. Damien pulled a bottle of Jack Daniel's from his backpack.

"We're gonna get proper pissed, mate!" Damien said, holding up the bottle.

"Aha!" Ramsay said, reaching over to take a swig.

"We'll see you at the bar later, yeah?" Damien asked.

"Yup, we'll be there," Ramsay replied, his lips still puckered from the liquor's aftershock.

It's a ritual in Blackpool: After the day's events are over in the convention hall, all the magicians congregate at the Ruskin, a low-ceilinged lounge with paisley-style carpeting and worn-in furniture, decorated like a grandmother's parlor. By the time we arrived, the place was already crawling with magicians. The bartenders worked feverishly, pouring foaming pints and fingers of liquor. Just after I sat down next to Ramsay on one of the couches, a commotion came from across the room.

"I brought my own moonshine!" yelled a guy with close-cropped hair and tattoos crawling up his neck, wide-eyed and smiling.[*] He was huge, barrel-chested with yardstick-wide shoulders, like

---

[*] Peter later got the word "Forever" tattooed in cursive script on his forehead.

a deviant lumberjack or a juiced-up linebacker. He held the bottle
of liquor in the air and walked over to us. It was Peter Turner,
a world-famous mentalist, a form of magic categorized by mind
reading and other impossible psychological effects. A gregarious
and audacious guy, he is also a skilled hypnotist. It's rumored that
he once went into the Grosvenor, a casino in London, hypnotized
the roulette dealer, and made off with £40,000 in five minutes. He
was nabbed by security before leaving the property and forced to
give the illegitimate winnings back. Since it was the dealer who
mistakenly gave him money (or so they thought), Peter left scot-
free. A couple years ago, I was later told, Madison heard of Peter's
abilities and asked him to demonstrate. After finding a skeptic in
the bar where the two met, Peter held his hand in front of the
guy's face and snapped his fingers. *Boom.* He fell to the floor—
hypnotized. Madison watched in disbelief.

"All right!" Ramsay shouted, clapping his hands together, ad-
dressing the group. "Let's go get some drinks!" We made our
way down the street to another bar. We danced, drank, and performed magic on clubgoers. I watched, amused and amazed as
they fooled the bartenders with simple illusions—ring magic, floating bills and straws—and garnered free shots in the process. A
dance circle eventually formed. Playing cards soaked in booze littered the floor. We threw handfuls of ice into the circle as Ramsay
danced in its center, tipping his hat with the beat, the party continuing into the night.

The next morning, Ramsay announced the day's plans. "Ian, we're
getting Blackpool Problems tattoos. You're getting one with us,"
he said matter-of-factly, interrupting a shuffling how-to session I
was having with Jeremy Griffith, a Los Angeles-based magician
in wire-rimmed glasses who spoke with a soft lisp. Jeremy's eyes

squinted when he smiled, which was often, his slight underbite clashing against his bubbly personality.*

Jeremy is truly a purist when it comes to cards—no frills, just raw table mechanics. His mesmerizing Instagram videos have garnered him more than 55,000 followers. Despite his popularity, he doesn't hesitate to sit down and give tips on sleight of hand with other, less savvy magicians. After telling him I grew up playing poker with my mother and knew a thing or two about cards and the basics of card cheating, he was adamant about getting a deck in my hands. But, before we could really dig in, Ramsay walked over and derailed our session.

The guys consistently referred to their antics in Blackpool as "Blackpool Problems"—the hangovers, the hookups in their hotel rooms, the drunken locals, the general debauchery. It was all summed up in that one phrase, and now Ramsay wanted to add it to his laundry list of magic-related tattoos—and, shockingly, he wanted me to join in on the outing.

I nodded without hesitation. "Sure," I said, like it was no big deal. One of the most influential young magicians in the world just asked me to join him for a matching tattoo. Of course I was going to say yes. What kind of journalist would I be if I refused, or showed even the slightest hint of hesitation? It was as if I had a nagging premonition throughout my time in Blackpool—that this was just the beginning of something much bigger. It was a strange feeling, like a bug burrowing its way under your skin. Even after just a few days, I felt like I was part of the gang. It wasn't so much that I was forcing myself to be cool with getting a random tattoo in this dumpy English town, but that I was surprised to be so calm at the thought of it.

---

* Whenever I call Jeremy on the phone, he always picks up with a lovable "Hey, boyo!"

"Yeah?" Ramsay said, smiling. "You'll do it? We're getting it on our ring fingers," he added, raising his into the air, pointing at the blank strip of skin. "Peter is going to get one, too."

"Of course, dude," I responded. "No sweat."

Jeremy began to laugh. "Oh man," he said, giggling. "You're really into it now if you're getting a tattoo with *these* guys."

After everyone finished eating, the group splintered. I went with Ramsay and Peter back to the Ruskin for a drink before we headed to the tattoo parlor. After ordering a round, Ramsay's phone beeped. It was a message from Laura London. She and Madison had ultimately declined to visit Blackpool—"I hate crowds," Madison told me in the bar when I asked if I'd see him the following day—and she was already back at her flat in London, prepping for her next gig.

Hey Chris, quietly put the feelers out for Shin Lim for the52. If you think he'd be game, I'll invite him and maybe you can get him inked in Blackpool. Hope you're having fun!! Lxxx.

Shin Lim, a short and soft-spoken twentysomething from Boston, is one of the most lauded close-up magicians in the world. He is the winner of the 2015 International Federation of Magic Societies (FISM) for Close-Up Card Magic, which is basically the Olympics for magicians. His winning routine, The Dream Act, which he also performed on the long-running televised competition show *Penn & Teller: Fool Us*, has been viewed more than fifty million times on YouTube.

Ramsay showed me the text message. "Whoa! Cool," I said.

"Yeah, dude. I had heard they were thinking about Shin for the52, especially after winning FISM. It's funny that they decided to pull the trigger on it while you're here," he said, phone in hand, typing back to Laura. He paused and shot me a glance. "Almost like, after meeting you last night, her and Madison wanted you to be there for an induction firsthand."

I had only heard whispers about the52. Ramsay, right before I came to Blackpool, had cryptically mentioned it: a secret society, founded by Laura London and Daniel Madison, comprising the world's most prominent young magicians, all of whom were pushing the craft forward and doing truly unique things.

"But Laura said 'inked.' What does she mean?"

Ramsay smiled and extended his middle finger, revealing a tattoo for the four of spades, the one I had noticed in the bar the other night. "You can't be in the52 without a tattoo," he said, smiling.

"But wait," I said, looking over at Peter Turner, who was sipping his beer across the table. He smiled and revealed a tattoo on his middle finger, too: the Jack of Hearts. Almost everyone Ramsay had introduced me to the past two days had one of these tattoos. Ramsay with the Four of Spades, Madison the Nine of Clubs, Laura the King of Diamonds. Jeremy Griffith, Damien O'Brien, Dee Christopher—they all had them, too. I had come here to write my story about how young magicians, Chris Ramsay chief among them, were changing magic in the internet age, but, with the52 now sitting at my feet, I saw this opening up into something entirely more fascinating.

Ramsay and Peter both tried texting Shin but with no luck since Wi-Fi was spotty. No one knew where he was. The nearest tattoo shop closed in less than an hour. We had to find him. I volunteered to run down to the convention center to look for him.

I hustled across town. A fierce wind, laced with salt, came off the ocean. That grit and sting in my eyes. I threw my hood over my head and kept running. I booked it into the event hall and found Shin. I pulled him aside. "You have to come with me right now," I said. "Ramsay and Peter have to speak with you."

"What's this about?" he asked, clearly confused—and a little worried.

"It's not my place to say," I said. "But it's important." It must've looked a little strange to Shin: this random guy, not even a magician, who he just met the day before, was ushering him to a bar without telling him what for. But I knew how monumental this invitation would be for him and wanted it to come from Ramsay directly. We walked over to the Ruskin and I realized how absurd it was for me to be there. I had just fallen in with these guys two days ago. And now I was about to be the first outsider to ever witness an induction into the52. We walked into the bar and Shin sat between Ramsay and Peter.

"So," Ramsay started, "I got word that we got the okay to invite you into the52. You want in?"

"*Yeah!*" Shin yelped. He clenched his fists and threw his arms into the air. "What card do I get?"

"I have to find out, but we have to get tattooed in about twenty minutes before the shop closes."

"I can still do my act?" Shin asked, referring to his headlining performance the following day at the convention, nervous that a finger tattoo could hinder his dexterity.

"Of course you can," Peter told him.

"Yeah, let's do it," Shin said, laughing. "Fuck it!"

Peter turned to Ramsay. "See if the Queen of Spades is available." It was Shin's favorite card. Madison replied quickly, "QS, GO!" We finished our drinks, threw on our coats, and walked down the street to the shop. We told the artist what we were after: the card symbol for Shin, Blackpool Problems for Ramsay, Peter, and myself. Shin was up first, the needle buzzing.

"Here we go!" Shin said, extending his finger, the tattoo artist hunched over his hand, lowering the gun. Ramsay and Peter were first for our matching ink. While Peter was under the gun, a family from Holland, after a double take from the sidewalk, came into the shop to take a group photograph with Shin. A bandage concealed his finger's fresh ink. "You're with the world champion!" the mother said to her son after snapping a picture. (In September 2018, Shin won the thirteenth season of *America's Got Talent*. Watch his clips: Can you spot his Queen of Spades tattoo on the inside of his middle finger?)

The tattoo artist signaled me over. It was my turn. I sat down and let him grip my finger. The needle stung as he scratched the ink into my skin: "BP PROBLEMS." An abbreviation, yes, but proof of the role this city played in the lifestyle of these magicians—and now a memento of my adventure there, as well.

After getting our ink, we went back to the Ruskin. Word spread quickly among other members of the52 about Shin being the newest addition to the group. Jeremy found him and extended his praise.

"Welcome to the club," he said.

"Thank you," Shin replied, smiling. "It's an honor."

Darkness fell, and we left the Ruskin to go back to the club from the night before. Peter carried his homemade whiskey and, as we walked down the street, passed it around. The club roared as we entered. The dance floor swelled with women wrapped in mini-skirts and men clad in slim-cut jeans. Neon strobe lights sliced through the crowd and techno music boomed from the speakers. I followed Ramsay through the pool of clubgoers to the VIP section in the back of the bar. Bottles of whiskey sat in ice buckets and decks of playing cards were stacked on the surrounding tables. Magicians were everywhere.

Just after 2 A.M., Ramsay gathered up the group and ushered us outside to move to the next spot. Ryan Tricks, a London-based magician, stumbled out with the crowd. He wore a three-piece suit and, while chatting drunkenly with a local, Ramsay secretly snatched his pocket square and, surprisingly, passed it off to me. It felt as if Ramsay had forced my hand—a way for him to see, with very little lead-up, what kind of magical moment I could create with a piece of fabric and an unwitting rube. I was the first outsider they had ever let into their world, and I needed to make a mark.

I looked around, trying to find a place to hide the handkerchief. But then what? There's nothing special about stashing a stolen pocket square somewhere random on the street. Where was the magic in that? I wasn't sure what to do. I saw a poster frame tacked to the brick wall next to the club's entrance. I casually walked over to it, trying not to arouse suspicion, looking over my shoulder as if I were about to steal a stranger's wallet. The frame was broken at one corner, with cracks spidering toward its center. I tugged on its edge and slipped the handkerchief behind the glass.

As the group started moving down the sidewalk, I stopped Ryan, put my hand over the chest pocket where the handkerchief would've been, and pretended to throw the piece of fabric at the poster frame. He looked up and saw it behind the glass. His jaw dropped. The group started screaming and hollering, grabbing me by the shoulders and jerking me from side to side. Ryan slapped his hands to his forehead and turned around to look at Ramsay. As he faced in the opposite direction, I quickly removed the handkerchief from inside the frame and balled it up in my palm.

"Ryan!" I yelled. He turned and faced me. "Look!" I placed my hand on the frame and "pulled" the handkerchief through the glass. My hands jumped quickly—*pop!*—and there I was, holding Ryan's pocket square between thumb and forefinger, the fabric gently swaying in the seaside breeze.

Ramsay threw his arm around my shoulder. "Now you're thinking like a magician," he said, leading me to the next bar.

3

MAGIC IS DEAD

B radford is a shithole."

Daniel Madison was talking about his hometown, a former textile hub in northern England. He grew up in Buttershaw, a neighborhood in Bradford's southwest corner where crime was rampant. His parents were churchgoers and kept him sheltered during his childhood. "I grew up in a bubble," he said, "and that was a mistake." They split up when he was ten, and his mother turned to alcohol to cope with the divorce. His grandfather began caring for him but passed away two years later. By age thirteen, Madison started exploring his hometown's darker corners. Unsurprisingly, he fell in with a rough crowd and, within a few years, started stealing cars. "These guys would say, 'Oh, see that car? If you take it to this address, you'll get this much money,'" he told me. "That was a really fucked-up time. I always wanted out of that cycle."

In 1999, at age seventeen, Madison landed a job with his father working road construction: digging up highways and laying asphalt, though he was usually condemned to cleanup crew. His father, seeing his son going down a dark path—and perhaps feeling guilty that he wasn't as supportive during his early teens—wanted him to turn his life around, so he made sure he had steady work. Madison wasn't the nine-to-five type, though. The excitement of the streets was still in his bones, and he had been practicing sleight-of-hand card moves in his spare time—simple cheats he could utilize at the poker table. A friend tipped him off to local games where he could put his new nefarious skills to work. He started off with small buy-ins and marked high-value cards during play by slightly creasing or crimping them (only a marginal advantage, but an advantage nonetheless). "If I'm not going to a regular job, I still need a way to make money," Madison explained. "I figured out that I could do this fairly easily, but I needed bigger games with more cash on the table. And it became my life for a while, trying to find higher- and higher-stakes games where I could sit down and cheat."

Eventually he found a fat-stacks game at a country club in Huddersfield, just twenty minutes from his home. At first, the men refused to let him play, but after he lied that his father was a member—"He's always here. He drives that silver Mercedes. You *definitely* know him"—they let him buy in. Instead of crimping cards, Madison tried out different moves: dealing from the bottom of the deck, as well as a simple shift, where a card is moved within the deck. He got away with it. The golf buddies didn't have a clue. He played a few games with them over the next few months and built up a rapport. After one weekend game, one of the guys told Madison where to find the real money: The Talbot Inn in Barnsley, about fifteen miles away.

The next weekend, Madison went to the pub. He hung around until closing, sipping beers, waiting for the game to begin. Around two in the morning, after the last patrons left, the barman signaled Madison into the back room, revealing a table with five chairs. "It was real money—you couldn't sit down with less than five hundred pounds," Madison told me. After successfully working his subtle cheats at the country club, Madison's confidence was high. But on his first deal, ten minutes into the game, disaster struck.

"I fucked up," he told me. Another player saw Madison stacking cards to the bottom of the deck. Looking the man in the eye, Madison knew he was caught. Without saying a word, he bolted for the door. But it was locked—no way out. Madison got the shit kicked out of him. The men left him on the sidewalk, bloody and bruised, with a broken leg and collarbone, a handful of cracked ribs, and a concussion. Madison woke up in the hospital and he phoned his father, who offered to put him up. "I always joke that my hands were completely left alone," he told me, holding them out as if inspecting their survival. As he recovered, he kept practicing sleight of hand. But he found a new, less dangerous application for his skills: magic.

Madison has since become one of the most respected sleight-of-hand artists in the world—and one of the most elusive. A cult figure whose history of card cheating created a distinct allure and upped his street cred, he rarely makes appearances in public, and his presence on social media is equally sparse. He cloaks himself in an alter ego: an edgy, gravel-voiced, irreverent vagabond. His entire persona—viewed primarily on Instagram and other social media networks, which are crucial tools modern magicians use to brand themselves and interact with others in the community—is highly calculated and steeped in mystery. He treats his career as a piece of performance art and has dubbed the character he has created "the architect," a nod to the fact that the character may be building him—the one in control—rather than the other way around. In many respects, he doesn't even consider himself a magician, but rather someone dedicated to the art of deception, whatever form it may take. In magic, he is the epitome of the underground. This was the Madison I met, more than a decade into his career.

In 2013, Madison began to seek out other young guns who he felt were trying to redefine the notion of what a magician could be. "I wanted change, so I went looking for people who could be part of a movement," he told me. He felt magic was on the cusp of something monumental; the young generation had started to find their footing, and he knew, as the subculture continued to change, that he was becoming an admired figure—that he had the power to create a wave if he put together something big. Madison had an idea: if he could round up the world's best talent into one cohesive group, he might be able to influence how people approached and consumed the craft and highlight some of the most revered young talent in the game. He wanted to prop up those he respected, and also be seen as the ringleader of the next generation of magicians.

He decided to create the52, a secret society of the most innovative performers and creators of illusion, deception, and mystery, and quickly found a handful that impressed him. They performed difficult maneuvers in new or unique ways, invented their own tricks and routines, and were savvy with how they marketed their brand of magic: slick videos posted on Instagram or YouTube, an enticing element of character embedded in their persona, and the chops to back it all up in person. They were paving their own path, not following the hokey formula of traditional hacks.

First, Madison asked his close friend Laura London to help recruit new members and launch the now-infamous club. Together, they became cofounders of the group. As one of Britain's most successful magicians, Laura is a television regular, and even once performed for Queen Elizabeth. She has spent her entire career proving that a woman's role in magic isn't limited to that of a scantily clad assistant; they can fool you as good as anyone else. The duo had been friends for a few years, and confided in each other, not only about how they wanted their careers to progress, but about how they hoped magic would mature in the years to come. Laura was pioneering a woman's place in magic, and Madison trusted her judgment more than anyone. He wanted someone's vision to complement his own. She was the perfect partner in crime.

The52 quickly became known as the new generation, the ones beginning to shake things up in the world of magic. They took the antiquated image of a magician and flipped it on its head. They vowed to no longer associate with the stereotypes of top hats and scarves, rabbits, and doves—lame crutches that can dumb down magic from an art form to a joke. To them, magic was something to be revered, and magicians could embody a modern mystique. "Every single person in the52 has something special about them," Laura told me, adding that some members are not necessarily magicians, but have contributed to the industry in other ways. They have inducted photographers, artists, a professional forger, hypnotists, and reformed card cheats. "Everyone we choose to become a member is an artist in their own way," she told me, "and they each have a specific role in the group."

Madison wanted membership to be a lifelong allegiance. As in *Fight Club,* one of his favorite films, where wearing a black eye to work and coughing up blood demonstrated your dedication to the group's ethos, he needed his inductees to prove their commitment to the52. With only fifty-two spots in the club, one member for each card in a deck, being inducted was a serious offer. As he began asking other magicians to join, assigning each member a corresponding playing card—their identity within the group—he tacked on another induction requirement: For it to be official, you had to get your card number and suit tattooed on the inside of your middle finger. Madison, the Nine of Clubs; Laura, the King of Diamonds; Ramsay, the Four of Spades; and so on. The other members obliged, never doubting Madison and Laura's vision.

But the group didn't make an official public announcement. Madison and Laura always wanted it to be shrouded in mystery, as a means, primarily, to garner some hype in the community. It was teased to the magic world only through photos of people's tattoos and, when Madison would speak about it, through a simple but provocative mantra: *Magic Is Dead*. Madison and Laura built a website for the52, but it's merely a landing page showcasing a single disclaimer: *By invite only*. For the hundreds of thousands of amateur magicians who follow the members on social media platforms like Instagram—where the inclusionary finger tattoos are shown off and the hashtag #the52 is a signal to the public of membership—there was very little to grasp in terms of what it all meant. But of course, that just added to its appeal.

Within comment threads on Instagram, I saw some followers refer to the group as the Illuminati of Magic, while others tried to figure out what it takes to become a member. Many asked pointedly what the club was all about. Some fans even got their own tattoos, thinking it automatically qualified them for membership. (It obviously does not.) In the end, no one really knew what it meant, aside from the fact that some of the best young magicians in the world were members, and that it was likely founded by Madison and Laura. It was cloaked in secrecy, with only cryptic details teased out to the masses. Was it a club? A quest? Or something more sinister? No one knew for sure. While the mystery and exclusivity sparked curiosity, it also heightened members' influence over their fans and followers. Other magicians respected them.

For the52, you are sought out by the founders based on your approach to the craft. It's that simple. It's not uncommon, too, for members to be recruited for more than a year before being asked to join. Many of the members not only perform magic professionally but also invent new tricks for other magicians, acting as private consultants, an occupation that predates Houdini, or to be sold on the public market through online retail shops.[*] These are roles that, although technically behind the scenes, really run the game in the world of magic. Ramsay and Madison are hired to do both of these things, while Laura dedicates herself mainly to performance.

Their take on magic has garnered nods of approval from the industry's most legendary performers, including Penn Jillette of the famed magic duo Penn & Teller, who told me, "I've seen the best magicians of my generation and none of them can touch the younger guys." He appreciates the ideology behind the52 and how it differs from flashy, mainstream magic. "Criss Angel wants to be seen as something supernatural," Penn said. "These guys in the52 want to be seen as artists."

When I first learned about the group, there were forty-four members, leaving eight remaining slots. Laura and Madison told me that they had an idea whom they'd choose, and what their roles would be, but they needed to finalize their plans. It was hyper-exclusive, and admitting new members was a serious undertaking. In Blackpool, I pressed for more details about the club and its plans, but Laura only smiled and said, "We are very, very close. You'll see when the time is right."

From my left, Madison leaned in and, in a clear, serious voice, said, "We are out to change magic forever."

---

[*] Tricks have been for decades a for-sale commodity; thousands of books have been published over the past century detailing methods and, more recently, these secretive and insular how-tos have made their way onto the internet.

4

LOCKED IN

The brain stem is the smallest part of your brain, about three inches long, roughly the size of your thumb. It plugs into your spinal cord and is composed of three parts: the midbrain, the pons, and the medulla oblongata. The midbrain oversees your vision, hearing, and eye and body movement. The pons assist in motor control and sensory analysis. The medulla maintains more vital bodily functions, such as breathing and heart rate. The body does its job correctly because of the brain stem, which is flanked by two arteries the size of a shoelace. Another, the width of a pencil, drives right up its center. Blood flows from your heart and into your shoelace-thin vertebral arteries before bottlenecking into your pencil-thick basilar artery. The point where your vertebral arteries and basilar artery meet, at the brain stem's base, is shaped like a wishbone, with eight smaller arteries branching off and wrapping around the brain stem itself. These little creeks of blood feed the brain stem, granting you the opportunity to live.

Because the brain stem is a direct extension of the spinal cord, it acts more like a relay center than a rod-and-piston. If your brain is an engine and the spinal cord its wheels, the brain stem is kind of like a transmission. It communicates some of the brain's most basic directives to the rest of your body. It tells it how to behave. The brain stem houses all the regulatory devices that power, oversee, and dictate how the body operates, and when blood circulation is cut off from the brain stem, the loss of these simple yet critical functions results in a very specific clinical diagnosis: *brain death*. Your body isn't necessarily dead—it still works, with the help of a machine—but your brain's ability to tell it what to do is kaput. Once the machine's plug is pulled, your heart will stop beating and your lungs will stop working (the medulla already choked to death in the back of your skull), and your brain will invariably starve itself of oxygen and you'll die. In a weird and ironic way, your brain will kill itself—an organ-specific suicide. It's kind of like drowning but without the necessity of water.

And, so, when that blood clot—a dark, knotted, disgusting black gremlin of a thing—dislodged from somewhere in my father's body and jammed itself dead center into his basilar artery, the brain stem's lifeline, we knew it was all over. It permanently damaged the midbrain, pons, and medulla oblongata (the poor, poor medulla), and cut off any semblance of communication between his brain and body—the two sides of the human anatomy that made him whole. He had the stroke at home but would endure four days of breathing through a machine (again: the poor, poor medulla) before he was officially pronounced dead. But to me, my father died in our living room on that clear, sunny, unusually crisp Saturday afternoon in May 2001. It was two and a half weeks before my fourteenth birthday, just a normal day for all of us—until everything went wrong.

There is an unspoken rule in entrepreneurial, blue-collar towns: if you want to get ahead in this world, you have to work Saturdays. They were basically part of the regular workweek for my dad, and went like this: up at five, chug a cup of coffee and smoke a few cigarettes while the truck warms up, be out the door by six, and, if you could help it, back home by two to do chores for the wife and play with the kids. Ambition was a drug for my father, and he always worked Saturdays. He had to. In May 2000, a year before his death, he and my mother moved us from the one-story ranch near the center of our small Massachusetts hometown to, on its outskirts, a big house in the woods. My mother painstakingly designed the home—a broad, two-story colonial with an airy, open kitchen and high-ceilinged den—for two years preceding its construction, which my father participated in from foundation to finishings. It was their dream home. It was where they were supposed to grow old together.

This Saturday in May was not unlike many others before it. Saturdays in spring consisted mainly of family time: catching up on homework, watching television, or running errands with Mom or Dad. It was a day so ordinary it became almost trivial. Sometimes, after my father came home from his half day of work, we would drive his truck to the dump and unload that week's worth of trash. Growing up, this was one of my favorite activities. I felt like a man helping Dad unload the truck. He would sometimes even let me drive after we finished. The road at the dump beelined from the landfill to its exit along a four-car-wide dirt track, a straight shot with no turns and very little obstacles to avoid. My father would slide the seat back and let me climb up onto his lap. He took care of the pedals, my hands on the wheel. He'd crawl along the dirt road, foot hovering over the brake while his hands—big, thick, blue-collar hands, the hands of a man I wanted to become—floated above mine, ready to divert disaster if needed.

But I was in eighth grade now—nearly fourteen. We had a lot of trash in the garage, I remember, and I hoped that, after dumping it, maybe he'd let me take the truck on my own, with us sitting next to each other as equals. So, I lounged around, waiting for two o'clock. On that day, he came home earlier than expected, maybe around noon. He looked sick, in pain even. The small sacks of skin under his eyes hung off his sockets as if filled with water. His face glowed an off-white, like old milk. He told my mother that he was going to take a nap for a few minutes. Maybe that would help, he said. He went into the living room and lay down on the couch. I was in the kitchen when I heard him stagger to his feet and cry out for my mother in a slurred grumble, as if his mouth was full of rocks: *Pam.*

He hobbled toward the kitchen but fell into the wall before he could reach its tiled floor. He vomited everywhere. My mother screamed, latched on to his shoulders, and dragged him back over to the couch. She grabbed the phone and dialed 911. She gave the dispatcher our address but was afraid that they'd have trouble finding the house. She kneeled down next to my father, catching his vomit in a bucket, and told me to wait for the ambulance at the end of the driveway. I bolted out the front door, cut through our front yard, and ran down the driveway. I wore only a T-shirt and the shadows of the trees were thick and black. I felt very small standing there in the darkness thrown down by the trees. It was cold, and I was scared that the ambulance wouldn't see me. I stood out there for what seemed like a long while. Maybe they were lost, I thought. I heard the siren, a far-off screaming, before I saw the lights come around the bend. I waved them into our driveway like a parking lot attendant and chased after it back to the house. The lights flashed so bright that I had to look at the ground as I ran.

The eldest of five children, my father was born and raised in Middletown, Ohio. It's a foul, poverty-stricken city, the shell of a former steel manufacturing hub, a land of lost hope. My father grew up in a housing project, a broken home plagued by substance abuse and domestic violence. His father left his mother, Darlene, when my dad was a young kid. She drank and dated, a lot of both, after that. The home was a revolving door of different men who always treated her poorly. His family was quintessential white trash. And he always knew, if he wanted to survive, he had to get out.

In his early twenties, he moved to Houston, where he met my mother. She was tending bar in that junky roadside shack, having just finished her cross-country road trip. He took a stool and they talked. After her shift was over they talked some more. They shot a few games of pool together. They saw each other the next day and the day after that. They quickly fell in love and, one day, closed their eyes and threw their collective finger down on a map: LaFollette, Tennessee. They packed their bags and moved. They got married and quickly relocated to nearby Knoxville, where my father worked construction jobs and took business classes at the University of Tennessee. This was also where, in 1987, I was born. This event sent them back to Massachusetts, where my mother grew up. She had a big family, with a slew of brothers and sisters, and they saw an accessible support system while they built a life together. They raised my sister (born a few years later) and me in a series of small, dumpy houses in the area while my father started and expanded his tile business. They kept expenses low and saved money to build the big house in the woods. It was the perfect plan: a real family, the dream narrative, a true love story.

My father's family, who still lived in Ohio, kept in touch with us over the phone and through birthday and Christmas cards, but I didn't get to see them all that often. I loved my grandmother, Darlene, with her hillbilly accent and warm demeanor, who mailed me dollar-store trinkets and candy and whom my father flew from Middletown to Massachusetts to visit us whenever he had extra money. My father had a love-hate relationship with his mother. He hated what she represented—that selfish and self-destructive mess he came from, a stigma he found repulsive—but he couldn't help

but take care of her. My father was deaf in his right ear, a consequence, he always said, from battling mumps as a child. After he
died, my mother reviewed his medical record and found that the
real reason he was deaf was that, when he was a kid, Darlene hit
him over the head with a cast-iron frying pan. He never told her
the truth.

Darlene also acted as an anchor between him and his siblings
who, by the time I was born, had themselves succumbed to drink
and drugs. When I was an infant, he took me back to Middletown
so the family could meet me. We went to his brother's house, a
filthy trailer on the edge of town. Everyone in the house was high
on Quaaludes. My aunt clutched her pocketbook, nearly caress-
ing it, never letting it out of her sight. It was full of pills. Someone took me (my mother doesn't remember who) and placed me
facedown on the mattress in the bedroom. I couldn't breathe—
blue lips and purple cheeks. I nearly suffocated. My father's family
didn't seem to mind that he continued to try to distance himself,
at least geographically, from his identity as a lower-class Ohioan.
(He still couldn't shake off his Rust Belt vernacular, though, and
I chuckled and poked fun at his odd turns of phrase: how he pronounced "guitar" with two hard syllables, or how, when riled up,
he'd exclaim, "I seen it!")

My grandmother, however, seemed proud of her son and what
he was trying to become: a successful businessman, a model father, the rock of a stable home. She knew, deep down, that the
shabby small-town life in which she raised him was a disease and
that, if you stayed around too long, it would find its way into your
blood. She couldn't be angry at him for wanting to get out. When
I was nine, her house caught fire and she died. I came home from
school and found the kitchen table in our small home near the
center of town stacked with my father's laundry, an open suitcase
on the floor. He crouched down and hugged me, and we cried. I
remember wanting to know if the fire had burned her. He never

answered my question. In retrospect, one good thing came from the fire: she wouldn't be there for her son's death.

When my father was in the hospital, lying there like a pile of bricks stuffed into a bag of skin, my mother told me, "He can hear you. He can hear you. You can talk to him, Ian. He can hear you." I remember thinking how absurd that sounded. *Look at him*, I thought to myself. *He's already dead*.

But he wasn't.

In fact, he was very much alive inside that swollen, lifeless body. He had locked-in syndrome, a rare by-product of a stroke within the brain stem. The midbrain, pons, and medulla are no longer able to tell your body what to do, but, cognitively, the brain continues to function without error. You are, in effect, a prisoner within your own body. I had no idea that my father suffered from such a horrifying condition until my mother sent me his medical records years later. I've never heard anyone in my family speak of it. It was a secret that died with him. I asked my mother why she never told me. She let out a long sigh and said, "I don't know." And that was that.

It took fifteen years for me to find out that my father, lying in that awful hospital bed, was fully aware of everything going on around him, a man shackled inside the dark cave of his now-dead brain stem. I can't help but wonder if he accepted his fate, knowing that we were planning on letting him die, that the plug would eventually be pulled, that everything he had worked for had culminated to such a cruel end. What conclusions did he come to about his own life? What regrets did he have? A few years after he died, my mother confided in me that my father suffered from depression, which peaked in the years after his mother died. He carried a contempt in his heart for so long, and he tried to fend off his guilt by deliberately drowning himself in work and the ambition to build the big house in the woods. Yet he saved the last voice mail she left him and, over the years, listened to it over and over. A fracture between him and my mother opened up and continued to grow. He drank more and talked less. I sometimes would find him drunk and asleep in our basement. I'd help him up to bed.

C'mon, Dad, let's go to sleep.

One night, a month before he died, my mother found him staring at family photographs that hung in the hallway off the living room. He was looking at a photograph of himself as a baby, affixed next to one of me at the same age. She walked over and put her hands on his neck. They stood in the hallway and embraced each other. "Six months ago, I wouldn't have cared if I lived or died," he told her. "But today, I care. I want to live."

I wonder now how much of his past he replayed while he was lying in that hospital bed, trapped in his own body, or how much of a future he tried to envision for his family, a future he knew he wouldn't be alive to participate in. We kept him on the machine for four days. On the last day, my mother stood over him and grabbed his hand. She told him that he wasn't going to get better. She asked him if he wanted it to be over. *Blink once for yes and twice for no.* He blinked once. She told him that she loved him, and to get ready for the most incredible journey of his life. She pulled the plug.

He died on a Tuesday, just after four in the afternoon. The nursing staff walked me out of the room before they took him off the machine and, when I reentered, my mother's hand resting gently on his chest, his mouth slack and free of tubes and wires, I knew he was gone. A sickly green coated his skin like bruised fruit. I ran over and dove onto his chest, throwing my weight on top of his body. I grabbed his hospital gown and screamed. I am not sure who pulled me off him, but they dragged me into the hallway. I fell to the floor and howled. We didn't stay in the hospital for much longer. Everyone just wanted to go home. Some family and friends came to our house, but that night, after they left, the house was cold and quiet. My mother quickly went to bed, but I couldn't sleep. I walked into the living room and saw that my father's vomit had stained the carpet. I took a paper towel from the kitchen and scrubbed, but the stain wouldn't come out. It was permanent.

5

A BREAK FROM REALITY

I became obsessed with magic after my trip to Blackpool.

As winter turned to spring, and spring to summer, I rarely went a day without a deck of cards in my hands. I didn't have a hardened ambition to become a top-notch professional magician, though. To me, if I could learn some sleight of hand, dig into the methodology of how effects are created, and nail down a stable of tricks that I could readily perform, I would come to understand magic and deception in a more profound capacity. It was funny, too: The handling techniques my mother taught me with a deck of cards were becoming more useful the more I practiced tricks. I was surely digging deeper than what was needed for a magazine article, but I couldn't help it. There was something fascinating about how dedicated these people were to magic. And, with them giving me such unprecedented access, the most important thing for me, really, was cementing a connection with this new community. I wanted to see the world through the same lens as my new comrades.

I kept in regular touch with Ramsay, Madison, Laura, and

Jeremy. They laid out the foundations of sleight of hand, taught me beginner card tricks and routines, and explained basic magic theory as to why some effects are more impactful or deceptive than others. Madison sent me his entire library of tutorials—hours of video instruction and hundreds of pages of text—and I would practice at my desk, or on the subway, or anywhere else I could handle a deck of cards. Every few weeks, I'd force Jeremy onto Skype to critique my mechanics. "You're getting there," he'd say when I'd show him my progress. Or, when I nailed a move, I'd inspire a screech: "Look at you, you certifiable badass!"

It had been a few months since my trip to Blackpool, and, with steady work and some semblance of financial stability (in addition to more magazine assignments, I caught a stint on a weed farm in Oregon, which is a story for another time), I had made my way back to Brooklyn. As soon as I returned, Ramsay called me and told me I should link up with a New York–based member of the52: Xavior Spade (the Three of Spades). Another popular figure in the magic community, Xavior is a quintessential move monkey, a sleight-of-hand artist dedicated to mastering and innovating the hardest moves a person can do with a deck of cards. He is most famous for his flawless pass—where a stack of cards is undetectably and instantaneously moved from the top of the deck to the bottom, or vice versa, or from one area to another within the deck—as well as many other ultradifficult sleights. He also owned Lost Art Magic, a small but respected online retail outlet. After hearing about him from the gang, and seeing his chops on Instagram, I had to meet him.

Xavior rolled up in front of my house in his tiny red hatchback. He popped out of the driver's seat, a Newport perched between his lips, and gave me a wave. He was a hefty dude, black-bearded, with aviator glasses folded into the collar of his T-shirt and an iWatch on his wrist that intermittently spat out text message and Instagram notifications. He took a deck of cards from his pocket.

"Let's grab something to eat and jam a bit," he said. We walked down the street to one of my favorite sandwich shops, ordered a bite, and sat down.

"Ramsay said you grew up in the city," I said.

"Yeah, dude. Jamaica, Queens. I grew up in the hood. I'm still out there, but I got a really nice place now, and I am able to run Lost Art Magic out of my house—got all my video equipment there and shit. It makes it all super easy." He munched on his steak-and-cheese sandwich.

"I mean, I don't want to assume anything," I said, "but how does a guy like you get into magic? It seems super random, to be honest."

Xavior laughed. "Bro, you're telling me. It's weird to think about it now, but when I was a kid, I was in a gang—you had to be, going to schools in the city and shit. And I'm Puerto Rican, so it's even worse. You have to run with your crew and do what they do. And I had to be a tough guy, you know? I had to be hard, in order to survive, so that's what I did. One day, I was at school, and I saw this kid in the hall do a card trick. I walked up to him and said, 'If you don't tell me how you did that trick, I am going to beat the shit out of you.'"

"Holy shit," I said, laughing.

"I know. I was such a little fucker. But that's how you had to be, you know? And it's still with me, that mentality; people say I'm the Asshole of Magic because I tell it like it is. But back then, after that kid showed me a few things, I was hooked. I started buying magic books and learning. And, after a while, I realized that magic could be a way out of this life I was falling into. All the gangs and shit. I didn't want to do that. Magic gave me an opportunity that I didn't know was there. I could live a life where I wasn't looking over my shoulder, where I wasn't worried about someone shooting me or some shit. It was an escape from the reality that I knew—my life—which was the streets."

"Was your family supportive of magic, you know, as an alternative to being in a gang?"

"Yeah, of course, you know—anything for your kid to have a better life. But it was hard because, when I was a teenager, my mother got cancer. I used to go to her bedside and perform for her. And I could tell it made her happy, allowed her to escape for a bit. In that moment, she wasn't dying of cancer. In that moment, she wasn't sick. She wasn't the mother of an asshole kid who was hurting people with drugs. I think magic helps fill a void that people can't explain. It makes you feel, if even for a moment, something that you can't feel anywhere else. And for me, magic became a new life. It was the life I never thought I could have, that I never thought I deserved. Just before she passed away, I booked my first paying gig. Once I made that first dollar, I sold all my guns and quit the gang. I never looked back," he said. "I can say, without a doubt, that magic saved my life."

"It seems to be a theme with magic, you know? I'm starting to see that it can do remarkable things."

"It's true, man. It's really true. And it's great that you're wanting to get into it. Have you been learning any new moves?"

"Well," I said, "just small stuff. My mother was a poker player, so I've always been comfortable with a deck of cards in my hands, but some of the moves are super hard."

Xavior chuckled. "We've all been there, dude. But c'mon," he said, pushing his plate off to the side. "Grab your deck. Let me show you a few things."

The more I dug into magic, the more I began to move past seeing it as a story. As the weeks went on, it started to become a lifestyle. It was as if I had been swept up by a rushing wave, something I couldn't resist. I didn't want to just write about it for a magazine and be done; I wanted to keep going. I wanted the adventure to continue. I wanted to learn more, for it to maybe change me the same way it had changed others. But, as time went on, a strange tension appeared. The more methods and secrets I learned the less, well, *magical* tricks became. They went from a moment of astonishment thrust within with a memorable experience, like a fat strike of lightning cracking open the sky during a thunderstorm, to just a series of moves, jargon choked and technical. I spent weeks still wanting to be the fool, to keep feeling like I had with Laura in that dark alley. Magic is beautiful because its inner workings—its organs and bones and muscles—are hidden from public view, encased in a skin of deceit. It's an art form built upon the concealment of information; secrecy is a core element of magic's DNA. It's what makes it come alive.

As I kept practicing I realized that this understanding of magic's blueprint is what I admired most about my new gang of friends. They were an outlier on the artistic spectrum; instead of clay or paint or dance, they worked in the medium of the human mind, knowing full well that they could reach in, twist some hidden knob, and alter a person's concept of reality.

With every passing day, I became more like them, if not in skill then in mentality. It wasn't that they could no longer fool me— I was still getting roasted all the time—but they could now enthrall me by their sheer dedication. I was wowed by the time and energy it takes to become truly *good* at magic, and to really understand its potential as an art form: to leave someone flabbergasted, to make a lasting impression, to create an authentic *moment*. What pulled me to them, more than anything, more than magic as a tangible thing, was the fact that I felt like I was falling in with people who were like me—a family of misfits, that we understood each other, that being drawn to deception says something about your outlook on the world. A love for magic maybe forms a bond not found in other passions. And so, I kept on.

Deception is a powerful psychological tool that we carry with us throughout our entire lives, and the grip starts early: it's scientifically proven that children learn to lie before the age of three. Moreover, many children by age six can deceive adults without being detected. "As a species, we are so well practiced in the art of deception that it comes to us almost as naturally and effortlessly as breathing," David Livingstone Smith writes in *Why We Lie: The Evolutionary Roots of Deception and the Unconscious Mind.* "Human society is a 'network of lies and deceptions' that would collapse under the weight of too much honesty." Robert C. Solomon, former professor of philosophy at the University of Texas at Austin, mirrored this sentiment in *Lying and Deception in Everyday Life.* "Deception is sometimes not a vice but a social virtue," he writes, "and systematic deception is an essential part of the order of the (social) world." University of Massachusetts psychologist Robert Feldman found that, on average, people tell three lies for every ten minutes of conversation.

"Lying is universal," Mark Twain once wrote. "We *all* do it; we all *must* do it."

A completely unique thing happens, however, when deception is applied within the context of performance. A new goal forms: astonishment. In the months after going to Blackpool it came to me that, throughout our lives, we are continually searching for a sense of mystery and an aspect of wonder—results of the "honest" deceptions seen in magic.

Sit down with any parent and bring up the topic and I'm sure you'll get similar anecdotes of their kids going through a "magician phase": the magic kit they begged for, the nightly living room shows, the scarves and top hats, the awkward-but-lovable card tricks, the glimmer in their eye when they correctly performed a routine. And, sure, maybe it was just a summer-long fad, but maybe it would stick with them for their entire lives. "There's a moment in your life when you realize the difference between illusion and reality and that you're being lied to," Teller of Penn & Teller once said, referring to childhood figures such as Santa Claus and the Easter Bunny. "[But] if you're sufficiently preoccupied with the *power* of a lie, a falsehood, an illusion, you remain interested in magic tricks." With magic, anything seems possible. With magic, deception has a happy ending.

Deception, misdirection, and ideological sleight of hand plays out all around us—in politics, romance, advertising, drama, media, sports, the list goes on.* And the instances are becoming more and more mainstream, and higher concept. In Netflix's 2017 documentary series *Abstract: The Art of Design*, award-winning stage designer Es Devlin described using magic tricks to control light during U2's stage show. Similarly, she recounted how she used mirrors in the production of *Macbeth* and the play *The Nether*. "People who came out of [*The Nether*] described having seen a glass box, but actually there was no box. There was nothing there." The mirrors she used altered the audiences' depth perception— a classic illusion that has been utilized in magic for centuries.†

On the critically acclaimed docuseries *Chef's Table*, Grant Achatz of the Michelin-starred restaurant Alinea described how patrons enter his Chicago-based hot spot through a hallway soaked in red light. It seems as if the corridor goes on for nearly a hundred

---

* Calculated trickery is even utilized by man's best friend. A 2017 University of Zurich study proved that dogs deliberately deceive their owners to get what they want. "These results . . . indicate the flexibility of dogs to adjust their behaviour and that they are able to use tactical deception," the findings read.

† Legendary playwright David Mamet once said, "Magic is using the mind to lead itself to its own defeat. The same thing is true in drama: You set up a proposition, so the audience is going ahead of you, trying to figure out what's going to happen next. So, at the end, just as in a magic trick, it's surprising and inevitable—inevitable because you knew it was going to happen and surprising because it happened in an unusual way."

feet, but the entrance to the dining room is only eight paces in front of you. It's the first of many cognitive and sensory illusions embedded within Achatz's dining experience.

"You realize they are totally going to mess with you," said food critic Francis Lam in the film, laughing giddily, visibly replaying the experience in his mind. "They are totally going to screw with your brain. And for however long you're there, you really don't know what's going to happen." Lam explained that, when conceiving a dish, Achatz asks himself unorthodox questions: *Can I make that float? Can I make that invisible? Can I hide the food in front of the guest?*

"I want the guest to have a sense of wonderment—what's going to happen next?" said Achatz, sitting in Alinea's dining room, dressed in his chef whites. "You should expect the unexpected. At every turn there's a little twist. The thing that's important for me is that the guest has the *aha* moment, where they feel that they have discovered something." For Achatz, the concept behind his world-famous restaurant is simple: "It's a magic show," he said, staring directly into the camera.

The government has even hired magicians due to their knowledge of deception. One of the most interesting examples occurred in 1953 when Sidney Gottlieb, chief of the Central Intelligence Agency's Technical Services Division, contacted magician John Mulholland. He had a special request. The United States was neck-deep in the Cold War and, in response to Russia's continued use of clandestine tactics, Dr. Gottlieb was asked to oversee MK-ULTRA, a highly classified (and extremely controversial) operation tasked with developing innovative ways to get a leg up on their communist adversaries. In the program file, CIA director Allen Dulles instructed Gottlieb to develop projects for "research and development of chemical, biological, and radiological materials capable of employment in clandestine operations to control human behavior."

Gottlieb, however, saw a snag in his assignment. He could develop these new techniques—including exploding cigars, poisoned pens, and hallucinogenic sprays—without much hassle. But if they couldn't be applied in the field, they would be useless. The CIA's team of field officers and undercover agents needed a how-to manual regarding the implementation of these new tools. In Gottlieb's eyes, a magician would be the ideal teacher: a master of illusion who could deceive you right in front of your face and walk away clean. That's when he called famed magician John Mulholland and gave him free rein on MK-ULTRA Subproject Number 4: Operational Applications of the Art of Deception.

Gottlieb told Mulholland to consider "the applications of the magician's techniques to clandestine operations, such techniques to include surreptitious delivery of materials, deceptive movements and actions to cover normally prohibited activities, influencing choices and perceptions of other persons, various forms of disguise, covert signaling systems, etc." Mulholland developed two manuals: *Some Operational Applications of the Art of Deception* and *Recognition Signals*. The first was based on close-up, sleight-of-hand moves used by magicians, adjusted slightly for in-field use, such as concealing a vial of poisonous powder in the hand that could be subsequently dumped into an opposing spy's drink. The second was a list of covert communication tactics that could be used by CIA operatives. Mulholland was also introduced, under suspicious circumstances, to Frank Olsen, who is alleged to have been a guinea pig for the CIA's LSD experiments and subsequently assassinated by the agency in an inside job. (Mulholland is mentioned in *Wormwood*, a Netflix documentary about Olsen, directed by Errol Morris.)

Outside of Mulholland's specific contributions to the covert intelligence community, principles conceived by magicians were utilized in many other high-stakes political situations. One of the most famous is the legendary deception from 1980 when six U.S.

diplomats were covertly smuggled out of Iran under the guise of Canadian filmmakers. The story was re-created in Ben Affleck's Oscar-winning film *Argo*. "[CIA Technical Operations Officer] Tony Mendez's improvisation was performed within carefully rehearsed scenes, meticulous paperwork, backstopped stories, and exhaustive research," wrote magic historian Jim Steinmeyer in a review of Mendez's memoir. "If the six Americans seemed to saunter effortlessly through the Tehran airport, it was because the stage had been beautifully set and the scene masterfully presented. It was a demonstration of Kellar the Magician's famous boast that, once he had an audience under his spell, he could 'march an elephant across the stage and no one would notice.'" The CIA and British intelligence outfit MI6 used similar techniques for more than 150 operations, the latter even hiding covert maps and other bits of coded intelligence within playing cards that were then shipped out to agents.*

---

* Another strange and juicy tidbit of magic's influence in politics: Matt Patterson, a former professional magician, applied his background in deception to his support for Donald Trump while the reality-television personality and businessman campaigned for president. While a working magician, Patterson self-published a book on the craft. *The New Yorker*'s Peter Hessler parenthetically exhibited lines from the literature to contextualize Patterson's political ideology: "The manual was written long before Patterson entered politics, but any candidate would recognize the wisdom of sleight of hand. ('A good friend once told me that the only difference between a salesman and a con-man is that a salesman has confidence in his product'). In July 2016, Patterson bet a friend two hundred dollars that Trump would win the Presidency. His conservative Washington friends didn't take Trump seriously, but Patterson believed that the candidate's ability to connect with voters was uncanny. ('Remember that you will be performing for people of varying degrees of education, in varying degrees of sobriety, and your routines must be easily understood by all of them')." Patterson's background and unique approach to politics proved successful: He held a brief stint as the Trump campaign's Colorado regional field director and now works for conservative nonprofits in Washington, D.C.

But deception is not something that exists in a vacuum. It is contingent upon human interaction; it's a by-product of social intercourse. "The lie is a matter of mutual engagement and not just a malevolent act perpetrated by one person upon another," Robert C. Solomon wrote. Deception experienced in everyday life binds us in ways that we do not notice and sometimes to extents that we do not understand. The same goes for a great magic trick. Moreover, magic—the romanticism of the inexplicable, the awe and admiration of the unexpected—is an underlying force in how we view the world and its myriad possibilities. We are all on an instinctive search for the extraordinary. It's a universal truth: all humans want to be amazed. And, ironically enough, deception is a useful tool to achieve this effect.

Like social deception, the most important facet of magic is this: a magic trick cannot exist, even in its most basic form, without someone on which to perform it. Magic's purpose is not initially predicated upon the execution of a trick, but rather a mutually consented interaction between magician and spectator. Magic's existence is contingent upon someone willing to be deceived. Moreover, magic is exceptional because a performer isn't merely trying to create a fantasy for a spectator (like movies or novels, which are also illusions of truth), but striving to alter their sense of *objective* reality.

People likewise instill a profound element of trust in the magician. They want that person to lie to them in a way they have never been lied to before, and in a way that may bend their understanding of what is possible in the world. Even if we know that it's just a trick, that there is some sort of hidden explanation, the momentary detachment from reality felt through a magic trick—through the art of being deceived—is riveting. It's captivating. It's unlike any other experience with which a human can take part. A gorgeous piece of magic is something we will always carry around with us, and the moment of astonishment is something we will never forget. It becomes a crease in your heart. Our natural fascination with deception is part of what makes us human. It's no wonder, then, that people naturally gravitate toward magic. It is the only situation where people willingly say, without hesitation, *Yes, please trick me, please lie to me—and don't tell me how you did it.*

And let's face it: Who, even as an adult, doesn't want a break from reality once in a while?

6

A VESSEL FOR
SOMETHING BIGGER

During our trip to Blackpool, Ramsay was employed by Murphy's Magic, the largest wholesaler of magical effects in the world. His main job was to invent tricks for Murphy's online store, which sold exclusive offerings and products produced by other, smaller companies.

Red Pill was one of Ramsay's most successful creations for Murphy's. For the trick's climax, the spectator's chosen card appears faceup inside the cellophane wrapper of a different, sealed deck—a deck they were holding in their hands for the duration of the trick. Ramsay then gives his audience member a choice: you can either tear the wrapper off to inspect the card—and have no proof that this magical event occurred—or keep the deck sealed as evidence of what you've witnessed. To many, the trick was truly indicative of what a magical moment should be—an enthralling and emotional experience, truly astonishing. Everyone was talking about it on online forums, people were sharing performances of it on Instagram, buyers approached Ramsay in public to congratulate him on the release, and fans were flocking to his social media pages. Inventing magic is the community's ultimate stamp of approval. More than high-paying performance or starring in your own television show, creating new magic is a way of legitimizing your skill, and Red Pill's popularity thrust Ramsay into the limelight as an important figure of magic's next generation.

When guys like Ramsay or Madison (or other members of the52) release an effect that they have invented, fans clamor to buy it. These tricks range from simple sleight-of-hand moves for $10 to more complex card routines for $25. Single-run printings of physical books, exclusive gimmicks, and other high-end products can fetch upwards of $100. For decades, the secrets behind magic tricks were disseminated two ways: in person and through books. But that all changed with the internet. Now magicians can just visit an online magic shop and pay to see how individual tricks are done. This also allows personal brands to be built, amplified by the accessibility and intimacy of social media.

Custom decks of cards have also become a prominent offering. Famous magicians like Ramsay, Madison, and other members of the52 come out with signature decks—think Michael Jordan's shoes for Nike—whose sales numbers reach into the tens of thousands. Many of these are intricately designed, with foil stamping or embossed boxes cast in thick stock.* Ramsay's first namesake deck, Memento Mori—highlighted by colorful, low-poly-design skulls—dropped on Murphy's store just after our trip to Blackpool and sold out instantly. Subsequent runs led to sales well north of 50,000 decks. At ten dollars a pop, that's nothing to sneeze at, and with magicians needing fresh decks all the time, high-quality cus-

---

* There are a few companies that print custom playing cards for magicians, but the United States Playing Card Company is by far the most popular. Founded in 1837, USPCC is the largest producer of playing cards in the world. They crank out 85 million decks a year—that's roughly 4.7 billion individual cards. If you ran them end to end in a straight line, you'd be able to circle the globe ten times.

tom cards have become a backbone of the industry. Only a handful of other magicians who release their own namesake decks drive numbers that high—Dan and Dave Buck, Chris "Orbit" Brown, and Alex Pandrea (another member of the52; he's the Seven of Spades), for example. Madison's decks, which he releases through Murphy competitor Ellusionist, also juice sales above 50,000.

Over the years, Madison has released dozens of versions of his namesake cards—stamped with his custom logo, the typical portraits on the court cards swapped with his face and those of his friends. Madison is always the king of diamonds (if you look closely, the Nine of Clubs, his identity in the52, is stamped on the king's palm). His cards solidified his personal brand as one of the strongest in the magic community. Having your name on a deck of cards that other people use is a big deal—it is a tangible object that people can buy and use to show their support of an individual magician—and strong personal brands have become a driving force in modern magic in a way that is as powerful as that of a YouTube star or an Instagram model.

By summer 2016, Ramsay became a hot commodity. His social media presence exploded, his skills as a photographer and self-marketer became more refined, and his product offerings to the magic community proved lucrative. And so it was fitting for Ellusionist to offer Ramsay a job, to help with marketing and trick development. They successfully poached him from Murphy's and he joined the Ellusionist team. He was now working alongside some of the strongest creators in the industry, including his friend Daniel Madison and other members of the52.

Buying and selling magic is a convoluted system heightened by the fact that, with online stores, tricks are no longer available exclusively at brick-and-mortar magic shops. When you're dealing in secrets, especially via the internet, things can get complicated. "We are magicians selling to magicians, right? So, if you can fool them, then they are going to buy it," Adam Wilber, general manager at Ellusionist—Madison and Ramsay's boss—told me back in Blackpool. "And of course, I am not going to expose it: 'This is how the trick is done. Do you want to buy it now?' It doesn't make sense." In essence, a magician will buy an effect online and not know the method—the secret to how it's done—until they've paid in full. "That's usually the fine line," Adam said. "How much do we show without giving it away?"

If done right, however, a single effect can make serious dough. Adam himself created PYRO, a $174 gimmick that allows a magician to shoot fireballs from an open palm. It has sold over 20,000 units since debuting in 2014 and raked in over $3.5 million for the company. Big-hit gimmicks, well-taught card routines, and custom decks from the community's best-known magicians have made the online magic retail sector a multi-million-dollar industry.

A good chunk of time and energy is put into the marketing of all of this, too. These businesses are selling a product, after all. When a magician goes on Ellusionist or another online store to buy a trick (there are many companies to choose from, all with their own brand and style of offering), it's presented to them as a trailer video, many with high production values. For PYRO, Adam is standing on a cliff at the edge of the desert. Dramatic music and graphics weave into the footage. Adam wears aviator sunglasses and an Audi R8 roars by. "You want to be a superhero?" he says, pointing to the camera. "This is PYRO." That trailer racked up more than 1.5 million views on YouTube and has been reposted by a host of viral-video and tech-gadget websites. It's a strange caveat that has forced itself into modern-day magic: to be a successful magician or magic retailer, you also have to be savvy with photography and video production.

Historically, many of magic's most successful illusions have become instant for-sale commodities. In 1921, the British illusionist P. T. Selbit debuted Sawing Through a Woman, the quintessential woman-in-a-box stage illusion that would instantly captivate the world and forever change stage magic. After word spread, American magician Horace Goldin claimed the idea was his and, in June of the same year, presented his own version in New York City. Six months later, in early 1922, Goldin began selling the method and necessary apparatus for $175 ($2,500 in today's money). You could also buy a how-to book for just five bucks.

Obviously, all of this is very new. Magic has only recently come to be dominated by young social-media-savvy artists, selling their wares with slick presentations online as they blow up hokey stereotypes and replace them with the belief that their profession is a truly modern craft. It seemed like magic was going through a much-needed renaissance, and I wanted to be there to soak it all in, to document the evolution and rub shoulders with the players who had become my friends.

Every few weeks, Madison and I would jump on Skype to catch up. It would usually be nighttime in England when he'd call, and I rarely had any notice. Madison wasn't the kind of guy who planned his day—it certainly went against his brand. Our talks ran the gamut. They were all rooted in magic, of course, but were free-ranging and philosophical. We talked about magic as an art form and Madison's opinions of deception and other magicians. Many lasted well over an hour: him talking, weaving from subject to subject; me listening, trying to understand his ideas while articulating my own points of view. One night, while I was doing the dishes after eating dinner, he called me.

"What's going on, dude?" I asked.

"Nothing much, man. Just been thinking."

"Thinking?"

"Yeah, you know. About my career, my place in all this. I think about it a lot."

"What do you mean? You're on top of the world."

"Well, I've always thought that magic is a vessel for something bigger," he said. "Like, I sometimes feel misrepresented by being labeled a magician. I've always wanted to be seen as a performance artist, more than anything else," he continued. "David Blaine did it. I think that's why he and I get each other." I heard that he and Blaine were close friends but hearing him speak about one of magic's most iconic figures made me feel like I was in on a secret.

"What do you mean?" I asked. "Are you saying Blaine isn't really a magician?"

"Well, it's complicated, you know? He did the street magic specials to make enough money, so he could do the performance art," he continued. *Frozen in Time* and *Vertigo*. To get to that level, he had to do the magic thing."*

"I mean, it's like writing," I told Madison. "It's like any other artistic pursuit—your career will evolve over time." He exhaled slowly, filling the receiver with static. He was still fixated on the environment in which he had found himself: the magic industry, something that he understood but with which he didn't truly connect. He always came back to trying to find his own role in a world in which he feels out of place. Madison is obsessed with deception but not necessarily magic. To him, they are two different things.

"I stay away from magicians, to keep it pure," he said. "I only hang with Ramsay and Blaine and a few others. That's it. At one time, I had four hundred to five hundred tricks that I could do, that I had mastered. But at the end of the day there were only six

---

* I remember reading an old article in *The New Yorker* where Blaine said, "All my work is about honesty. Magic card tricks—we have to get beyond that. If magic is just magicians doing card tricks to impress other magicians— I'm not interested in that anymore. I don't want magic that looks real. What I want are real things that feel like magic."

of them that meant anything. I found my way to those six, and now I know, if I meet someone, those are the only six I will ever need to show them."

"It still feels like, to me, you're getting something out of this as an art form," I said.

"But is there any more excitement in knowing and mastering all that an art form has to offer? What's *new* there? It's like, you just turned up and started asking questions; it was all new and exciting to you," he said, adding that he always respects relationships that sprout organically. "It's just one of those natural things." Madison drew in a breath and let out a puff of laughter. He was clearly thinking of something, but I couldn't tell what. A moment passed, and he said, "What I have enjoyed seeing most, though, is your connection to magic and what you'll get from it—and what we'll get from you."

A few days later, I headed back to Portsmouth, New Hampshire— this time, just to visit. My air mattress was still in the office building and, in a strange way, I enjoyed reliving my carefree months of squatting. I thought about my conversation with Madison while I was there. His words swirled in my head. What did he mean, *What we'll get from you?* Had I been designated some sort of role? It was a strange, stressful feeling, like my friends had an assignment for me that I wasn't yet aware of.

I went swimming every day, to shock my system. I'd drop down to my knees in the shallows of the coast, the sun beating down on my back, and close my eyes. The undertow would pull the water out, its surface falling from my chest to my thighs just before the wave came crashing down, sending me under, throwing me to the ground. I never brought my phone to the beach—just a book and a towel. I'd leave everything else in the car. One day I stayed out on the sand for longer than normal, reading and sleeping. When I got back to my car, I checked my phone. Madison had sent me a text message.

We have the52 deck in the works, but I don't want to print it until we have a full deck, with everyone in, so that we can get each person's name on their related card. I'd love for you to be in. Would you join, and get the tattoo?

"Holy shit," I said to myself. I didn't know how to respond. My heart raced. I began to text back:

Wow.
I don't know what to say.
Of course, I'll join. It would be an honor.
I'm a little speechless, to be honest. Haha.
So, what's my new identity? Which card?

Madison responded a few minutes later:

Ha, don't think too much. Let me list the cards that aren't taken, and we can choose one. You'll be a monster of a member, your role in this is bigger than you think. Thank you for being a part of it. Welcome to the underground.

It was settled the next day: I would become the Two of Clubs. Madison told me that no one aside from Laura knew that I was now a member.

"Keep it to yourself," he told me over the phone. "Don't tell anyone."

7

CHEAT

Jeremy Griffith called Laura London not long after he picked me up at Los Angeles International Airport. Jeremy had invited me to check out the West Coast magic scene for a few days before driving to Las Vegas for Magic Live, the largest magic convention in the United States. Ramsay planned to fly from Canada and join us for the road trip.

We sat in bumper-to-bumper traffic as we chatted with Laura on speakerphone. She had just started her one-woman show, *CHEAT*, a residency performance in Edinburgh, Scotland, based on a fictitious female card hustler. For the show, the stage is adorned with a square felt table surrounded by wooden chairs—a makeshift gambling parlor. A framed photograph of Geraldine Hartmann, the female cardsharp character, sits bathed in light from a lamp on an end table off to the side. After the audience takes their seats, Laura enters the stage in a black Prohibition-era cocktail dress embellished in translucent beads and silver sequins, her bright red hair cutting a line just under her jaw. She's holding Geraldine's diary. She invites two spectators onto the stage for a game of cards and, as if sitting for a true backroom poker game, embodies Geraldine's character: a whiskey-slugging cardsharp who can pull aces out of the deck at will and deal winning hands to any player of her choosing.

There are elements of theater throughout the show, with old-timey music and character-driven monologues. It's a magical twist on vaudeville, a throwback to magic's golden age. Laura scripted the entire performance herself. The finale, she told us, really knocks the audience on their asses. "The greatest gift in cards is to know what your opponent is thinking," she said as Jeremy and I drove to his house in Irvine. "So that's what I'm doing with this. At the beginning of the show I have a spectator think of a card and write it down. And then at the end I call on them to keep thinking of that card and, as I say that, I am dropping cards onto the table one by one, and then the last card I am holding in my hands is the card they were thinking of. It's great. It's really, really great."

It was her first crack at the show, a full-month run, and she was hoping to take it to London and then the States. Laura was clearly excited about the opportunity. In the past, she has held walk-around residencies at numerous high-end clubs in London, including the Hippodrome Theater, a well-respected venue in which Houdini had made numerous appearances. She gets paid well, too, nearly £1,000 per gig, a comparable fee to her male counterparts. *CHEAT,* however, was a peak moment for her. It was what she had been working toward as a performer; it was definitely harder for a woman to land a headlining show, especially by just doing card magic, and she was beginning to break through the glass ceiling. Sitting in the car, I smiled as I heard the enthusiasm in her voice. But although Laura presented herself as a hardworking magician chasing her dream—and breaking the mold for women in magic—the truth is that she was born a millionaire and had a childhood full of rock-star decadence and luxury before it all fell apart.

Laura's mother, Pauline, was a dancer in her youth. She toured the world, entertaining British troops in various Middle Eastern countries, including Lebanon, where she met Laura's father. He was a young freedom fighter, part of a rebel faction on the run from the government. "He was a gambler, he drank a lot, and was a womanizer," Laura told me later. "I definitely take after him in a lot of ways." Her mother and father moved back to London together. Pauline became a well-known figure in the city's bustling nightlife scene and, in the late 1970s, she bought Speakeasy, a famous club in town, and renamed it Bootleggers. She had worked there as a hostess before going to Lebanon and told the owner that when she returned she was going to buy the place and turn it into the best nightclub London has ever seen. And that's exactly what she did.

The club had always been a celebrity hangout, chock-full of London's most notable musicians and bands, including Ringo Starr, the Who, the Rolling Stones, and King Crimson. Its notoriety held on during Pauline's tenure as owner, and she became close friends with London's celebrity elite. She often had to baby-sit musicians, such as Motörhead's Lemmy, who always seemed to take the drinking and partying too far. "She once kicked out Phil from Thin Lizzy because he was passed out on heroin," Laura told me, laughing. In 1987, however, everything took a dark turn. Laura's father passed away from cancer. Pauline spent hundreds of thousands of dollars on treatment, and even sent him to a cancer institute in Texas. A few months after his death, Pauline's business partner died in a car crash—two tragedies in one year. Laura was only four years old.

Pauline isolated herself: too proud to ask for help from her posh friends and too traumatized to keep the nightclub afloat. The club was closed within a year, the lease on their penthouse in Westminster ran out, and they were forced to move into a subsidized housing project in Hendon, a neighborhood in London's grimy North End.

Laura had previously attended the same private nursery school as Prince Harry. Now she was hoofing it by foot to the nearest public school. "Pride is a shitty thing," Laura said about her mother.

Laura's mother briefly dated an alcoholic clown who, during his gigs for children, performed some magic. "His tricks were really terrible," admitted Laura, who was eight at the time. "He wasn't a great performer, but all the kids were having the best time in the world. I have always been able to see things differently, so I could see through the trick and figure out the method. *I could do that!* I thought. And if I could do that, I could make kids smile. And I loved the secrecy of it all."

Laura started buying gimmicks and props from magic shops in town, including Davenport's, London's oldest magic store, which was founded in 1898 and is still in operation. When Laura was twelve, she forced her mother to introduce her to their neighbor, a man with a curly mustache and a pointed beard who Laura was convinced was a magician. Laura was right: the neighbor was the Great George Kavari, an old-school London performer. He gave Laura a slew of magic books and elevated her knowledge of the craft from sad party tricks to real-deal performance and routine. "That was the first time I saw proper magic," Laura said. "And it was over after that: *Well, obviously now I am going to be a magician!*"

Laura became obsessed with magic during her teenage years. She likewise became entirely defiant of authority and rejected the rigidity of school. "I had my own little gang of nerds—the punks and goths," she told me. She hacked into her school's computer system and sent threatening messages to kids who bullied her. She was expelled. She never got back into the swing of things at school and, by age sixteen, started selling drugs, ditching class, partying, and practicing magic. She got kicked out of another school and never returned. "It didn't matter because I was going to be a magician," she said. "What magician needs to finish high school?"

It's no surprise that Laura constantly argued with her mother.

She would run away from home for days at a time, and eventually moved into a nearby youth shelter. She stepped up her drug dealing; dove into London's goth, punk, and fetish scene; and kept at magic. She'd perform only for those in her social circle, including her best friend Amber, who is now one of London's most famous dominatrix and fetish models.*

Laura also became a regular at Slimelight, London's biggest goth and punk nightclub, and the clubgoers were her primary clientele. Everyone who wanted drugs knew where to find her, and Laura was soon running a robust operation with numerous distributors, until one of her associates was arrested. She was banned from Slimelight.

"It was my life, my everything," Laura told me about the club. She was heartbroken. Stuck in her flat far away from the heartbeat of her social scene, she practiced magic even more intently. But she had no connections in that community. It's never been easy for a woman to find her place in magic, especially for someone like Laura, who, at the time, rolled around in a spike-covered leather jacket, a massive mohawk jutting from her head. With her old life crumbling, she decided to go in a different direction. She decided to join the Magic Circle. Formed in 1905, it is one of the oldest members-only clubs for magicians in the world.

---

* Laura's home, a large, two-story industrial flat in northeast London, is a dream for both magicians and fetishists alike. Laura lives on the top floor—stacks of magic books, shelves stuffed with cards and other memorabilia. A portrait of Mona Lisa secretly palming a playing card hangs on the wall. The basement, in which Amber takes clients and does photo shoots, is a full-on BDSM dungeon: a catacomb of dark rooms with specific themes, including a white-walled prison cell and a doctor's office, each with its own closet of whips, chains, and other sadistic tools. When she took me on a tour of the space, I turned the corner to find a stunning blonde woman in a one-piece latex suit. Six-foot five in her knife-sharp heels, she towered above me—I'm five-foot seven—but bent down and greeted me with a firm handshake and a gentle smile.

The Magic Circle hides on a nondescript brick-lined street in the Kings Cross neighborhood of London. Magicians gather in the lounge, share drinks, and talk shop. There's a small theater, and the basement houses a musty, low-ceilinged library with thousands of books. An elderly woman, the resident librarian, who normally wears a pink cardigan, can be seen restocking vintage periodicals. On any given day, handfuls of old men in tweed jackets and dark slacks pore through old papers and magazines. Another room houses stacks of vintage posters and props from legendary performers, including Houdini.

Laura walked in for her membership audition. She was a bit on edge, but had practiced her stable of tricks for weeks, and was eager to show the judging panel her chops. They weren't the most mind-blowing effects, but the Great George Kavari had given her well-known material, and she figured the judges would be pleased to see that she was pulling inspiration from classic routines. Despite her nerves, her audition went off without a hitch and she was granted membership. After being banished from Slimelight—effectively losing the only family she had at the time—Laura hoped she might find a home here, in the world of magic.

Laura started hanging out at the Circle, but no one dared interact with her. She stood out like a sore thumb: the mohawk, the platform leather boots, the outlandish punk gear, the gritty street-kid demeanor. But Laura kept coming back, waiting to break through, to find acceptance. One day, Barbara Astra, an older female magician, saw Laura from across the room. She stomped over and confronted her.

"If you are going to come to this establishment, you need to start dressing appropriately," she told Laura sternly. Laura looked down at herself. She was wearing her signature black leather jacket, covered in spikes, and her hair was gelled into a mohawk. She was hurt by Barbara's comment—and angry. She glared back up at the woman, clenched her jaw, and bolted for the door. She felt rejected, the snub made infinitely worse because she loved magic so much.

Fuck this, Laura said to herself as she made her way toward the exit. *I'm never coming back here. I don't need these people.* But another female magician, Fay Presto, spotted Laura rushing for the door.

"Hey! You!" Fay called out. "What's wrong? Why are you leaving?"

"I guess this place just isn't for me," Laura told her, on the verge of tears.

"Are you fucking kidding me? They're all a bunch of *assholes!*" Fay responded. "But I'm the rebel here. You couldn't have bumped into a better person."

"Really?" Laura said.

"Oh, yes, darling. Magic, you see, has never truly accepted the people who want to change the way things have always been done. But you and me," she continued, placing her hand on her chest, thrusting out her hip, "we're different, darling, we're the ones who will keep magic exciting—who'll keep it *alive.*" She had a point, Laura thought. Fay was boisterous, unapologetic, and, Laura would come to find out, a real trendsetter: Fay was born a man, and had just recently come out as transgender. Fay had been a magic influencer in London throughout the 1990s, spearheading high-paying restaurant residencies for close-up magicians, but caught a lot of flak when she fought for fair treatment of women in the craft—equal to men, with a fifty-fifty say in where the art form was headed.

"You just stick with me," Fay went on, taking her by the arm and leading her back into the building. "I'll show you the ropes, how to navigate this place. I'll teach you all you need to know. And I'll make you a star."

Fay became Laura's mentor. She taught her new tricks, explained the nuances of routine, and gave her the business tactics needed to gig for a living. Fay kicked Laura's ass into gear, preparing her not only for life as a professional magician but also as an adult. She championed Laura's quick wit, but also smoothed out her anger issues. "Fay helped turn me into a woman who could live out in the real world," Laura said. In some ways, Fay became a surrogate mother. With Fay's help, Laura performed regularly throughout her twenties, nabbing residencies at some of London's most popular restaurants and nightclubs. She took much of her act from Fay, who was grooming Laura to take over some of the city's regular spots. Eventually, Laura was able to charge more than £500 for a single night's work. "Then I met Daniel Madison," Laura told me. "And I started seeing magic very differently."

Laura had been gigging under Fay's guidance for a few years when she had been chosen to audition for a major television show. She packed her bags and made her way to the production studio. But she was underprepared and flopped. Although she had worked steadily over the past half decade, she became bored with the material she was performing. Much of it came directly from Fay's repertoire and Laura no longer felt inspired by the gimmick-heavy, old-fashioned routines: ropes and scarves, sponge balls and other props. Her passion for magic had begun to wane.

Dejected by her performance at the audition, she went to a pub down the street with a couple of friends. A few magicians hung around the bar, including a rough-looking guy with black hair and a scruffy beard: Daniel Madison. He started chatting with Laura, but she didn't know who he was.[*] She spent so much of her time in Fay's circle, she didn't have any insight into the new things going on, and the burgeoning talents behind them, within her industry. To the older magicians Laura had surrounded herself with, the young guys taking the reins were bastardizing magic.

---

[*] Laura carried with her a small suitcase, stamped in the Union Jack and stuffed with gimmicks, that Madison later described to me as "a little box full of stupid shit."

But Madison and Laura connected that night and vowed to keep in touch. After Madison left the bar, another magician came up to Laura and said, "Do you know who that was?! That's Daniel Madison, the creator of all this amazing magic!"* They kept in frequent touch over the succeeding months. Madison began teaching Laura more advanced card tricks and introduced her to the ways in which the industry was changing.

"It was kind of perfect really, the timing of it all," Laura told me. Madison convinced Laura to alter her routine and focus specifically on card magic. No more props, no more stereotypical patter, no more old-school tricks. He championed a transformation, both in Laura's brand and skill, and instilled a sense of confidence in Laura as a magician. "I had a great reputation amongst older magicians, not realizing there are these younger magicians that are making far more headway and changing magic. This is what it's about, and what's it's going to be. This is the future of magic," Laura told me. "It changed everything. I am a completely different person entirely. I love what I do. I got back into loving to practice, loving to read, loving the history again. All of the things I truly wanted to do, I started doing."

A couple of years later, as they both became more popular, Madison and Laura wanted to collaborate on something big and special, something that would hopefully change the industry, but not necessarily impede on each other's trajectory: Madison as a creator of magic, Laura as a full-time performer. They wanted to

---

* Ironically, the magician who said this, Ollie Mealing, later started a beef with Madison over Instagram. He posted a photo with the hashtag #MADISONISDEAD, labeled Madison an egotistical narcissist, declared his videos "nonsensical drivel," and called his *Magic Is Dead* tagline an embarrassment to the art form. Madison clapped back with a photo of an early Derren Brown promotional poster (Ollie always bragged about having worked for him, one of the most famous magicians in England) that read, in big bold letters, "MAGIC IS DEAD."

bring all the friends they had met into one space, the ones who seemed to love magic and deception as much as they did, the ones who wanted to forever change the art form.

Thus the52 was born.

Jeremy and I cruised south down the highway, toward his house, and Laura continued to share details about her show. But then, as if she had just remembered something, Laura switched gears.

"Oh!" she exclaimed. "Ian! We are so excited to have you in the52!"

My heart sank, and I stayed quiet. Jeremy glanced over, clearly stunned.

"*Yeah*," I replied, after a beat, trying to reciprocate her excitement. "I'm thrilled." In reality, I was devastated. Laura had thrown a wrench into my plan.

"When are you going to get your tattoo?" she asked.

"In Vegas," I said. "I have a little something planned."

"We are really excited to have you, Ian," Laura said, before hanging up. "You're a perfect fit."

Jeremy and I sat in silence for what felt like an eternity.

"You have *something planned*?" he asked, finally breaking the silence.

I turned and look at him. "Well, of course," I said, trying to muster a smile. "I have to make an event out of it, right?"

I hadn't wanted to just go to a local shop in Brooklyn for my membership ink, and have it revealed on social media. It didn't seem dramatic enough for what was, to me, a monumental occasion, nor did I want to waste a great opportunity to demonstrate to other members of the52 that I was worthy of the invitation. Moreover, I had wanted to create a moment around my induction—especially since Madison had asked me to keep it a secret. The trip to Las Vegas for Magic Live felt right. I'd be going with Jeremy,

Xavior, and, most important, Chris Ramsay. He was the one who had ushered me into this world, and the first to tell me about the52. He should be there when my membership was revealed—he should be the centerpiece of what I had in mind.

When we first met, Ramsay didn't try to impress me by drowning me in magic. In fact, he did only a few tricks for me. To him, magic shouldn't be flaunted; overdoing it could diminish the impact. But once, back in Blackpool, Ramsay had performed an effect just for me.

It was the last night of the convention and we had just eaten dinner. We made our way back to the Ruskin for a drink, as we had done every night. By 11 P.M., some members of our group started heading back to their hotels. Many of them, including us, had early flights the next morning. As Ramsay finished the last of his beer, we stood up and headed for the stairs. But before we went up, he pulled me aside and took a deck of cards from his back pocket. He shuffled and started to speak.

"I want you to imagine that we are in a room much like this. There is a table in front of us and on this table is a deck of cards. We are going to select a card together." He fanned the deck. I chose a card. He motioned for me to hold it facedown in my palm and told me to not look at it. He put the rest of the deck back into his pocket. "If you had the choice to remove red or black from the deck of cards, which would you choose?"

"Black."

"Leaving us only with?"

"Red."

"I want you to imagine that we are going to put all the diamonds here"—he motioned to his right hand—"and the hearts here"—he motioned to his left—"and I am going to drop one of these two piles on the table. Either diamonds or hearts. You choose."

"Diamonds."

"Leaving us only with?"

"Hearts."

"In the heart cards, there are number cards and picture cards. You're going to imagine that the number cards are here"—he again gestured to his right—"and the picture cards are here"—to his left—"and you are going to toss one of these piles up into the air. Which would you choose? Numbers or pictures?"

"Pictures."

"Imagine the picture cards leaving and, right here"—he looked up into the space above our heads—"they stop in midair. You have the jack, queen, and king levitating right in front of you, right here." He raised his hand into the space between us. "I am going to grab two of them. Which two did I grab?"

"Jack and king."

"Leaving only the . . . ?"

"The queen of hearts."

He nodded to the card in my hand. I turned it over. I held the queen of hearts. I stared at the card and smiled. He grinned, too, and modestly shoved his hands into his pockets. We stood there in silence for a bit and then he said, "Let's go," and that was that.

This moment—shared between the two of us—came back to me when Madison and I were discussing my tattoo and subsequent announcement. I wanted to give Ramsay something like what he had given me. I wanted to give him an experience. And so I prepared for Vegas—a secret privy only to me.

Jeremy pulled off the highway, and we stopped at a red light. "So," he started, "are you going to tell me what you have in store?"

I smiled. "You'll see. Let's just say I'm going to create a magic moment."

8

HAPPY PILGRIMS

Our first order of business in Los Angeles was to check out the Magic Castle, a cornerstone of magic history in the United States. Built in 1909, and a magician hangout since 1963, the massive venue is propped up on a small hill and built like an actual castle: a chateau-like structure with lattice-rimmed gables, wraparound balconies, and spires thrusting above the tree line. It glowed a bright yellow in the dark as Jeremy pulled his car up the steep driveway. We got out and he gave his keys to an awaiting valet. You must wear a suit to enter and, as I waited to get in, tightening the tie knotted around my neck, the evening sun burned through the smog hovering over downtown Los Angeles.

"Absolutely no cameras!" bellowed the bouncer. "No selfies, food porn, cocktail porn, belfies, Pokémon Go, Periscope, Twitter, Instagram, Snapchat, or anything that involves taking pictures with your phone! If you take photographs inside the Castle, we will show you the door!"

"A little strict, huh?" I whispered to Jeremy after getting past the doorman.

"Well, it's a club for magicians," he said. "You can't keep a club secret if everyone is taking pictures inside of it!" We checked in at the front desk and Jeremy led me over to a bookcase.

"Where do we go in?" I asked.

"Right here," he said, smiling.

"But there's no door. This is a bookcase."

"See that owl?" he said, pointing to the shelf. "Lean in and say, 'Open sesame.'" I smiled, gave him a condescending glance, approached the shelf, and said, 'Open sesame.' The bookcase shot left, revealing an entryway into the club.

"After you," he said, smiling, and I led the way.

Inside the Castle, men and women congregated around the main bar, which, dimly lit and lined in metal stools, anchored the room. I felt like I was in some sort of off-kilter church: stained-glass windows hovering above doorways, nooks and cabinets holding strange trinkets, the floors coated in dark paisley carpets, everything highlighted in polished wood and exposed brass. An air of quiet reserve engulfed the small pods of people—women in flashy low-cut dresses, men in eccentric suits, black on black or an eye-catching red—as if someone were watching their every move. Although it held a definitive panache, the Castle honestly felt kind of stuffy—hulking doors and narrow passageways packing in loads of people—making the place feel, at least at first, more claustrophobic than magical.

"Let's go over here," Jeremy said, gesturing toward an adjoining room at the rear of the bar. "I want you to meet Irma." We walked into a small parlor. A black baby grand piano sat in the corner.

"Well, ask her to play something," Jeremy said.

"But no one's in here."

"Oh, Irma is here. Watch." He stepped up to the piano and said, "Irma, play a song by the Beatles." A moment later, the keys began tinkling, despite the instrument's seat sitting empty, and "Hey Jude" filled the room.

"Oh, right, a ghost," I said, laughing. "Of course! I should've known!"

Jeremy smiled. "All right, let's keep going," he said, signaling me to follow him out of Irma's parlor and down the hall, the piano's hulking chord progression fading into the background.

"I basically grew up here," Jeremy told me as we walked around the venue. "I had always been a huge magic geek as a kid, and I was part of the Junior Club in the 1990s."

"I mean, yeah, magic is a big deal for kids, so I'm not surprised there's a program here for them."

"Exactly, it gives them structure, and access to history—the old-timers to talk to, the library downstairs, great shows on the weekends. But, as I got older, I kind of grew out of it," he said. "I'm not really sure why, but it didn't captivate me much anymore." We cut left into another small room and took a seat on a sofa. "But then my dad passed away about five years ago, and I started getting into it again."

"You know," I started, "my father also passed away—I was a kid, but still."

"Then you know what it's like. I was very angry after he died, just pissed off at the world. You feel like you've lost a part of yourself, that a guiding force in your life is gone. It took a long time for me to come to terms with it, and to try and move on."

"That's the hardest part, moving on, realizing that you can still become your own person."

"Well, that's the thing—it's weird really," Jeremy said. "Turns out, my father actually practiced magic himself. He just never told me! He kept it a secret. He'd always critique my moves when I was a kid, and I'd always brush him off—I was a know-it-all. But after he died my mother told me that he was once a magician's assistant. That really got to me. And with Instagram, I had a public outlet to showcase my progress. I could practice in private, feed my energy into this thing, and then film the final product and post

it on social media. And I guess I've gained some semblance of notoriety from doing that," he continued, flashing his Ten of Spades
tattoo on the inside of his middle finger, "but I've also found
something I was once passionate about, and that I'm now passionate about again. It feels really good, to know there are things out
there that you can fall back on, that you can use to find yourself."

"I mean, there is such a community in magic, like a brother-
hood," I said. "Just look at this place," I added, looking around.
"It's kind of remarkable."

"I mean, everyone has a soft spot for the Castle," he said. "You
can't deny that. For decades, the best minds in magic came here,
sat down, and progressed the art form. But, you know, it is still a
business, and you have to be realistic sometimes in that regard.
I hate to admit it, but sometimes it can seem more like a tourist
attraction than a secret enclave. It's very Disney-ish now, the way
it presents magic. But it's still a place for people who love magic
to come and hang out. A lot of celebrities come around, too. Hell,
Neil Patrick Harris, you know, the actor, has been a magician forever, and comes here all the time. He was once president of the
board of directors."

We continued to walk around the Castle. A small two-person
sofa sat at the far end of the main room. A painting of an old man
hung above it, all white hair and chunky-framed glasses. Clad in a
gray suit, he held a deck of cards with a cigarette perched between
his fingertips.

"You know who that is?" Jeremy asked me.

I squinted at the painting's accompanying plaque. It read: *This
couch reserved for Dai Vernon when he's in the club.* "Oh yeah," I said.
"Of course. I was reading up on him, actually."

"He is, without a doubt, the godfather of modern magic," Jeremy said. "He died in 1992. He was ninety-eight years old, and he
basically lived here for the last two decades of his life."

It seemed, whenever I read anything about magic's history, I came across Dai Vernon. He was a sleight-of-hand artist so intrinsically dedicated to magic that his every waking moment was spent obsessing over the innovation and perfection of routine, theory, technique, and performance. "Dai Vernon is to conjuring as James Joyce to the novel and Einstein to physics," legendary magician Max Maven once said. "It's a person who comes along about once a century and just changes the way people approach that field." Everyone knew his name but over time he earned the moniker "the Professor." In the nearly sixty years since he rose to fame, no one has come close to dethroning the hyperactive, quick-talking master magician who completely revolutionized card magic.

Born in 1894 in Ottawa, Canada, Vernon discovered an interest in magic at a young age after his father showed him a few simple card tricks. By the time he could read, Vernon had bulldozed through all the magic books at his local library and, once he was exposed to the stage acts of prominent touring magicians, he focused on card manipulations. By the end of World War I, fired up with the ambition of becoming a full-time magician, he moved to New York City. His ultimate goal was to elevate magic to the realm of high art—respected, revered, forever remembered, and forever changed. He became a premier entertainer for the city's aristocratic elite, but when the stock market face-planted and the Great Depression hit the city, Vernon's life as magician to the rich and famous fizzled out. And so he advanced his chops with a deck of cards largely in private or alongside the company of other top-tier magicians. By the 1940s, Vernon was consistently inventing new card tricks or refining other magicians' work, and gaining more and more notoriety in the community.

By the end of the 1950s, Vernon had become more than a household name in the community—he was a living legend. He began hosting private lectures, earning a living by teaching other magicians his techniques. "I went to one with my friend, and we were astounded by what we saw. Our mouths just hung open," magician Herb Zarrow once said, adding that Vernon was using sleight-of-hand moves that no one had seen before. His work made the moves more indecipherable, the performances more refined, and the magic more astounding for the spectator. To Vernon, true magic existed close up and in tight quarters, an experience far removed from the stage and replaced by a more exclusive and more impossible set of circumstances. If it was happening right under your nose, it must be a miracle, right?

Over the years, Vernon's influence continued to flow not only outward, engulfing his peers, but likewise trickled down to subsequent generations. In the 1970s, he moved to Hollywood and took up residency at the recently opened Magic Castle, altering the geography of magic as an art form. "Vernon made happy pilgrims of us all," famous magician Ricky Jay, who died in 2018 and studied under Vernon, once said. "He literally had the power to make people get up and move. We must have all felt it at one particular point: There was no choice, this is what we must do, and this is what we did."

Jeremy touched the painting's frame. "Yeah, man, this has been here for years. It never gets moved. He's been dead for over twenty years, but you can't do card magic without being influenced by Vernon. A lot of what everyone has been performing for the past fifty years or so came, in one way or another, from Vernon."

The room had filled up around us, and Jeremy looked at his watch. "Oh, shit. We are going to be late for the show!" I followed him toward the front, around the bar, and we got in line for the next performance. I was eager to see a show at the Castle. There are a handful of performances every night in different rooms, each with a different style: the Close-Up Gallery, the Parlor of Prestidigitation, and the Palace of Mystery (the largest of the three, built for stage illusions). Paul Gertner, a legendary sleight-of-hand artist in his fifties, held court in the close-up room and Jeremy insisted that we see him.

We entered the tiny theater and grabbed a seat in the third row.

Other patrons filed in, the lights dimmed, and the show began. Gertner, affable with spectators and comfortable onstage, presented some of his most memorable material, including his renowned Cups and Balls routine using steel balls inside steel cups (both a nod to his hometown of Pittsburgh as well as a distinct logistical hurdle, since you could potentially hear the balls knocking around under the designated cup before the reveal). He also performed Unshuffled, an effect he created that bowled over Penn & Teller on their television show *Penn & Teller: Fool Us*. The deck's edge is drawn on with black marker and, after shuffling a few times, the scribbles magically transform into letters that spell out the spectator's chosen card. He also performed Namerology, my favorite effect of the show.

For this he had a few spectators join him onstage. Each person chose a card, swapped cards with one another at random, and then switched seats at random. Next, everyone put their cards back into the deck. Gertner, using the number of letters in each person's name, spelled down to each person's chosen card—moving down the row in the order of their new seating arrangement. I was in awe. I couldn't begin to figure out the method. If he was tracking the cards the entire time, he was doing so effortlessly. But the trick wasn't over. When he flipped over the small piles produced from spelling each name, the cards of each small stack produced a Royal Flush.

"Oh, fuck that," I said, turning to Jeremy and laughing in disbelief. He just raised his eyebrows and smiled, as if to say, *Yeah, dude, I know.*

I loved Gertner's performance, but it also brought the fracture between current and past generations into focus for me. It wasn't that Gertner was a bad magician—far from it—but there's much more involved than skill these days if you want to be an ambassador of magic. The fact is, in terms of substance, the blueprints of magical effects have largely been the same for decades. There is only so much you can do with a deck of cards or a certain type of illusion, and many effects are just reiterations of old material. It is the presentation that has changed. "Performing magic is like ballet—all of the moves have already been created and there's no changing what you can do," magician Derek Hughes, who performed on season ten of *America's Got Talent*, once said. "But how one choreographs these moves and effects into ballads of your own, makes them unique to us as individual performers. That's how original magic is created." How magic is given to an audience is what prompts its evolution.

Although magicians like Gertner are extraordinarily talented, it's hard to imagine someone like Gertner—a middle-aged, happy-go-lucky dude who still uses a magic wand—crafting a brand that embodies the charisma and connectivity necessary to disseminate a contemporary take on magic to a broader (and much younger) audience, especially through a medium as judgmental, nuanced, and fast-paced as the internet.

Jeremy and I filed out of the theater and made our way outside. "Well, your first trip to the Magic Castle is complete," Jeremy said. "What did you think?"

"I think I'm becoming obsessed, to be honest."

9

AN ACTOR PLAYING
THE PART OF A MAGICIAN

It's a fact: humans have forever been fascinated with individuals who possess powers beyond that of the common man. And although the notion of weaving deception into entertainment has always been present, magic—and the brand associated with the art form—has, like other types of performance art, continually evolved. But unlike dance or opera, magic has forever been under a cultural requirement to continually push the boundaries of illusion. Magic is only as good as how much better it was than the trick that came before it. "Magic cannot stand still," legendary nineteenth-century magician Nevil Maskelyne once wrote. "It must either advance with the times or fall behind." For magic to thrive—and survive—it's become mandatory for the craft to be questioned, dissected, and innovated by the next generations of conjurors. As with Dai Vernon (and, now, the members of the52), those who propel magic forward—in both substance and style— are the ones who are revered.

The first "magician" is said to be a man named Dedi, who lived in ancient Egypt around 2590 BC during the reign of King Khufu.

Dedi is credited with creating magic's oldest routine, the Cups and Balls, which is still performed today—by magicians like Paul Gertner. This trick, which anyone who has seen magic performed knows, is a series of effects where the magician presents three cups and a small ball (or in the case of Dedi, a stone) on a table, and makes it disappear and reappear under different cups. With the cups stacked atop one another, the magician manipulates the stone to move *through* the cups, and at the end of the routine, the stone turns into a larger object, like a piece of fruit.

Dedi also performed supernatural feats, which captivated Egyptian royalty. During one memorable performance for Cheops, the pharaoh who oversaw the Great Pyramid, Dedi demonstrated his ability to bring a decapitated animal back from the dead. He carted a live goose into Cheops's palace and, standing in front of the pharaoh, ripped off the bird's head. Blood squirted everywhere. He placed the goose's limp body on the floor and held the head in his hands. After a dramatic pause, he grabbed the body and rejoined the two. The goose came back to life and scurried around the room, stunning the pharaoh. The story of Dedi, written in Hierac on a papyrus scroll, was discovered in 1823 by English-born Henry Westcar. The tale, titled "The Tale of King Cheops' Court," however, did not reveal the secret behind Dedi's illusions, only that they were seen as feats of someone more powerful than an ordinary man.

For the proceeding 3,500 years, magicians were largely viewed as people with supernatural powers, not performers. "When guys back in the caveman days figured out how to make a stick disappear, they didn't do it to make money; they did it to foster a belief in the supernatural, or to be perceived as godlike, to deceive people and make them believe they had real powers," David Copperfield once said. "That's how my craft began."

As time went on, that reputation inherited unfortunate consequences, both for the art form itself and those who practiced it.

With the explosion of Judeo-Christianity beliefs across Europe during the fifteenth century, magic was directly linked to the occult and magicians were persecuted as witches and practitioners of the Black Arts. It was not uncommon for magicians to be tortured, executed, or exiled. "When the colonies began in Jamestown, Virginia, magicians were instantly banished," T. Ian Flinn states in *Conjuring Curiosity*. The way of life during America's infancy was "traced back to their strict Christian lifestyle," Flinn continued. "Only letting Christ in their lives would lead their path to righteousness." It would take two hundred years and widespread cultural evolution in both Europe and North America for magic to become a respected and highly coveted skill.

Magic began its transformation into its modern-day incarnation at the start of the Victorian era. "By the early 1840s, magic had gradually but successfully emerged from the clutches of traveling mountebanks and showmen who worked their hanky-panky in the booths of outdoor fairs," writes magic historian Walter Gibson. Magic, accepted by intellectuals and no longer associated with the occult, was now legitimate entertainment worthy of a stage and a paying audience. The most popular early iterations of modern magic, however, still relied on the intrigue of séance and spiritualism, which played off (especially in America) the general public's fascination with people who could seemingly communicate with the dead.

In the 1850s, Buffalo-based brothers Ira and William Davenport developed their séance act and toured around the country labeled not as magicians but something more spiritual—something *ethereal*. "The appeal of the Davenports' act, its mix of religion, agnosticism, science, superstition, and fraud, was a magnet for controversy," Jim Steinmeyer concludes in *Hiding the Elephant: How Magicians Invented the Impossible and Learned to Disappear*. "They started riots in many of the cities where they appeared. They were booed from the stage as fakes, hailed in the press as mediums, threatened, bloodied, cheered. At a time when the Victorians prided themselves on science and rationality, the two quiet young men from New York began a confusing debate about just how honest a magician needed to be or could afford to be."

These sorts of routines, however, were largely frowned upon by dedicated magicians who wanted to present stage illusions and perform deceptions without holding the belief that what they were doing was otherworldly.* Luckily, this type of supernatural act fizzled just as quickly as it exploded in popularity, replaced by more traditional, intellectual, and honest conjuring. In the early days of magic, trends changed with the speed of a magician's hand.

It sounds strange, but a clockmaker from France ushered in magic's golden age. Jean Eugéne Robert-Houdin, France's most famous magician (and from whom, in 1891, Harry Houdini sourced his stage name) used his background as an engineer to revolutionize magic not only in the ingenuity and complexity of props, but in the presentation of the craft. He saw it as something that could combine illusion with plot, character development, and narrative tension.

Robert-Houdin was famous for declaring that a magician is merely "an actor playing the part of a magician." His inventions and innovations in presentation put that mantra front and center. Robert-Houdin used his knowledge of clocks to create mechanical apparatus called automata, the analog inner workings of which could be built and programmed to execute seemingly impossible acts, such as an orange tree growing from a pot, or a hand writing out messages on a piece of paper. He combined his penchant for sleight of hand with these props to create the foundation on which many vaudeville acts were built. His model of stage conjuring extended well into the twentieth century, some aspects of which are still being utilized today.

---

* Houdini crusaded for years against mediums and spiritualism in general.

Robert-Houdin also revolutionized the brand of a conjuror, specifically how magicians dressed. Instead of embodying the image of a robe-clad mystic, Robert-Houdin dressed like members of his audience. He wore traditional evening clothes: coattails, starched shirts with a high collar, sometimes even a top hat or white gloves. It goes without saying that aspects of Robert-Houdin's sartorial influence live on today as cringeworthy clichés.[*]

As the twentieth century rolled along, however, magic began to change. "During the past twenty years, magic has suffered a good deal," magic author Will Goldstone reflected in 1933. He blamed "the Great War, which turned the world, and people's ideas, topsy-turvy. The demand for entertainment, after the war, was for noise and excitement. Those magicians who were able to adapt their programmes to meet the new condition did well, but they could not re-establish magic in all its old prestige."

Just as Robert-Houdin played off the intellectualism of the late nineteenth century, magicians in the 1910s and the 1920s were paying attention to the mind-set of the general population in the United States and Europe. Like all art, the greatest magic has always reflected the current state of the human condition. Whereas magic in the late nineteenth century focused on subtle and intellectual routines and effects—á la the Victorian era—World War I, which left more than 40 million dead, altered people's perception of the world. Life was changing, and magic had to change with it.

One trick perfectly encapsulated this shift in magic: Sawing Through a Woman. Invented by the British illusionist P. T. Selbit, it first debuted on January 17, 1921. It was an overnight success. "Selbit auditioned the perfect product for the decade which would

---

[*] Alexander Hermann, another style influencer, invented the sly-eyed and sharp-goateed devilish look that has been an equally pervasive and laughable stereotype. When exactly the fedora became a staple for magicians, however, is unclear.

be later said to roar: impulsive, aggressive and thrilled," Jim Steinmeyer writes in *Art & Artifice*. "With it, he made a clean break
with the Golden Age mysteries . . . and in a logical and significant
step, changed the development of stage magic."

Selbit incorporated grotesque publicity stunts into his shows:
ambulances parked out front of the theater, sirens and lights ready
to whirl, stagehands dumping blood-filled buckets into drains on
street corners near the venue. The effect succeeded not only because of its shock value but also because it incorporated a woman
as a prop (another cliché that would cling to magic for decades
to come). "The world had lost its innocence, and crusading ladies
had forfeited their innocent charms," Steinmeyer states. "Even
entertainment had changed—the threat, the hero, the victim—
and magicians were in unique positions, dramatizing fantasies, to
demonstrate those changes." Selbit's initial offering spawned dozens of spinoffs, torture-style illusions that stood the test of time
and became a centerpiece of stage magic. Criss Angel, in his show
at the Luxor in Las Vegas, does a modified version of the effect (he
uses a massive buzz saw); David Copperfield in 1988 performed
Death Saw on television, where he was sliced in two; and Penn &
Teller also perform an effect where they each have to reach into
bear traps without losing a hand.

These cultural forces came together most impactfully in the
most famous magician of all time: Harry Houdini. A gruff-spoken
Hungarian immigrant from New York City, Houdini didn't have
the sleight-of-hand chops or the performance grace to succeed
as a traditional magician, but his penchant for escapes and innate
ability to generate frenzied publicity created the perfect storm for
his rise to fame in an era where spectators wanted their magic
more thrilling and dangerous than ever before. He became known
for his stunts, like removing himself from a straitjacket while
hanging upside down from a crane, and his death-defying stage
escapes, such as the Water Torture Cell, which he invented and

constructed with his longtime assistant and engineer Jim Collins. For this trick, Houdini locked himself upside down in a container full of water and raised a curtain, concealing the vessel from view. After building tension for a few minutes, they dropped the sheet to reveal Houdini perched on the edge of the tank, arms raised in defiance. He magically escaped.

Houdini soon became magic's most recognizable figure—and one of the most egotistical. He publicly boasted that no magician could fool him if he saw the effect three times. Many magicians tried and failed to best the king of their craft. That all changed in 1919, when a young man approached Houdini and asked to show him a card trick. He had Houdini choose a card and place it into the middle of the deck. With a snap, the card jumped to the top. The young gun did it again and again—eight times in a row, in fact. Houdini was in shock. He'd been fooled. He'd never seen someone so deceptive with a pack of cards. Although Houdini would never acknowledge it, the man he met that day—not yet famous for his contributions to magic—was none other than Dai Vernon.

After the sensationalism created by the sawing craze and Houdini's outlandish escapes, magic went into a lull. Moving pictures and radio programs captivated audiences, the Great Depression ravaged the country, and, with World War II consuming much of the public conscience, neither the United States nor Europe had much time for magic. But that doesn't mean the art failed to progress. In fact, because it became so isolated, many magicians had time and space to innovate—especially in close-up magic, which required only everyday objects or a deck of cards rather than cumbersome and expensive stage props—with Dai Vernon and his peers leading the charge.

As time went on, however, Vernon's approach fell by the

wayside, with hokey illusions, cheesy funnyman routines, and lack-luster gimmicks taking center stage. Harry Blackstone Jr. comes to mind, with his black goatee and bedazzled tuxedos, whose 1997 obituary in the *New York Times* notes that "his hat and sleeves had yielded 80,000 rabbits." It's unclear why magicians, during the mid-twentieth century, became so enamored with these types of clichés—the top hats, the bunny rabbits and doves, the magic wands—but magicians have always respected those who came before them. And that's a good thing, but it quickly became as much a detriment as it was an asset. Although there was much to learn about the theory of magic from legends past, their out-dated branding concepts were equally embraced. Robert-Houdin's eveningwear and Alexander Hermann's goatee merged with the kid-friendly tackiness of the 1950s into this magician-specific brand—the ultimate stereotype. And, once the public accepted this image as what a magician should look and act like, it unfor-tunately stuck.

Moreover, the façade of being a "magician," by the stereotypes' standards, allowed lackluster performers to hide behind the cli-chés and operate as if they were true ambassadors of the craft. For some it created an existential crisis for the art form. "There are no set qualifications for being a talented magician," Daniel Madi-son told me once. "As long as the spectator *believes* that you are a magician, even if you're bad, it's enough to pass muster." But, as time went on, many magicians didn't seem to mind that they were dumbing down the craft and embracing clichés (audiences liked the image and it paid the bills, so why fight it?), and it would be years before magic, and those who practiced it—especially mem-bers of the52—started questioning why they were being shackled to the most outdated parts of their past.

In the 1970s, magic's visibility began to skyrocket because of one thing: television. Like the Victorian era, or Sawing Through a Woman, the small screen would forever alter how magic is presented to the public and—up until the internet age—limit the ways in which people came in contact with the craft. For much of the 1970s, Doug Henning was North America's best-known magician. He was a charismatic and comedic entertainer, and he connected with large audiences because of his personal brand. He was a straight-up hippie: fuzzy mustache, long Allman Brothers–style hair, bell bottoms, and tie-dyed shirts. His image fit snugly into the trendy, New Age mysticism of the time and, between 1975 and 1982, he cranked out seven seasons of his television show *Doug Henning's World of Magic*. He also made regular appearances on *The Tonight Show with Johnny Carson* and other programs. He even crafted a Broadway show called *Merlin*. "The really successful magicians are the ones who are able to resonate with their audiences," writes magic consultant Charles Reynolds. "Henning was one with his audiences, the flower children, the hippies. He somehow convinced them that he really believed in magic." Starting with Henning, television became the go-to vessel through which a general audience could see magic.

With the 1980s came David Copperfield, arguably the most famous magician in the world.[*] His performance style was (and to a large degree still is) quintessentially eighties: loud, brash, fast-paced, and flamboyant, his stages filled with beautiful women, engulfed in loud music, and buzzing with over-the-top pyrotechnics. He wanted to be a household name, with the largest illusions and the most outsized personality, and quickly merged the entertainment of magic with the life of a rock star. After bringing his brand of conjuring onto television, he became the de facto archetype of a magician: an impeccably tanned dude clad in tight leather pants, a matching high-collared jacket and motorcycle boots, with a puff

---

[*] And the wealthiest; he's on track to hit a net worth of $1 billion.

of brown hair floating above a chiseled jaw. His large-scale, televised illusions became massive hits. But to some magicians they weren't really magic.

"I didn't like the Statue of Liberty vanish. It meant nothing to me," Penn Jillette once said of Copperfield's 1983 television special, which labeled itself "the illusion of the century." Penn added that the simple fact was this: He wasn't making the monument disappear. Nothing magical was happening. It was merely a trick—the audience was on a rotating platform and, while the curtain was in place, they were simply swiveled away from the monument—enhanced by the fact that those watching from home were forced to see it through the lens of a stationary camera, a caveat that undoubtedly helped the illusion's execution.[*]

With television bottlenecking magic's visibility to the public, the art form seemed to be tumbling down to one of its lowest common denominators: flashy, headline-grabbing, one-off illusions only seen on a screen, the concepts for which were approved by bigwig executives focused more on ratings than the quality of the magic being created. Most important, however, was the enduring effect this phase would have on how the public would come to define magic as a whole: if it wasn't big, wasn't flashy, wasn't on prime-time television, it wasn't truly good magic.

But then, in the 1990s, a breath of fresh air—a renaissance moment. David Blaine emerged on the scene with his brand of

---

[*] After the vanish, an on-screen spectator wearing a priest uniform said, "I was amazed. It was there and now it's not there anymore. I have no idea where it went." A 2017 NPR investigation found that the on-screen audience were stooges and privy to the trick's method. NPR also discovered that the trick was filmed at least three times. Copperfield's team denied these claims. Regardless of the circumstances on set, folks watching at home were fooled to hell and the stunt further established Copperfield as America's most popular magician.

street magic—a stripped-down, spontaneous approach that, when filmed, focused heavily on spectators' reactions. Blaine had aspirations to be a big-named magician, but his ticket to stardom came through gigging like any other young gun trying to make a living. It was during his time in the trenches that it dawned on him that close-up performance, not big illusions like Copperfield's, was the future of magic on television. He wanted to bring it back to the days of Dai Vernon, who could blow a spectator's mind in a casual setting with everyday objects. "Their reactions to the magic were so animated and intense I instantly recognized that this is what magic on television should be—magic done to real people in real places," Blaine writes in his 2002 book, *Mysterious Stranger*. He later said, "[A reaction is] the thing I'm searching for more than anything, finding that unfiltered—that person inside. The layers are all being peeled away: guards down, vulnerable. You're seeing a real human being."

His first hour-long television special, *David Blaine: Street Magic*, dropped in 1996. The show was intensely simple: Blaine scuttling up to people on the street and, with his signature deadpan demeanor, performing simple card tricks or other types of illusions, such as making himself levitate. It reinvigorated the art form, made Blaine a celebrity, and gave him the platform to not only keep releasing street magic specials, but perform more and more extreme endurance stunts such as *Buried Alive* (locked in a casket for seven days on 68th Street in Manhattan), *Frozen in Time* (encased upright in a block of ice for over sixty hours in Times Square), and *Vertigo* (where he stood atop a hundred-foot tall pillar for thirty-five hours in Bryant Park). Blaine's more organic approach, however, was followed by the overproduced *Criss Angel Mindfreak*. Television executives were drooling for more magic programming, and Angel's show is widely believed to have used camera tricks and stooges to enhance the effects. Penn Jillette,

speaking on *The Opie and Anthony Show,* once likened Angel to
Samantha Stevens from *Bewitched.**

By 2010, magic was once again far removed from serious performance art. Criss Angel's pervasive character had embedded itself
into the psyche of the typical American entertainment consumer
and merged with magic's already-established clichés. Blaine was
still making captivating specials, but with a multiyear lag between
shows, his take on the craft seemed like something exclusive to
him—something he solely owned—rather than a widespread mentality being adopted by young magicians. Magic was in a cumbersome if not altogether highly complex transition period and, with
young magicians vying for a fast track to stardom on the silver
screen, magic started sprouting up on NBC's *America's Got Talent,*
and the show quickly became a hot-button issue in the community.

It's widely agreed that the main problem with integrating magic
into shows like *AGT* is that it confines the art form's performative
flair within the context of competition. This, to many magicians,
is the antithesis of magic's purpose. Moreover, routines are determined based on the wants and needs of the shows' producers and
the network that pays them. The criteria by which the magicians
are judged, too, is constructed based on parameters set by the
television industry, not other magicians. This in turn influences
how people at home come to evaluate magic. In a way, these are
the same problems magic encountered in the past—the dumbing
down of a much larger artistic vision for television's tried-and-true
model.

---

* More than anything, though, the show's success relied on Criss Angel's
  hyper-cringeworthy and notoriously clichéd goth-rocker branding, no doubt
  exacerbated by the alt-metal music that ruled Middle America in the early
  and mid-aughts. I mean, I think we can all remember the opening credits,
  where Angel is just screaming "Mindfreak" over and over and over.

Young magicians hoping for a breakout moment have likewise lost the ability to curate their presence if they go the route of an *AGT*-type competition show. Eric Jones, part of our friendship circle, performed on *AGT* in 2017. When Eric—who is black—showed up wearing a blazer and slacks, the producers told him to change. They gave him new, stylish streetwear clothes to wear while he performed, including Y-3 shoes, Off White jeans, and Kanye West shirts.* "The producers liked me because I gave the show variety. I am not sure if that's because I had the anti-showmanship presentation, or if it had something to do with my race," Eric told me. "It was never overt, but they did use words like 'hipster,' 'urban,' and 'swag,' and those were words that were also given to Tyra Banks to use in her script when dealing with me."

The producers also forced an intrusive backstory onto Eric, where his estranged son was the driving emotional force behind his appearance on the show. "I fought hard against them integrating my son because I didn't want him used as a prop," Eric told me. "I wanted to focus on the positive things about my life." The producer who crafted this docu-style vignette dug into Eric's relationship with his son, as well as the death of his father. "He starts down one path, finds a sensitive core, and then prods it to make you emotional—to try and make you cry," Eric said.

Eric eventually conceded to the producers' incessant demands to have his son fly out to their filming studio in Los Angeles, mainly because he knew it was unlikely he would advance to the final round, and he wanted to create a moment his son could remember. Still, the entire experience left a sour taste in Eric's mouth. "The producers see us more as actors on their show, even though we see ourselves as artists," he said.

For *AGT*, a magician puts their entire image—and their career—in the hands of producers who see their talent as expendable fodder

---

* They made him return the clothes after he got kicked off the show. *Savage*.

for a television audience, easily manipulated for ratings and on-line clicks. Moreover, magic's ethics come into question when the craft is put into the hands of television producers.* Like with Criss Angel stooging spectators for *Mindfreak*, it's an open secret that some segments on *AGT* are dramatized for added effect.

Demian Aditya, Indonesia's most famous magician (also a member of our friendship circle, and someone who eventually became a member of the52), fell into this conundrum where, for a buried-alive stunt on the show, the producers botched his secret escape tunnel. Demian was supposed to appear behind the judges, with the audience across the way. But the audience was set up *be-hind* the judges, a last-minute decision by the producers, and the tunnel, unbeknownst to Demian until he walked on set, was diverted to another location. Demian was forced to employ a bit of misdirection—and toe an ethical line in the process—to distract the audience.

His wife (a professional actress who knows how all his tricks are done) was folded into the story line at the final hour. "The only option was for my wife to be the misdirection for me to get out," Demian told me. During the stunt, she ran to the site of the burial and screamed, "Get him out! Get him out!" She fell to the ground and howled, the camera zooming in on her tear-soaked face. When Demian emerged unscathed, she ran over and embraced him, the audience fooled into thinking her actions were genuine.[†]

Despite Demian's heart-thumping routines, his time on the show was short-lived. An apparatus for his next stunt—a tower

---

* I'm sure we all remember *Breaking the Magician's Code*, first aired in the late 1990s, where the Masked Magician divulged methods for no reason other than to reveal information long kept secret.

† But, hey, the effect racked up 13 million views on *AGT*'s YouTube channel and advanced Demian to the next round.

that suspended him, handcuffed in a coffin, over a flaming bed of spikes—malfunctioned. When the coffin was supposed to fall onto the spikes, it got stuck halfway down, a consequence of *AGT* producers refusing to pay for Demian's personal builder, replacing him for a contractor of their choice, who, testing the device without Demian present, bent a piece of the delicately engineered rigging.*

He still went through with the reveal, shuffling up behind the judge's table—a humiliated look plastered across his face—as they scowled at the mishap. The judges didn't say anything when he emerged, just smashed that loud honking button, red X after red X beaming from their panel, and killed his dream of winning the show. "It's frustrating when a lot of people thought it was my fault," he told me. "The people at *AGT* think they know about magic, but, eh, not really." He packed his bags and went home.

Far too many people think the magic they've seen on television is all that the craft can offer. "Many people have not felt real, live astonishment," Chris Ramsay told me during one of our many conversations. "Part of the art form is to make them *feel*."

---

* How about this for adding insult to injury: Demian had to pay $10,000 out of his own pocket for the faulty apparatus to be built.

10

THE RULES OF THE GAME

For a long time, magic was confined to a stage. Then it found its place in private parties and spontaneous, close-up situations. Then it was stuck on television. But with the dawn of the internet age, the rules of the game have changed, and social media has emerged as the most important catalyst for magic's current progression.

Social media is in many ways a tool to live vicariously through people whose lives are seemingly better than your own. You follow a fashion blogger because you want to dress like her, you stalk the fitness vlogger because you wish your dedication to the weight room was as forthright as his, and you gawk and awe at the mother on Pinterest because of her perfectly curated domestic life. The same is true for magicians. Ramsay has always said that his take on social media isn't to strictly disseminate the performance of magic, but to show people what type of life can be attained by being a magician—jet-setting, traveling to the biggest cities in the world, mingling with celebrities, lecturing to the masses, and cashing six-figure checks as a successful new-media entrepreneur.

Truly, a successful magician has never been solely defined by his or her technical ability. A magician who wants to make it, especially in the present, needs to not only be talented but also gifted in self-promotion, performance, video and photography production, trick invention and innovation, and personal branding. And in many ways, this has always been true. Just look at Houdini's or Blaine's rise to fame: Houdini performed his most dangerous stunts in public places and whipped a city into a frenzy before the stunt by giving newspapers early access into how the event would go down; Blaine also utilized public spaces for his performances and marketed himself kind of like the antimagician—no frills, just raw astonishment. But the internet has made these aspects of a magician's career even more crucial. Because, the truth is, anyone eager for magic is only one click away from someone bigger and better—someone who best fits their own archetype of what kind of magician they want to see perform, or they themselves want to become.

In present-day magic, you not only have to harness the technical prowess that people can aspire to, but you also have to encompass lifestyle and aspiration, where success and influence is charted through Instagram followers and YouTube views. In any art form, people have been equally fascinated not only with the skill of a practitioner but also the lifestyle embodied by the artist. For me, great writers come to mind: Truman Capote, Hunter S. Thompson, Jack Kerouac, Joan Didion, James Baldwin, Ernest Hemingway. People loved these authors not just for their books, but for the way in which they lived their lives while they created these memorable bodies of work. The two become inextricably linked. On a completely customizable platform like Instagram, a person can become anyone they want without the threat of their brand being diminished or strangled by outside forces—an almost mandatory concession for a magician contracted into a big-time television deal with a billion-dollar media corporation.

The person who has emerged as one of magic's most heralded ambassadors to the outside world—the go-to archetype of a twenty-first-century magician—and the master of utilizing social media for the benefit of his career is also the person who first introduced me to this fascinating world: Chris Ramsay.

In 2012, at age twenty-eight, Ramsay decided to release his first piece of exclusive material. The project, Praxis, was a simple but effective card control and peek hybrid, where the performer could move a card from one spot in the deck to another while simultaneously catching a glimpse of its identity. He wanted to release it through Ellusionist (though this was long before he worked for them full-time). But without a reputation in the industry, Ramsay had to find another way to catch the eye of magic's largest and most powerful retailer. "I didn't look at the content people were creating, but at the creators themselves," Ramsay told me. He saw a crucial flaw. There was a major gap between what the magic community thought was cool or acceptable for a magician's brand and what everyday people thought was cool or acceptable when they imagined a public figure. He knew he wasn't the most astounding in terms of skill, but he had a more evolved cultural taste level than most magicians. He was plugged into millennial culture—he followed fashion trends, had a penchant for tattoos, dedicated himself to the latest hip-hop releases, understood the nuances of social media and digital marketing—and, so, instead of waiting around for the industry to discover him, he took matters into his own hands.

He hired a cameraman and filmed the entire Praxis project himself, complete with an intriguing and well-produced trailer: Ramsay, his face not yet covered in his now-signature beard, wandering around an abandoned building in Montreal, a deck of cards in his hands. The video cuts back and forth to artistic b-roll shots and close-ups of the sleight itself. More than anything, however, it lathered Ramsay in a layer of swagger rarely seen (at least back then) in the magic industry. Because the industry had be so insular, the approach to filming projects revolved around the trick—the product being sold—rather than the magician performing it. But with Ramsay's video, that point of view began to shift; it was as much about him as it was about the sleight. Ellusionist loved everything about Praxis and offered him a contract to release it on their website. Ramsay was ecstatic.

With his first release secured, Ramsay immediately put more effort into building his brand on social media. He knew he needed to create hype. By 2013, Instagram had emerged as the core social media platform for magicians. Magic is an inherently visual enterprise, and Instagram's simple, photo- and video-centric interface was a breeding ground for the community. It shifted the entire subculture. It became their beating heart. "As in the best social media, the artifacts are not the innovation on Instagram," Virginia Heffernan puts forward in her book *Magic and Loss: The Internet as Art.* "Instagram images have become units of speech, building blocks in a visual vocabulary that functions like a colonial patois, where old-school darkroom photography is the native tongue and digitalization is the imperial language." This broader simile of visual media's confluence with digital communication is directly mirrored in magic's breakneck evolution at the time: out with the old, in with the new—and hurry up.

Another by-product of Instagram's influence on magic is cardistry, a card-handling offshoot categorized by flourishes, riffles, and complicated shuffles—balancing intricate shapes of cards with the fingertips, flipping cards into the air and having them fall seamlessly back into the stack. Cardists can handle a deck with incredibly graceful ease; it's as if the cards are dancing in their hands. They are hypnotizing feats of dexterity that take years of dedication and creativity to master. *Wired* wrote a feature on cardistry in 2015 and called it "the elegant, mesmerizing subculture of card juggling."

The practice of flourishing cards has been around for decades, but its modern inclination has become so popular that cardistry-only meet-ups have blossomed into annual events, the flagship of which is hosted by Dan and Dave Buck, the godfathers of the movement. They were the first, in their 2007 DVD *Trilogy*, to offer tutorials on complicated flourishes. "We never thought it would get as big as it's gotten," Dan told me. "When we first started, we could count the people doing it on our hands." More than 350 kids from all over the world traveled to California for CardistryCon 2017; tickets sold out in less than one minute.

The movement has blossomed into its own subculture, now only tangentially related to the magic community. "A lot of guys from cardistry are only interested in cardistry. They don't care about magic. And I think that's really cool," Dan Buck told *Vanity Fair* in 2015. "It's fun to integrate the two, which is what [my brother] Dave and I are known for. But we want cardistry to be a separate art form because it could stand on its own." Cardistry's popularity has likewise been compounded by the nature of content on Instagram and YouTube; as soon as people were able to post videos of themselves doing cardistry, more and more people started adopting the pastime and it continued to grow.

Although many magicians themselves practice cardistry, a lot of newcomers to the activity didn't practice magic previously. It's a fast-growing community centered around a love for playing cards, an offshoot dedicated strictly to sophisticated handling and a pursuit of style. Cardistry doesn't seem to have a specific performative purpose but exists rather to see what is possible with two hands and a deck of cards. "It does seem quite pointless from time to time to just be super skillful at one thing that you can't really use, other than just to show people or do videos," Oliver Sogard, founder of the cardistry-focused playing card company dealersgrip, told me. "But because cardistry is such a small community, the internet plays a very big role in the subculture. Without Instagram, without the internet in general, the cardistry community would have a tough time surviving. We need the technology to communicate with each other and show each other our stuff—which, in the end, has influenced the artistic mentality behind it." Charles Bukowski once said, "Style is a difference, a way of doing, a way of being done." This seems to be the core ethos of the cardistry movement.

Previously, the online magic community had lived in private forums and Facebook groups, which were heavily regulated by moderators and guarded from the public—online extensions of the exclusive backroom meet-ups of yesteryear. But with a blank, hyperpublic canvas like Instagram, magicians had the chance to build constraint-free personal brands that anyone could access and be influenced by. It was the perfect opportunity for magic to snuggle up alongside the widespread sociological revolution the platform produced. Any magician now had the ability to truly be an individual—to try new tricks, to innovate, to truly connect with others in their community. Finally: *total freedom*.

Ramsay was one of the first magicians, alongside Daniel Madison, to take advantage of this sea change in digital consumption and curate his social media presence, using it as a tool to build his reputation in the industry. He added an element of lifestyle to magic: themed, well-lit still-life photographs of playing cards, and tasteful shots of himself in cool clothes—slouching irreverently on a street corner in a bomber jacket, gazing at the camera while adjusting his wide-brimmed Goorin Bros. hat, or, clad in a chunky gray cardigan, flourishing a deck of cards in a snowy field. (Ramsay's style has since evolved into a more high-end streetwear, hypebeast-esque aesthetic: A Bathing Ape jacket, Supreme cap and hoodie, adidas by Pharrell Williams NMD sneakers, etc.)

It was this take on self-branding that first caught my eye when I stumbled across Ramsay in the summer of 2015. I was surprised—befuddled even—that a magician seemed so tapped into the cool-kid self-marketing tactics of social media influencers. Weren't magicians supposed to be nerds? I was pretty straight-up when Ramsay and I met, telling him that he didn't fit the part. "Yeah, dude. That's the whole point," was his telling response.

The new generation's ability to not *look* like magicians in any traditional or stereotypical sense had become their greatest asset, and Instagram allowed that viewpoint to rapidly disseminate. "Magicians used to have this unattainable factor about them," Ramsay told me. "But with Instagram, that veil was lifted. Magic became a culture people could access and be a part of, and allowed Daniel Madison, me, and others to put out our vision of what we thought a magician could be."

This approach—understanding that magicians can be cool; that they aren't inherently geeky or cheesy—laid the groundwork for magic's branding evolution. Just as Robert-Houdin changed the perception of a magician from an otherworldly wizard to the everyday gentleman, young magicians in the twenty-first century were taking current trends and fusing them with an age-old art form for which they had immense love and respect. Guys like Ramsay were now able to replace outdated clichés with a more acceptable notion of who is, and who gets to be, a magician. That was one of the things that intrigued me most about magic once I knew where to look: it now resembled a truly modern subculture. The guys I had fallen in with could be anyone mingling in the crowd at a hip-hop concert, or shooting hoops on the basketball court, or taking down a few whiskeys at the bar on a Friday night. For an art form drowning in stereotypes, that seemed like a massive development—perhaps even its biggest change yet.

After reading about Robert-Houdin and juxtaposing his influence with that of Ramsay and Madison, I saw that building a connection with an audience is reliant not only on the effect itself, but on the understanding that the magician and the audience have so much in common. And Instagram, a platform nearly everyone today is familiar with, made that requirement easier to obtain. Not only does a heightened sense of relatability make the art seem that much more impossible—*Wait, this dude is just like me; how is he so good at magic?*—but entirely more psychologically accessible to a contemporary audience. Part of Ramsay's goal was to take the magician off his self-carved pedestal.

Instagram prompted a change not only in the general aesthetic of magic, but in the innovation of the field. With idea-sharing and chops-boasting no longer confined to members-only forums or private clubs, magic on Instagram (especially after the company integrated video in June 2013) became the main vein of inspiration for young magicians and, therefore, innovation in all areas of the craft. "When Instagram came around, it was a branch for magic," Ramsay explained. "We could now use this platform to be creative and do things no one else had ever done before. A virtual audience brought in a whole new set of rules for how to operate as a magician." Instagram did for magic what no stage or television screen had done before. Magic, previously structured like a monarchy, with kings and lords and princes and gatekeepers, had finally transformed, with the help of the internet, into a democracy.

In addition to content on Instagram, Ramsay also released performance compilation videos on YouTube, as a kind of moving-picture portfolio. His street magic video, from 2014, is still one of the first videos that pops up when you type "street magic" into the search bar (it has since garnered more than one million views). Ramsay didn't know it yet, but being a "YouTuber" would eventually become his full-time job. Back then, though, social media prowess quickly became synonymous with the name Chris Ramsay.*

While pioneering the movement for high-quality, mainstream-friendly content on social media, Ramsay also kept pumping out for-sale projects—making sure to film and direct the videos himself. He released Slipshift, a highly technical color-change sleight—where one card instantly changes into another. Then came Red Pill with Murphy's Magic, which, alongside his growing social media presence, made him a household name in the magic community—and prompted Murphy's to present Ramsay with an offer: become a member of the team. In under two years, Ramsay now held a coveted position as a full-time employee of a magic retail company—an official *creator*—tasked with inventing effects and developing tactics to market, advertise, and brand them online, especially for Instagram. He would continue to make strides, and climb the professional ladder, but back then his quick ascent seemed remarkable.

Around this time, Ramsay also caught the eye of another trend-setter in his world: Daniel Madison. "He was the guy you wanted to know and be friends with, but who no one was actually friends with," Ramsay told me. After linking up on Instagram, Ramsay and Madison chatted frequently over Skype, not necessarily about

---

* When *MAGIC* magazine's Jamie D. Grant profiled Ramsay for its January 2016 issue, he wrote: "Chris Ramsay is what the youth of today would describe as 'crushing' social media with nothing more than a camera, a pair of hands, decks of playing cards, and a unique understanding of how a new art form has been created that mixes magic, cardistry, and personality. One where the fans, supporters, and spectators don't have to leave their homes to see miracles or marvels. They don't even have to buy tickets. The show is free, it's on 24 hours a day, and you hold it in the palm of your hand."

magic but about online branding. They both wanted to carve out strong personas through their social media feeds—with Madison more reliant on an alter ego—to help boost their reputations. They brainstormed in private and coached each other along as their individual influences began to grow. Over time, they became close friends.

One day in 2014, Ramsay sat down at his computer. His Skype pinged. It was a message from Madison: "Pick a card." Ramsay knew what this meant. It was his invitation into the52. He typed back: "The Four of Spades."

"Ah, good," Madison responded. "The devil's bedpost."

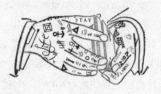

11

CARDSHARPS

The middle-aged man wore a charcoal blazer. He stood in the back of the room and watched the younger magicians mingle about. He didn't speak to anyone, just hung around with his hands in his pockets, quietly observing.

Jeremy Griffith hosts a weekly magician meet-up in Los Angeles called Monday Night Jams. After visiting the Magic Castle, the hangout was next on my SoCal to-do list. They hold court in a backroom section of the dining area at Mimi's, a nondescript restaurant in a strip mall outside Irvine. It's a big meet-and-greet for young magicians in Southern California, and more than two dozen upstart card junkies and illusionists normally roll through. They eat, drink, talk shop, and present their new moves. Many show up just to meet Jeremy—a local celebrity for magic geeks—but once in a while someone surprising makes an appearance.

"That's David Malek," Jeremy whispered, pointing to the back of the room. Malek was the man in the blazer. He was well dressed, with tailored jeans and leather shoes, his brown hair combed back, hands still in his pockets. He gazed around with wide, sharp eyes. After Jeremy introduced us, Malek sat me down at a booth in an adjoining room and took out a deck of cards.

"I spent the majority of my life as a cheat," he said, gazing up at me, smiling. His teeth, wolfish and glazed, reflected the room's light. He reminded me of a comic book villain, reveling in some sort of evil plan, always seeking a way to deceive the guy across from him. Malek, grown tired of grinding away at being crooked, had transitioned from hustling into the world of gambling protection, advising casinos across the country on the methods employed by cheats. He also performs magic professionally. Because of his history on the wrong side of the law, he has, like Daniel Madison, found himself a popular figure in the world of magic.

"Let me show you something," Malek said. He began to shuffle the cards in casino fashion, riffle-style, which prevents the bottom card from being seen by players. He dealt a nine-hand Texas hold 'em game—two facedown cards for each player—and punched out the flop, which are the first three of five faceup communal cards used to make the best hand: seven, deuce, deuce. He turned over his two hole cards: pocket aces. He nodded for me to turn over mine: a seven and a two. I had a full house—a monster hand.

"What do you think the turn and river are going to be?" he asked, referring to the last two communal cards, beaming that sly grin again. I just smiled at him.

"You're right," he said, raising his eyebrows. He dealt the remaining cards: two aces. That gave him four of a kind, crushing my full house. He smiled again and said, "I never lose."

Magicians have long held a fascination with card cheating. Despite both being around for the better part of a thousand years, with obvious overlaps in technique, it took centuries for the two to officially cross paths. Since the early twentieth century, though, sleight-of-hand moves that originated at the card table have been heavily adopted by magicians—for performance and showing off alike—and the lore of con men is delicious fodder for card-magic geeks. Many magicians don't have the gall to sit down at a real card game, put a stack of cash on the table, and pull off a swindle. Utilizing the same techniques for entertainment, though, is the next-best thing. And for me, a guy with poker in his blood, magic's overlap with card cheating is irresistible.

One of the earliest known references of card table artifice came in 1552 when English author Gilbert Walker wrote *A Manifest Detection of Diceplay*, an exposé and cautionary tale of duplicity at the dice counter and card table. He wrote that cheats "have such a sleight in sorting and shuffling of the cards that play at what game ye will, all is lost beforehand." A cardsharp who wasn't dexterous enough, however, was known to hire an old woman to sit behind the sucker and transmit the identity of his cards through the speed and style of her knitting. Back then, no game was safe.

Forty years later, in 1591, Robert Greene published *A Notable Discovery of Cozenage*, which likewise detailed the risks of play during Elizabethan England, an age where "high unemployment and scams were plentiful; thieves, rogues, vagabonds, gamblers, beggars, whores and madmen all lived by their wits and a well-turned trick," writes David Britland in *Phantoms of the Card Table: Confessions of a Cardsharp.*[*]

In Greene's book, he embellished a tale first told in Walker's *Diceplay* about an *Ocean's 11*–style con, in which a group of thieves

---

[*] Card-game duplicity was also prevalent in Italy, as chronicled in Caravaggio's 1594 painting *The Cardsharps*, which showcases a boy hiding cards in his waistband. The painting ushered in many fine-art representations of cheating at the card table, including French painter Georges de La Tour's 1620s masterpiece *The Cheat with the Ace of Clubs*, which is currently on display at the Louvre Museum in Paris.

targeted an oblivious farmer. The tale goes something like this:[*]
While at a local tavern, one man in the group convinces the
farmer to play a card game, under the guise that they are going
to work together to cheat his friend, with the wager being a pot
of wine from the bar. They have two runs at the game, with the
man pulling off some sleight of hand for the benefit of the farmer.
They win, and the second man buys a round of drinks. The first
man then reveals to the second that he and the farmer had played
a trick on him, and the three laugh it off. The stakes were fairly
low, after all. But then another man, right on cue, saunters past
the table and demands a try, himself betting a pot of wine. The
farmer agrees, knowing that he will win because of the ruse. And
he's right: His friend, whom he has just met, pulls off the cheat
for the farmer's victory. But then the third man says he wants to
play again and throws down a large cash wager. The farmer, coincidentally having just unloaded his crop in town, has a pocket-
ful of money. His confidence boosted by a belly full of wine, he
bets it all. But this time his "friend" does not pull off the ruse.
The farmer loses everything. The three men, having successfully
duped their mark, take their winnings and exit the tavern, leaving
the farmer penniless and devastated.

Card cheating showed up again three hundred years later, this
time on American soil, ushering in the advent of modern gambling subterfuge. Just before the Civil War took hold, vagrants and
vagabonds boarded steamboats that cruised up and down the Mississippi River, playing perhaps the first incarnation of present-day
poker. James McManus, in his book *Cowboys Full: The History of
Poker*, writes that poker's increased popularity was natural for the
time, and was a game whose "rules favored a frontiersman's ini-
tiative and cunning, an entrepreneur's creative sense of risk, and

---

[*] It's worthwhile to note that its choreographed structure and scripted role-
playing could be applied to many situations.

a democratic openness to every class of player." In many ways, McManus aruges, poker and the United States grew up together.

By the 1840s, poker emerged as a mainstream American pastime, and in 1875, the *New York Times* declared that "the national game is not base-ball, but poker." Chester Arthur, president of the United States from 1881 to 1885, was an avid participant, and dozens of proceeding presidents likewise played the game competitively, including Dwight Eisenhower, Harry Truman, and Richard Nixon. In 2007, when asked by the Associated Press to name a secret talent, then-senator Barack Obama replied, "I'm a pretty good poker player."

By the mid-1800s, the rules of five-card draw became standardized, Mississippi River steamboats transformed into unregulated on-the-water casinos, and thousands of cardsharps flocked to America's jugular vein, eager to put their deceptive practices to use. Most used sleight of hand, but some cheats, like P. J. "the Lucky Dutchman" Kepplinger, who hailed from San Francisco, developed intricate card-holding contraptions. Kepplinger wore a metal slide hidden within his sleeve that held high-value cards. The slide attached to a rod under his jacket, with wires running to his knees. By clamping his knees together, a card of his choosing would shoot from inside his sleeve and into his hand. This device, called a "holdout," has for decades also been a popular utility for magicians, both to have an object appear in—and vanish from—the hand.

Swindlers like the Lucky Dutchman emptied the pockets of down-and-out travelers and well-to-do businessmen alike, sometimes with disastrously morbid effects. In *Cowboys Full*, McManus describes how, in 1845, a riverboat captain lost a two-thirds stake in his vessel to a cardsharp who beat his four-of-a-kind kings with four-of-a-kind aces. The captain left the table, went to his bedroom, and shot himself through the heart. Many men suspected of being cardsharps suffered a similar fate. In 1835, in Vicksburg,

Mississippi, five hustlers were lynched by vigilantes. "Being hung, shot, stabbed, tarred and feathered, or thrown overboard were not uncommon fates for blacklegs," McManus concludes.

No sooner after cheating became a rampant problem in American gambling were manuals published and speaking tours organized by reformed cardsharps detailing their immoral tactics. In 1843, former hustler Jonathan Harrington Green began giving gambling demonstrations across the country. These quickly transformed from a cautionary tale into magic-esque entertainment. "In its own way his performance was every bit as entertaining as watching a magician at the theatre," David Britland writes in *Phantoms of the Card Table*. "Perhaps more so, because unlike the magician, Green let the audience into the secrets of his illusions."

Aside from describing sleight-of-hand moves, divulging to audiences that cardsharps used marked decks was one of Green's most captivating revelations. When a deck is marked, the design on the back of each card is inlaid with a coding system that reveals its suit and value, a secret language decipherable only by those privy to its alphabet and vocabulary. But cardsharps didn't just come to a table with their own tricked-out deck. In the early days of American gambling, they flooded the entire market with coded cards.

By 1860, an estimated 25 percent of all cards used in America were marked during manufacturing. In 1895, the *Fort Wayne News* reported that a gang of cheats, posing as card salesmen, disseminated large quantities of marked decks to general stores across Ohio, Indiana, Kentucky, Illinois, and West Virginia. The group amassed $15,000 in winnings during a three-week run in Indianapolis alone—more than $400,000 in today's money. In 1844, after one of Green's marked-deck demonstrations, the New York Anti-Gambling Society sent out a newsletter proclaiming that Green showed "that all, or nearly all cards are marked by the manufacturer, some of which were so strongly marked that he told the suit at the distance of twelve or fifteen feet by gaslight."*

Even more so than holdouts or similar devices, marked decks became a staple for magicians. Today the majority of custom decks designed and produced by magic companies implement some sort of intricate marking system. But very few tricks demand marked cards as a core element of its method, so now they are implemented more for nostalgic commodity rather than logistical asset. Still, the level of detail and pure ingenuity that goes into these systems is jaw-droppingly impressive.

While at his house, Jeremy took a deck of cards from his bookshelf (he had hundreds of them, both collectibles and those used for practice), opened it, removed an ace, and told me to stand ten feet away. "David Malek designed this deck—just look." He slowly oscillated the card so its back caught the sunlight coming from the window. "You see that?" he asked. I did—it was plain as day: an obvious band appeared every time the ray of light hit the card.

---

* A few modern-day casino scams also involved marked decks. In 1999, the Caesar's Casino in Johannesburg, South Africa, discovered that nearly every deck used in their casino was marked by the manufacturer. In-the-know hustlers plunked down at the blackjack tables and siphoned more than $300,000 from the establishment. "When you have a new move that the casino isn't looking for, it fools the hell out of them. They aren't defending against it. They don't even know it exists!" said Ron Conley, a legendary casino protection expert and former card cheat whom Jeremy and I visited during my time in Los Angeles. "If you are trying to rob them," he continued, "that's the optimal situation." We sat in Conley's living room, listened to his stories, and watched him work a deck of cards. Conley explained that, back in the 1970s, casinos started using automatic shuffling machines, which revealed opportunities for advantage play. He obtained one of the machines and fed it a few decks, with each card labeled numerically. "The way the machine shuffled, you wouldn't see the top forty cards for hours," he said, adding that, for blackjack, that could give a player a distinct edge against the house. A player would know how the machine *thinks*.

The system of incorporating these markings, which are faint lenticular treatments, is called "juicing." This system is even more covert than traditional markings because it can only be detected if the object is in motion—like when a dealer tosses cards across the table, or a player lifts his hand to take a peek.

Design-based coding systems, however, are more common, and the first set of marked cards produced for magicians was released by Theodore DeLand in 1907. Called Devil's Own, it was a ten-card product used for a specific trick. Six years later, in 1913, DeLand came out with DeLand's Dollar Deck, the first fully marked deck of traditional playing cards. Since then, dozens of custom marking systems have been invented, all using different methods to decipher a card's identity, developed both for custom designs and standardized decks.*

Aftermarket tools for secretly modifying honest cards are also used by both cardsharps and magicians. There's punching, also known as pegging, where a small indentation is placed on a given card via a small pin secretly affixed to the thumb. If a cheat receives an ace from the dealer, they'd punch the card. A few hands later, when it was their turn to deal, they could feel the card's

---

* For modifying well-known cards, like Bicycles, a magician could, for example, implement the Farmarx System. "The areas to be blocked out are the four daisy patterns, two at each end of the back," Kirk Charles instructed in *Hidden in Plain Sight: A Manual for Marked Cards*. "There are eight petals and a center dot in each daisy. These nine spots are filled in to represent the values and suits of the cards. The daisy on the left signals the values, while the daisy on the right signals the suits." The Farmarx System uses shape to discern value—petals left unblocked in the shape of an *A* represent an Ace, for example—but loads of other image-based languages can be used for a common brand like Bicycles. All you need is the right color ink to illicitly modify a deck that anyone could have lying around their house. "Harry Riser suggests using Pelikan Drawing Ink, No. 3, Vermillion," Charles continued, referring to red Bicycles, "and No. 10, Prussian Blue," for blue Bikes, "applied with an 00000 sable or camel artist's brush."

identity—a kind of swindler's brail—and do with it as they wish. A magician can utilize the same process during an effect, or pre-peg specific cards before a routine.

There's also daubing, a system where special goop is secretly smeared on a chosen card before or during play. It creates a slight discoloration that is virtually invisible to the untrained eye. After David Malek demonstrated his skill as an advantage dealer at Mimi's, he reached into his pocket and pulled out his cell phone. "Let me show you something," he said. He opened a text message. It was from a man who was in search for a special kind of daub.[*]

"You see that?" Malek said, standing up, swiveling around, pointing at the message. "He wants me to make him a daub that can only be seen through special glasses. You'd make out any card you want, clear as day. You wouldn't even have to try. This guy plays for big money in Monaco—*big*."

"But I thought you helped casinos?" I asked him. He beamed a sly, glazed-over grin.

"Sometimes, my friend," he said, putting his hand on my shoulder, his voice falling to just above a whisper, "you have to play both sides."

Some contemporary magicians use daub, and many more implement old-school marking systems into their custom designs. Jeremy's first deck, Royal Reserve, which was sold through Ellusionist, utilized the juicing system for value range only, a system best used in blackjack rather than poker: the aces are marked with a single band through the middle; ten through king are marked with two bands that are close together; seven through nine are marked with two bands that are far apart; and two through six have no marking on them at all. Almost all of Madison's namesake decks—the Dealers, Rounders, and Gamblers, to name a few—use

---

[*] Malek requested I not use his name for fear the guy "would probably get killed."

simple marking systems popularized by cardsharps in the 1800s. Even David Blaine's decks are secretly coded. It was believed for a long time that all the different ways a deck could be marked had already been invented. There was only so much you could do to covertly code fifty-two pieces of paper, right? But, in 2016, Ondřej Pšenička, a young magician from Prague, Czech Republic, came out with Butterfly Playing Cards.

He spent four years designing a marking system that gave the magician the unprecedented ability to know the exact position of any card in the deck, even when the deck had been shuffled by the spectator. It also allowed the magician to instantly know the identity of a card that had been removed from the deck. Or even better: a card that had been removed from the deck *and put back in.*

With his system, a spectator could literally pick any card, take a peek, put it back into the deck, shuffle the cards themselves, and hand the seemingly indecipherable mess back to Ondřej. He'd then be able to announce the chosen card without having to do anything but quickly glance at the stack. Seeing the face of an individual card wasn't necessary. How beautifully simplistic is that? How supremely magical in its impossibility? How flat-out remarkable in its conception—that it came from the mind of one man, a magician with a goatee and round glasses and colorful socks?

It was a groundbreaking achievement—a contribution so ingenious that, once Laura London and Daniel Madison became aware of Ondřej's invention, they immediately invited him into the52. Laura took Ondřej to get his ink while he was visiting England. He became the Ace of Hearts.

Magicians began adopting techniques pioneered by cardsharps as early as the 1860s—some even sold holdouts based on the Lucky Dutchman's design—but it wasn't until 1902, with the release of a curious book by an anonymous author, that sleight of hand pioneered by cheats completely changed how magicians approached the craft. *The Expert at the Card Table*, written under the pseudonym S. W. Erdnase, has stood for more than a century as magic's most thorough and well-regarded text on playing card sleight of hand. If you are serious about magic, reading the book should be first on your to-do list.

The book is a hard-core instruction manual, as thorough and meticulous as any medical journal. "The wording is wonderfully precise, with every finger position of every sleight and move thoroughly described," David Britland writes in *Phantoms of the Card Table*. "They are framed by many insights into the psychology of sleight of hand and the mind of a cheat. . . . It retains its position as one of the most detailed and rewarding books on cheating with cards ever written."

The book did not set the world on fire. It wasn't until 1909, when it was first featured in conjuring journals, that it began to gain traction within magic circles. But I'll be completely honest: it's damn hard to read. The prose is so chock-full of jargon that, when I first attempted to muscle through it after returning from Blackpool, I had to constantly refer to the list of nineteen technical terms at the start of the book to understand what the hell was going on: *stock, run, jog, in-jog, out-jog, break, cull, blind, upper cut, under cut, crimp,* and so on. I'd call up Jeremy or Ramsay, venting my irritation. "What the hell does this shit *mean?*" I'd say. It was like I was reading the *Infinite Jest* of magic. The prose was dry and clinical. I found practicing frustrating.

As I met more magicians, though, I saw the book's influence. The terms Erdnase used, although originating with cardsharps, now form the backbone of card magic's modern-day lexicon. The book created a pivotal shift in magicians' approach to card magic, not only because of its precision as an educational tool, but also because, frankly, no one had any idea who the hell S. W. Erdnase was. Magicians were fascinated not only with the quality of the text, but the anonymity and elusiveness of its creator—and because no one understood what prompted the author to divulge his secrets.

After decades of obsessive digging by magicians, the widely accepted theory is that Erdnase's real name was Milton Franklin Andrews and, shortly after publishing *Expert*, he was accused of murder and went on the lam, living as a down-and-out fugitive and squatting in a San Francisco halfway house. While there, he got into a scuffle with another man and tried bashing in his head with a hammer. But Andrews didn't kill him, the cops were quickly on his trail, and they soon raided the building in which he was hiding. Before they could bust through his door, however, Andrews murdered his girlfriend before shooting himself in the head.* Because of his shadowy and untimely death, it cannot be wholly confirmed, even to this day, if Milton Franklin Andrews was really S. W. Erdnase. "He remains, however, a phantom at the card table, an anonymous figure who plays and wins and then takes his leave," Britland writes in *Phantoms*. "And, as the door shuts behind him, like a great magician he keeps you guessing." If anything is certain about an art form rooted in deception, it's that S. W. Erdnase—a murderer, fugitive, and con man—changed magic forever.

Over the years, the cultural myth of Erdnase and the technical advice he crafted slowly descended upon the world of magic and has never left. We see remnants of his influence on the skin of those in the52: Ramsay has one of the book's figure diagrams tattooed on his arm, and Madison has the year in which it was published permanently scrawled on the faces of his knuckles. Madison and Laura admitted magician and professional (legal) forger Chris Dickson into the52 (the Five of Spades) because of his uncanny

---

* Some theorize that they were gunned down by police and the murder-suicide plot was planted by local authorities.

ability to reproduce duplicates of the book's earliest known copies, or those with annotations written by famous magicians. He has gifted these reproductions to the likes of David Blaine, Ricky Jay, and the Magic Castle. Dickson also created the diary used for Laura's show *CHEAT*.*

Finding the book was life changing for many magicians—especially Dai Vernon. One of the earliest and most aggressive evangelists of *The Expert at the Card Table*, he was obsessed with the lore and lifestyle of the cheat (not to mention the moves in the book, which he quickly mastered—and used to fool Houdini). The book was also the seed that grew into his philosophy toward magic, a point of view dedicated to the naturalness of action during a routine: no clues and no flashes, impeccably seamless movement, operating as if nothing were happening during a sleight. It was the same methodology that dictated a cheat's behavior at the card table. "When you do a trick move of any kind, whether dealing a bottom card or making some kind of pass," Vernon once said, "all eyes are focused on you and it has to be faultlessly executed or, needless to say, you will wind up in an alley with a broken hand."

In the 1930s, Vernon became increasingly obsessed with finding cardsharps who would teach him sleights that could be applied to magic. Any rumor of a new cheat sent him off to far-flung destinations, including a jail cell in Wichita, Kansas, and the back roads of Missouri farm country. He frequently brought to New York those he corralled on the road and presented them to his friends as specimens of unusual skill. "I never aspired to be a gambler," Vernon once said. "I never wanted to cheat anybody, but I was still fascinated by the work of these people." Over the years, he

---

* In an occupational twist, Dickson is also an air defense artillery warrant officer for the United States Army, tasked with pushing the button on the THAAD missile system in Guam if North Korea were to lob a ballistic missile at the island.

counted many swindlers as friends. Although Vernon met many a cheat during his travels, another cardsharp made a more lasting impression on the magic community—a card mechanic so fluid, so devastatingly deceptive, that Vernon's closest friends admitted that he may have bested the Professor. His name was Walter Irving Scott.

Scott lived in Providence, Rhode Island, and was a former cheat who could not only flawlessly handle a deck of cards across a spectrum of techniques but also had reportedly developed an approach to the second deal, where the card second from the top is dealt instead of the first, not seen in Erdnase. After hearing of his skills, the best magicians in New York City arranged a meeting for June 14, 1930. They wanted to see Scott work.

Scott was a slick-dressed man in his thirties, hair combed back, with a gentlemanly swagger that disarmed the skeptical magicians. Before the demonstration began, however, the gods of sleight of hand had one request: Scott had to show his skills with a black bag over his head. He had to do it blind. Scott warmed up, worked the cards a bit, and asked someone to shout out a number. "Six," one of the magicians in attendance replied. Scott then dealt a six-handed game of five-card poker. After all the cards were laid out, they turned over Scott's hand: four-of-a-kind aces with a king kicker. The magicians couldn't believe their eyes.

"Without a doubt Walter Scott is the cleverest man with a pack of cards in the world," *The Sphinx*, the most prominent magic journal at the time, wrote shortly after the meeting. "I am as much at sea as anyone. Can't explain or give any clue. There is simply no explanation." Two months later, the publication wrote of Scott again: "I cannot begin to tell you of the miracles of Scott. . . . Dai [Vernon] to me is the greatest in cards but now I have to pass the crown to Scott and the others all agree with me." Vernon had, for at least the time being, been kicked off his throne as the king of cards.

Scott didn't care much about being famous with magic's in crowd; his true passion was music. Supremely deceptive feats of card handling were just things he had acquired throughout his life. He wasn't necessarily secretive, either, just simply modest regarding his penchant for sleight of hand. After his short-lived foray into the world of magic, Walter Irving Scott vanished. His legend, however, lived on. His otherworldly abilities, and the lore associated with his demonstrations, continued to steal the hearts of card junkies and move monkeys for decades to come.

One magician who still idolizes Scott: Daniel Madison.

In 2011, Madison was invited onto *Penn & Teller: Fool Us*. It was the show's first season, and Madison was one of magic's rising stars. It was around this time, too, that he began solidifying the alter ego that would eventually encompass his entire public persona—the secretive and cryptic cheat, chock-full of internal demons.

Madison took the stage in a black short-sleeved button-up, its collar held tight to his neck by a matching black tie. He opened his skit by telling a story. "June 14, 1930. There was a card cheat called Walter Irving Scott," he said. "He managed to fool some of the world's most amazing magicians by demonstrating an ability to deal winning poker hands from a shuffled deck of cards. And he did this blindfolded. A lot of speculation followed these stories as to whether the deck that he used was borrowed or his own. Any magician can deal aces or a winning poker hand from his own deck, but tonight I am going to attempt to deal a winning poker hand from a deck of cards that I've never handled before. And in honor of Walter Irving Scott," he continued, pausing to take a large black object out of his back pocket, "I am going to attempt to do it wearing a blindfold."

Madison had Penn & Teller join him at the card table onstage. The duo inspected and approved of Madison's blindfold, took out their own deck of cards, and gave it a thorough shuffle. Madison strapped the blindfold to his face and took the deck from Penn. He began dealing cards into a single pile, one by one, pausing inter-mittently to deal himself one card as he went through the deck. His actions were slow and methodical, as if he were trying to read the identity of the cards through touch alone. A minute later, Madison had a five-card hand in front of him, the rest of the cards discarded to his right. "If I've done this correctly, the five cards that I've dealt to the table will be a Royal Flush, all diamonds." Penn flipped them over: ten through ace, all diamonds.

"Wow," Penn started. "I think we might be more impressed because we know what you did. A good friend of mine, Jerry Camaro, did the move that you did when you were dealing out the cards. And his move was so perfect, he would teach it to ma-gicians, but they could never learn it, and the reason they could never learn it was because he spent fourteen years in prison for Murder One and practiced every day." The crowd laughed. "I have never seen anyone who did not do hard time in prison do that move that well."

Madison later confessed to me that he never intended to fool Penn & Teller. What he was really trying to communicate with the performance was his idolization of Walter Irving Scott and his own, hopefully comparable skill with a deck of cards. All he wanted was for Penn & Teller to know what he was doing, and he wanted them to respect him for doing it so well. In some ways, you can win that show without necessarily fooling its hosts. But it's slightly unclear, at least to me, if Penn & Teller truly knew the method behind the trick.

The secret behind the performance is really quite simple and rooted entirely in nineteenth-century card cheating: Madison stashed the winning hand in his pocket before coming onstage and secretly placed it on the bottom of the deck when Penn handed him the cards. He dealt the Royal Flush from the bottom of the deck. Called bottom-dealing, it's a classic move taught in *The Ex-pert at the Card Table*. But there was one crucial glitch in his plan.

"I had no idea if they were going to give me a red Bicycle deck or a blue one!" Madison told me, laughing. Seconds before he went out onstage, a producer tipped him off on the deck's color, and Madison strode out and dealt the impossible. It was a quasi-landmark moment for Madison as a magician (he personally couldn't give a shit if he's on television), but also one of very few instances where he would make such a public appearance. After that, he went back underground, continuing to practice his mechanics in private, and presenting himself exclusively through his well-curated social media feeds. The performance, however, nodded to the thing that got Madison into magic in the first place: cheating at cards.

The next day, in California, Jeremy was scheduled to film his second official offering to the magic community.* Ellusionist asked that he compile nine moves detailing the secrets and methodology behind his most famous tricks—all of which were first seen on Instagram. We traveled down to San Diego to film the project, and Ramsay, having just been hired by Ellusionist and tasked with producing the segment, flew in from Montreal to meet us. Dan and Dave Buck, the San Diego–based twin-brother duo who own their own magic retail companies Art of Play and Art of Magic,† let us use their studio for the day. Jeremy sat down and got to work.

They called the project the Instagram Sessions.

I was always in awe of Jeremy's skill, but seeing him work for the camera was mesmerizing. The moves were raw sleight of

---

* His first was a false-shuffling technique put out earlier in the year through Xavior's company Lost Art Magic.

† Art of Magic was overseen for many years by Elliott Terral, a dapper magician and fashion aficionado from Louisiana who became a close friend of mine.

hand, many of which were contemporary riffs on old cheating techniques: mucking, where a single card on the table is replaced with another after a quick swipe of the hand; ditching, where one or more cards—or the entire deck—is dumped into the lap; the one-handed top palm, where the top card is seamlessly taken from the deck and hidden in the hand; and the Arthur Finley Steal, a variation of the Diagonal Palm Shift—a move first taught in *The Expert at the Card Table*—where a card is secretly removed from the middle of the deck. The project was a perfect example of the evolution of card-cheating moves, and how they've found a place in magic's contemporary, social-media-fueled landscape.[*]

The day after we filmed Jeremy's project, we piled into his car and pointed east, careening along Route 15, past Barstow and into the desert. The road boiled in the heat and stretched out to the

---

[*] Cheating at cards likewise holds an element of intrigue in today's mainstream culture. In 2017, for the fourth season of *Penn & Teller: Fool Us*, Richard Turner duped the famed duo with a gambling demonstration, including second-dealing and false-shuffling. He even let the guys shuffle the cards and subsequently dealt Teller four-of-a-kind kings in a hand of Texas hold 'em. The catch? Turner is blind. (The performance racked up over four million YouTube views and landed on the front page of reddit; Turner was also the subject of the acclaimed 2017 documentary *Dealt*.) For his one-man show *In & Of Itself*, which ran in New York City throughout 2017 and 2018, innovative young-gun magician Derek DelGaudio incorporated an anecdote of a card cheat, using the metaphor of a wolf to introduce his skills with a deck of cards—including the infamous middle deal, where cards are dealt from the middle of the deck. In 2016, New Jersey–based magician Mark Calabrese (who eventually became a friend of mine) was featured on VICE's cable television show *Black Market*—masked, with his voice distorted; Mark told producers this wasn't necessary, but VICE made him do it for added dramatic effect—where he talked about deceptive tactics used to cheat at underground poker games. His identity was never revealed by VICE, and no one knew that the guy talking about stacking the deck is also a well-respected member of the magic community. And so, almost all current mainstream gambling demonstrations are conducted by magicians, not reformed card cheats.

horizon like a piece of hot black taffy—110 degrees outside, the sun sinking in front of us like a ship ablaze, lighting the scrubby expanse on fire. I sat in the back while Ramsay took the front seat. Just after the sun fell beneath the hard black line of the horizon, we saw the lights: a sea of flickering white and green and red, the Las Vegas Strip, an oasis of degradation stuck in the middle of nowhere. At that very moment, thousands of magicians from all over the world were flying to Sin City for Magic Live, the largest annual convention in the country. I stared out the window knowing that, at some point in the next few days, it would be official: me, the journalist who stumbled upon this world, would become a member of the52. But the most delicious part of the whole thing was that Ramsay didn't have a clue.

All I would have to do, I told myself, was stick to the plan.

12

AT THE TABLE

Two years ago, my mother and I took a weekend trip to Foxwoods Resort Casino in Mashantucket, Connecticut. It's pretty convenient for both of us. She drives down from Massachusetts and I take a bus up from Brooklyn. She begins her time at the casino playing slots, the cheap ones, a penny or nickel per spin. It's really just an excuse to smoke cigarettes and have a few free beers. (Maybe she'll even win some easy cash.) You can't smoke cigarettes in the poker room, which is the real reason why we make these trips. We try to get together at least once a year and play some cards. It has almost become a pilgrimage, a ritual we've allowed ourselves since my father died. It's our time together.

The poker room is in the basement, away from the buzzing slot machines and crowded blackjack tables. It's a wide, low-ceilinged room with red carpet. We try to not sit at the same table but every couple of hours I'll take a break and walk over to watch her play, to see if her stack has grown. Halfway through our second day, she was on a cold streak and, folding most of her hands, spent her time observing the other players. What were their tics? Their personality traits? How could she figure out things about them that, despite being at the poker table, they couldn't hide from other players—that they couldn't take away from themselves? At the poker table, people try their best to conceal who they are from those around them, but a lot of the time, the poker table is where the truest form of you is revealed.

It's strange to think that she's been playing since before I was born—back in her Houston days. It must've been a strange sight, my mother in those dimly lit rooms, stacking chips with her slender fingers. But she enjoyed proving people wrong, I think, and, in a way, when she sat down at those tables she was able to become someone else, if even for just one night. She grew up in a strict, no-nonsense household, an environment where she couldn't break the rules or engage in risky behavior. But when she first found poker, she realized she could shed that good-girl veneer. She could be the villain and get rewarded for it. "The biggest draw for me with this game was that I could go out there and be blatantly deceptive, which is very unlike me," she told me once. "But, with poker, the entire premise is to sit down and lie to other people. It's almost liberating. There's just something about it that speaks to me. And I'm *good* at it."

Moving back to Massachusetts was more a strategic decision than one rooted in loyalty. My father refused to return to Ohio, and New England held stability and promise. My mother initially stayed home to take care of the house and us kids but eventually became my father's secretary when he founded his tile company a few years later. He always wanted more, both materially and metaphorically, in an effort to be as far removed as possible from where he'd come from. My mother found that her life had quickly latched itself on to an immovable track. Her life—and the decisions associated with it—were driven by her emotional and logistical obligations to the ideals of stable family: her children, her husband, his business. They had a plan. The plan meant everything.

But she still made time to teach me about cards. We would sit in the living room and play out hands together, wagering with pocket change or flimsy plastic chips. We played both five-card draw and Texas hold 'em. Her teeth are narrow and sharp and, even against me, her smile would creep out from behind her thin lips as she fanned out a winning hand—a full house, say, or a king-high flush. We lived in the small, one-story rental near the center of town then, and the kitchen had cheap linoleum floors. My mother refurbished most of the furniture herself and sponge-painted the hallway that bisected the house, running from the kitchen down to the bedrooms. She was in her late thirties when I was that age, nearly twenty years since her real playing days. But now she was married and the mother of two children. She had a dream house to save for, goals to achieve. She had responsibilities. The only thing left over from that period in her life were those playing cards. They were a relic from her past, signaling a lifestyle she had since given up but not forgotten.

After my father died, she started hosting games in our base-ment with a group of friends. With Texas hold 'em exploding in popularity, her circle of players quickly grew. She also started taking frequent trips to casinos, playing in larger and larger tournaments and against better and better players. She won con-stantly. I started playing, too. I'd fold into her games or schedule a tournament with kids from my high school. While my friends and I squeezed in rounds on weekends, she was playing regularly, sometimes five or six nights a week. The schedule became nor-mal for me: I'd get home from school and, a few hours later, she'd kiss me good-bye, leave some money for dinner, and head off to a game. She would always make sure she took care of her respon-sibilities at home first—a clean house, food in the fridge, emo-tional upkeep of her pubescent teenagers—but she always fed the need to play cards, to once again sit in those dimly lit rooms, to grasp at the fragments of a life she once had, before everything changed.

She'd come home after midnight, long after I went to bed. Normally, on my way out the door for school the next day, I'd find $100 bills laid out on the kitchen table, a trophy from a good night's work. One night, though, I woke up around 1 A.M. to the crack and sizzle of oil in a pan, the smell of fried eggs wafting through the house. I came downstairs from my bedroom and found her hunched over the skillet. Tears ran down her face as she sucked her lower lip. I walked over and hugged her. "He's gone and I'm just so sad," she said. Her chest shook against mine—that spastic shuddering of pure despair. I said, "It's okay," after every sob, my arms wrapped around her. Behind me, a stack of money sat on the counter next to the sink.

I noticed that poker was making things easier for her. It gave her an outlet that required concentration and mental clarity. It also allowed her to make decisions solely for herself, to be a little selfish, to take risk at her own expense. And while poker may seem like an unorthodox pastime to heal the loss of a husband, to her it became a release, an opportunity for her to take control and be rewarded for being unabashedly herself—for being the risk-taking person she once was, for letting loose the part of herself that she put away when she became a wife and mother. She created a new obligation in life: herself. She was trying to find a way to be happy again, or at least forget the ways in which her life had derailed itself from the previously chosen track. She wanted to escape. And, so, I make sure we always set aside time to go to the casino together.

My mother moved tables after her cold streak at Foxwoods. A guy in his late twenties sat across from her and kept reaching over his chest to tug at his shirt just below the collarbone. He must've played basketball, she thought. Only basketball players adjust their shirt that way, a habit made from wearing a uniform with tank-top-like straps. I did the same thing as a kid when I played. She folded hand after hand and watched this man play. She watched the way he touched his cards, the way he grabbed his shirt. His hair was cropped short, like an athlete, but his hands were thick and calloused. What had happened to him after the dream of professional sports faded away? How did he get here, at this table, with me? What was *his* plan and how did it fall apart?

We cashed out our chips late, after two in the morning. She said she wanted a beer before going to bed and asked if I would sit with her. We went to the bar and I bought her the drink. We sat down, and she lit a cigarette. She told me about the guy she thought was a basketball player. It took her a while, but she finally asked him, and it turned out that he had in fact played college ball. She didn't ask about the rest of his life. She didn't have to. She stared off as she told me the story, tapping the end of her cigarette on the rim of the ashtray in front of her. I felt like she wanted to say something, something that she knew to be true not only about the player sitting across from her, but also herself. After nursing a long sip, she put down her beer and looked at me. She took a drag from her cigarette. "You can't change how ingrained your past is within you," she said. "You can't leave that behind no matter how hard you try, even when you're at the table. You just can't."

13

THE TWO OF CLUBS

Jeremy's rumor spiraled out of control. I swear I had nothing to do with it.

During our visit to the Magic Castle, one magician after another asked me to perform. I told them I wasn't a magician and that I didn't know any tricks. One performer, Lauren, was sure I was just being modest and later asked Jeremy what my deal was. "Oh, Ian? He doesn't like to show people stuff, but he's incredible," he told her. "Maybe one day he'll show you his Diagonal Palm Shift." He was describing a sleight where the performer can seamlessly remove a card from the center of the deck and either palm it (keep it in the hand but hidden from the spectator) or move it to the bottom of the deck for easy access. It's one of the more difficult maneuvers that magicians use. The seed he planted in Lauren's brain continued to grow and, by the time we got to Las Vegas for Magic Live a week later, had planted roots. She was a woman on a mission. She needed to see me perform it.

"Ian, when are you going to show me your DPS?" she asked,

referring to the move by its acronym. This was the third time she brought it up in the past two days.

"Okay, fine," I told her, pulling a deck from my pocket. "Come over here. I'll show you." I took the top card off the deck with my right hand and showed it to her: the ten of spades. I threaded it into the middle of the deck and moved my left hand down the pack's edge—this is where the move is supposed to happen—and then, after a moment, showed her the bottom card: the ten of spades.

"Wow," she said. "So smooth! It's almost like nothing is happening!"

And she was right: Nothing *was* happening. Jeremy and I had set up the deck that morning. I placed a duplicate ten of spades on the bottom, and the one I had taken off the top of the deck and shown her was still in the middle of the pack. I had found my own way to deceive other magicians: not through technical skill but by using my own reputation against them. An insider with the community's most famous cast of characters, I was now viewed as someone special, and I had to keep up the act. I felt no shame in my deception; any other magician, given the opportunity, would have done the same thing.

"Do it again? Please?" she asked. I rolled my eyes.

An actor playing the part of a magician.

"Okay, fine." I took the top card—the eight of hearts—and slid it into the middle of the deck. After squaring up the cards, I showed her the bottom: the eight of hearts.

"This is the only time I'm going to show you," I said to her, getting up to walk away, knowing she would never suspect that I set up *two* duplicate cards in the deck. "Never again."

We all hung out at the Mardi Gras bar in the Orleans Hotel and Casino—surrounded by sloppy tourists, grubby gamblers, and dejected dealers—and it became our de facto clubhouse for the duration of the trip. The true convention, however, was upstairs in the event hall: endless tables of gimmicks and props and how-to manuals, vendors shouting for your attention, hawking their latest release—just like Blackpool.

Have you seen this one?

Come close!

I'll show you something! It kills!

But none of us had bought tickets. Ramsay and the guys treated the convention in the same way they did Blackpool: a social event, not a glorified magical flea market. We were scheduled to be there for four days. I figured that I had plenty of time to pull off my scheme.

My plan was to lure Ramsay to the nearest tattoo shop under the pretense of touching up some of my ink. Once in the shop, I would perform a trick for the tattoo artist and, after fooling the shopkeeper, turn to Ramsay and divulge that Madison had made me a member of the52. The trick would use cards, integrate the Two of Clubs, and the reveal would not really be about the tattoo artist at all, but rather about Ramsay and what we now shared. From there—*buzz buzz*—I would get my ink and it would be official.

My planned trick was Angle Zero (widely known as Angle Z), an effect that Madison had invented. It was actually one of his claims to fame—a trick that has been touted as one of the most influential card routines of the past decade, and solidified Madison's place in the hierarchy of magic's elite creators.

After its release in 2007, David Blaine started performing it on television. It made an appearance in his 2013 special *Real or Magic*, but he also performed it the same year during a one-on-one ABC News interview to promote his show. After the reveal, the host sat in his chair, slack-jawed and stunned, and stared at the playing card in his hand. He eventually muttered, "Wait a minute. Are you serious? How did you . . . How did you . . . Well now you freaked me out. My wallet is still with me, right?" he said, checking his back pocket. "Okay, when the cameras are off, you'll have to show me how it's done." Blaine just smiled, shook the man's hand, and extended thanks for having him on the show.

After Madison's violent confrontation with the backroom gamblers, he was a wreck. He decided that his days playing poker, or any kind of nine-to-five life, were over. He wanted to put his skills into magic. He wasn't someone who had grown up idolizing David Copperfield, or playing with a kiddie magic kit, but he did love cards, had a knack for sleight of hand, and had done a short stint as a card cheat. The slide over into magic, he thought, should be easy.

He started booking gigs in Bradford and was soon discovered by Dynamo, another upstart magician from the area. Dynamo was just a scrawny blue-eyed kid back then, in the early 2000s, but would eventually go on to become one of England's most famous magicians, and star in one of the most successful magic television series in the country's history. His brand is mysterious and otherworldly—he once walked on water over the River Thames in London—but also honest and humanistic. Dynamo has Crohn's disease, a crippling gastrointestinal disorder, which stunted his growth as a kid. Despite being bullied, he became famous. His aspirational backstory, that you can do anything you want if you put your mind to it, made him an idol to kids and adults alike. But back in their early days, Madison and Dynamo were both just young guys trying to make a living. Madison confessed to Dynamo that he didn't know anything about the magic industry and, despite his skill with a deck of cards, was a newbie in that world.

Shortly after they first met, Dynamo invited Madison to visit the Magic Circle in London, and Madison decided to audition for membership. He saw, back then, a community he could become a part of—a way to be accepted. "I thought, *Wow, this whole industry exists, and there are places where magicians hang out and come together? And they share tricks? Yeah, I want to be a part of that!"* Madison told me, mocking a past version of himself.

Madison pulled together the nicest clothes he had and walked into the parlor for his audition. A panel of judges in front of the small stage waited for him to begin. They were examining not only raw technical skill, but also style of performance and if the magician was presenting any exclusive material. Madison introduced himself, said he was visiting from the Leeds area, took out his deck, and started his set. His routine was basically material copied from David Blaine's television specials, with a bit of his own stuff mixed in. They were effects he had never been officially taught, just things he picked up through reverse-engineering Blaine's work or routines constructed from moves he developed on his own—which, to be honest, is highly unusual. Most magicians are taught in a traditional way, from another magician or through educational literature, but not Madison. He had come out of the beating broken and lost, and, with no connection to the magic community but still a love for it, he spent much of his time alone in a room with a deck of cards. He found comfort in solitude, and in the challenge of reverse-engineering the tricks he was seeing on his television screen. In his own little world, he had a sense of purpose, a goal to accomplish, a new skill to master— perhaps something that could carry him into the future. With his prospects as a thief thrown out the window, and his family life unstable, he needed a new path.

After Madison performed a few tricks, he waited for the judges to give their determination. "Where did you learn? Did you learn from Dai Vernon's work?" the judging panel asked him. Madison had no idea who Vernon was, and confessed as much during their questioning. But they didn't believe him. "You don't have to lie to us," they told him, chuckling. "We are all magicians here." Madison pulled one of the judges aside.

"Listen, I almost died in a card game where I cheated, and I turned that into magic," he said. "And I really don't want to have to tell that story to people."

The man smiled back at him, nearly winking in his response. "Oh, so *that's* your story, huh?" he said, still grinning. Madison left feeling dejected. Despite being granted membership, he was put off by the encounter—"I saw pretty quickly how lame it all was"—and never went back to the Circle. Madison then began to write his own material and publish his take on effects and sleight-of-hand moves. In 2003, when he was twenty-three years old, he stuffed a dozen copies of his first instructional booklet, *One*, into his backpack and set off for the famed Blackpool Magic Convention. Madison explained to other magicians he met that he would demonstrate all the moves in his booklet the following evening at the Ruskin. Hyped up by word of mouth, nearly two dozen people showed up to watch Madison work, including a few actual names. They left in awe.

The collection of notes, a modest £10 each, sold out instantly and Madison went back to Bradford £100 richer. When he got home a few days later and checked his PayPal, which was linked to his online store, he found dozens of orders for the book. Word had spread through online forums about his performance, and everyone wanted a piece of magic's new creative mind. "When I put that first book out, I didn't know shit about magic," Madison told me. "I didn't read magic books. I had no history or point of reference at all. But people were buying it and that's all I cared about."

He came out with subsequent editions and sold them online as downloadable PDF booklets. Some of the moves he discovered himself, however, had already been developed and published by someone else: S. W. Erdnase. "When I first found out about Erdnase, my mind was blown," Madison said. "People have been doing this shit for a hundred years! I was like, *Fuck*. I naïvely thought that I was the first person to discover these things."

So, Madison did his homework. He started reading and researching the history of sleight of hand, both for inspiration and to properly credit his work's roots. "The more I wrote, the more I loved it, and the more I taught, the more I loved it," he said. He continued to put out his self-published mini-books and, in 2007, he released *Dangerous*, a two-DVD instructional video set detailing numerous moves—one of which was called Angle Zero. He became a household name in magic circles. "He has carved a genre and a niche and a space for himself where he doesn't care about performance; he cares about inventing new stuff and mastering the skills and the technicalities behind it," Dynamo told me. "Madison is a superstar amongst magicians."

But Angle Zero was only the beginning. Madison had a mission. Two years later he began to wrap himself in his alter ego, and then five years later he created the52.

Angle Zero is a relatively simple trick—no intense sleight of hand needed—but its impact on spectators is extraordinary. That's what makes it so special. After Madison showed me how it is done, I immediately began performing it to friends. And, after I was asked to join the52, I felt it fitting, for such a special moment, to pay homage to Madison's influence: the trick he invented, the group he created, and the acceptance he had bestowed upon me.

Having it all go down in a tattoo shop was a shoddy plan, though. For one, the tattoos I already had didn't need touching up (I had only three, the last the one I had gotten in Blackpool with Ramsay), and, moreover, it was deathly hot outside. August in Las Vegas, with its claustrophobic bubble of flickering lights, concrete, steel, and glass, was suffocating. No one wanted to leave the casino unless absolutely necessary.

I tried dropping subtle hints to Ramsay that we should hit up a nearby tattoo parlor. *It'll be fun. . . . Just like Blackpool . . . Got anything in mind? . . . It's Vegas!* But he wasn't biting. He didn't have anything he wanted to get done and, moreover, he had promised his girlfriend he would be a good boy while in Sin City: no tattoos, no gambling.

Plus, we were busy. We bopped all over the strip, filming some projects (which included getting kicked out of the Wynn), linking up with other magicians from around the world, and finalizing the imagery for Ramsay's next signature deck, Carpe Noctem, which featured a cereus flower—a desert-dwelling plant that only blooms at night—illustrated in white and purple against a black backdrop.

We also hung out with Penn Jillette, with whom Ramsay had become quite friendly. Penn & Teller perform five days a week in their namesake theater at the Rio in Las Vegas. Penn offered us VIP seats for that night's show and invited us backstage. Penn is a tall man, well over six feet, but no longer the long-haired, chubby loud-mouth that was his brand for decades. He recently lost more than one hundred pounds and his hair, freshly dyed a crow's black, is cut short. He is still just as boisterous, though, and speaks with an unmistakably loud bark punctuated by a gravelly chuckle.

Before the show, we headed toward the Monkey Room, Penn's private backstage lounge. We sat on chairs wrapped in zebra-print, and promotional posters and backstage photographs from the 1980s and '90s lined the wall. A monkey sculpture in a checkered vest and feather-stuck hat held a guestbook. The glass table in the center of the room also featured little monkeys lying on their backs, using their hands and feet as supports.

Penn spoke in one continuous stream. I said maybe six words the entire hour we were with him. He told stories about performers who inspired him, including Billy the Mime, who is known for his sociopolitical-themed performances, as well as Johnny Thompson, a legendary Polish magician. Penn also confided in us that he is not allowed into London's Magic Circle, even though the Circle contacted him and requested props from some of his most famous illusions to be showcased in their museum.

"Of course, I said yes," Penn explained. But when he asked for membership in return, they refused to let him in because in the past he and Teller had revealed secrets to how some of his tricks were done. The ethos of Penn & Teller has always been to make magic as interesting and accessible as possible, which sometimes includes revealing the secret behind their tricks. "Some magic tricks are better as an experience when explained," Teller explained to *Psychology Today*. "They're more interesting, more multileveled, more ingenious." One time, in a segment for *Animal Planet*, the duo showed how the legendary Cups and Balls trick is done by performing the routine with clear cups. The performance was both hilarious and riveting, despite the secret being revealed plain as day. The old guard of magic, however, did not approve of their progressive take. "Penn and Teller take the mystery out of magic," said David Berglas, president of the Magic Circle, when the duo first came to prominence in the 1980s.

"I don't give a *fuck*," Penn said plainly. He raised his arms in the air and shrugged. "But that shows you how convoluted and backwards some of these old-school clubs can be."

"That's how these groups have always been, though: not moving forward with the times," Ramsay said.

"I don't fucking know, man. But with young guys like you," Penn said, "I am hoping that will change—that we can move beyond this bullshit." A skilled musician, Penn plays jazz for the crowd before every show, and he had to prep for the performance. We said our good-byes and went for a bite to eat before the show began.

Penn & Teller are an unconventional if not altogether strange magical act. They met in 1974, and, in 1981, crafted the brand they have since become famous for: Penn, the bombastic narrator; Teller, the silent partner. Their off-kilter take on magic, comedy, and political and cultural commentary propelled them into stardom, and they have held court at the Rio in Las Vegas since 2001. We sat in a VIP booth, one tier up, center stage, and watched them run through a series of signature tricks, including removing an audience member's phone from the guts of a frozen fish.

Although I loved the entire set, the most beautiful act of the night—and probably my favorite magic trick of all time—was Teller's Goldfish routine. It's gorgeously simple yet seemingly impossible. The curtain opened to reveal Teller standing next to a table with a large glass box, filled with water, sitting on top. An empty chair sat to the table's right. He signaled for a woman to join him onstage, had her sit in the chair, and handed her a medium-sized fishbowl. She cradled it in her lap. Teller rolled up his sleeves and began transporting handfuls of water from the large tank and into the fishbowl. It took him nearly a dozen trips, small handful after small handful, to get a few inches of water into the container.

On his next trip from tank to fishbowl, a handful of quarters fell into the bowl—not water. He went back and forth again and again—sleeves rolled up, scooping water, dumping quarters, an impossible transformation of matter, from liquid to metal. He dumped at least thirty dollars' worth of quarters into the fishbowl before picking it up and showing the audience. Water sloshed around inside as quarters anchored the bowl's base like a metallic coral reef. He then walked back over to the large tank and turned the fishbowl upside down, dumping its contents. And sure enough, as the quarters hit the water, they transformed into dozens of swimming goldfish. Teller turned to the crowd, held up the empty fishbowl, and smiled.

I turned to Ramsay, my mouth hanging open. I was speechless.

Throughout all this nonstop action, I never even came close to convincing Ramsay to join me on a trip to the tattoo parlor. On our last day in Vegas, I was in a panic. Time was running out. I gave it one final try. Ramsay had just come down to the bar.

"Xavior and I are going to hit up the tattoo shop in a bit," I said to Ramsay. "Do you want to come?"

"I don't think I'll have time. We are going to go back to the Wynn to do some more filming. We need some more shots for my deck."

"Oh, yeah, no problem. Let me know when you want to head out. I'll come with you."

I tried to play it off, but inside I was a wreck.

I had practiced Angle Z incessantly since Madison asked me to join the52. I cornered my roommates nearly every day and forced them to endure the same trick over and over. I gathered feedback, watched their reactions, and tried to figure out ways to improve my approach. I crashed and burned more than once, but over time my performance became more refined. Then I started adding my own personal spin: changing the verbal patter, adjusting how the spectator chooses the card, and using a brand-new, sealed deck to heighten impact.

As I perfected the trick, I gained confidence amid the intense vulnerability that goes into performing. I also learned firsthand that when you're creating magic for an audience, they expect perfection—they want it to be real. I performed the trick for my friend Eric at a birthday party in Brooklyn the week before my trek to Vegas and, upon receiving the response "What the actual fuck, dude," I knew I was ready.

But here I was, my plan falling apart right in front of me. I was beginning to regret making things so complicated. I had two options, from what I could tell: perform the trick right now for Ramsay, or just tell him the news straight up. No surprise, no big reveal, no magic moment—but I knew, without even having to think about it, that that would be more devastating than flubbing an attempt at the trick.

It was now or never. I took a deep breath and got out of my chair.

I took a brand-new, sealed deck of cards out of my backpack and handed it to Ramsay. He opened it and gave the deck back to me. My heart rattled around like a grenade ready to explode in my chest. I did a quick false shuffle—a maneuver where you cut the deck twice, which looks genuine, but really reorganizes the deck back into its original order—as a means to gain composure. Jeremy, adjusting his wire-frame glasses, watched from behind Ramsay. He put his hands on his hips, a smile curling on his face. He knew this was all part of my plan.

I told Ramsay to pick a card, and he chose one from the deck.

"The two of clubs," I said. "Good choice. Now, let's take your card and just . . ."

I started to tear the top-right corner off the card. He smiled as I did it. He knew that I was performing Angle Z, and he seemed thrilled. He had never seen it done with a sealed deck before.

Before I completely tore off the corner, pinching that edge between my thumb and forefinger, the larger chunk dangling below, I had Ramsay rip the last portion himself. This added detail, a way for the spectator to be physically involved in the trick, was a necessity by Madison's standards. If a spectator can participate in such an important way, the trick becomes that much less possible. Now he was holding the larger portion of the card, with the torn piece still in my hand.

I slowly opened my hand. One finger at a time. The piece had disappeared.

"Check your back pocket," I said. Ramsay yelped as he reached in and found the piece. He brought its edge against that of the rest of the card. They lined up perfectly.

I put my hand out and told him to give me the torn corner. I brought it up in front of his face and pointed at it with my free hand. "This is *me* now," I said. "I'm the Two of Clubs. I'm in."

He eyes widened. He threw his right hand over his open mouth. "*No way!* You're in?!"

I smiled and nodded. "Yeah, man. Madison asked me to be in about a month ago. It's been hard, holding on so long to tell you." He opened his arms and I walked into him. We embraced each other for a moment and then he pulled away. "Ah! Holy shit! I can't believe it! Ian—in the52! This is going to be great!"

The casino seemed to go quiet: the dinging slot machines faded to a muffle, the dealers' mouths at the blackjack tables and roulette wheels moved but no sound came out, and the shuffling of cards from other magicians went mute underneath the weight of the moment. For a split second, the casino was ours to share.

It didn't matter that Ramsay knew how the trick was done. It was more so my ability to execute it in a new and interesting way—using a sealed deck—that made it my own, and to do so with an explicit purpose. Like all the other members, I had done something to prove that I could bring magic forward in a new way, even if just for Chris Ramsay. The purpose of magic is not to be the biggest or the best or the most technical all the time, but rather the most fitting for the situation at hand. It is here that a magic moment is found. The spontaneity of my performance—capturing the moment when I had it, cementing my friendship with Ramsay—may not have been the instance for which I had planned my reveal, but it was perfect nonetheless.

As we sat down at a nearby table, I thought back to what Ramsay and Madison and all the guys had been trying to explain to me for the past year. This was the gravity of a magic moment—one of astonishment, an experience layered in psychological and emotional revelations. The purpose of a trick isn't merely to fool the spectator, but to make them feel something they have not yet felt, and to give them a memory and an experience they can carry around with them. It was a turning point in our friendship and my place in the magic community. I looked over at Ramsay, who was still grinning, and I knew that this would be something he would never forget.

"So," I said, "let's hit up that tattoo shop." Ramsay laughed. He realized what I had been getting at the past few days.

"Well, looks like we have to go now, right?"

We immediately made our way to the nearest tattoo parlor, and Madison's words sounded off in my head as the artist fired up his gun: *You'll be a monster of a member. Your role in telling this story is bigger than you think.* It felt like I was in a movie.

What the hell had I gotten myself into?

EVERY ONCE IN A WHILE, THE LION HAS TO SHOW THE JACKAL WHO HE IS

Oh what a tangled web we weave,
when first we practise to deceive.
—SIR WALTER SCOTT

He is devoted to a theater that he alone sees.
—YEVGENY VAKHTANGOV

14

YOUNG BLOODS

Becoming a member of the52 changed everything.

For months I had merely been a hanger-on, a wannabe magic cool kid. I was always just *there* but without much purpose. I had begun to make occasional background appearances in Ramsay's YouTube videos, and got some shout-outs from Madison on Instagram; it was fairly obvious that fans and followers of these guys, and other members, had some questions about me. Sometimes I'd scroll through their comments and people would be asking who I was; some kids even said they thought I was cool. A few magicians started to follow me on Instagram. My profile said I was a journalist; what was my role in this world? Surely they wouldn't let an amateur into their inner sanctum for no reason, right? After I got the tattoo, the confusion and intrigue ratcheted up. Who *was* this guy?

After I got inked, we all grabbed some dinner at the casino and then made our way to the strip. We met up with Ramsay's friend

Andrei Jikh.[*] He had recently moved out of an apartment adjacent to the Aria casino and still had a key to its rooftop pool. We didn't swim but instead peered out at the endless landscape of pulsating lights, clusters of casinos, and towering hotels that stretched off into blackness. Ramsay took out his camera. "Put it up," he told me. I raised my finger in front of the window, my skin still swollen from the needle, the fuzzy red glow of the Las Vegas Strip gleaming in the background.

Click.

After the news was posted on Instagram that I had become the Two of Clubs, my stature immediately rose. Magicians flocked to my profile, convinced I was some underground figure, recently discovered by Ramsay and Madison, Jeremy and Laura, Xavior and everyone else. It was hard not to pay attention to all the hoopla, but when I got back to Brooklyn, I just kept practicing magic and doing my day job. I dug into more of the theory of sleight of hand, and routines I could perform, and continued practicing tricks to my roommates (who, by now, were calling me Gob, after the character on *Arrested Development* who is an aspiring magician). Shortly after I got my ink, I spent an afternoon with Ryan Tricks, the magician I had fooled so badly with his pocket square back in Blackpool. He was in the city to film some street magic. "So, you're in the 52, yeah?" he asked in his thick British accent as we walked through Union Square Park. I smiled and flashed him my tattoo, careful not to share any information about the group. He grabbed my finger to get a closer look. "Mate, that's *mental*. I wanna be in! It's like a gang, innit?" I just laughed.

---

[*] Andrei, a master card handler, worked behind the scenes of *Now You See Me* and *Now You See Me 2*. One of his main contributions was to guide the cast during the heist scene in which Dave Franco steals an all-powerful computer chip, affixes it to a playing card, and flicks it through the air to Jesse Eisenberg, who then hides it up his sleeve. We'll get more into consulting for Hollywood and television shows later.

Jeremy had given me a flyer before we left Las Vegas. "You should go to this," he said. "It's an old-timer thing, but they've been letting some of the young guys in the past few years." Every October, there's an invite-only event for advanced sleight-of-hand card magicians. Industry veterans come from all over the country to Buffalo, New York, to lecture on card deception and other sleight-based manipulations. I took the flyer with me and, when I got home, called Xavior. He told me he planned on attending, and that we should go together. I emailed Randy DiMarco, the event's organizer, and told him that it was my first year being invited and that I was coming with Xavior Spade. He gave me the green light.

Xavior and I booked adjoining rooms at a local Motel 6. It was, as expected, a dump, but we weren't there for luxury. As we lounged around Xavior's room that first night, eating pizza, Matt Whittaker, a local magician and friend of Xavior, stopped by and jammed with us. He showed me a few routines he was working on, and Xavior gave him some tips. I sat on the bed and tinkered with a few moves of my own. My execution had definitely become more refined over the past few months.

"We are going to get you doing routines soon, dude!" Xavior told me, smiling. He could see I was making significant progress. Matt asked that I show him some effects—perhaps something that I had invented myself. I shrugged him off.

"You can't be in the52 and not do magic!" he mocked, playfully frustrated, as if I were keeping a secret.

We drove to the venue the next morning, the West Seneca American Legion, a squat, single-story building on the outskirts of town. Laminated square tables filled the main lounge and a wooden bar anchored the south side of the room. A television broadcasting local news hung above the liquor shelf; the month's pinochle schedule, a holiday raffle promotion, and the funeral details of a member who recently passed away were tacked on the wall. A group of old-timers sat around showing each other moves, including one guy with an enormous potbelly and a Buffalo Bills cap who demonstrated a "control" he had developed, which looks like a messy shuffle but actually places the chosen card on the top of the deck for easy access. We mingled around the room and chatted with a few other young magicians. Someone complimented Xavior on his recent lecture for Murphy's Magic during which he offered his take on specific moves and ideas on performance. It was available online.

Dai Vernon, the godfather of modern magic, had traveled around the world in his old age, giving exclusive lectures in halls and theaters, sharing the secrets he developed to a select few. Although magic has become digital, and thus more democratic, in-person lectures are still popular because of their intimacy (audience members can also buy rare self-published books, how-to videos, and handmade props), and many young magicians still take up the opportunity to see older magicians share their wisdom, even if they don't always agree with their perspective; there is always something to be learned. The viewpoint is that maybe they could find something to apply to their modern take on the craft.

A few older magicians were scheduled to lecture in Buffalo over the course of the weekend. Many of them had solid information to share, garnering nods throughout the audience, but their best offerings were mainly technical. There was an obvious distance between the older generation and the current crop in how magic should be performed, presented, and disseminated. During one of the lectures, when the magician speaking recommended using a comedic crutch as a setup for a trick, Xavior leaned toward me and whispered, "And that's how I know magic hasn't changed. Some of these older guys say that they've been doing something a certain way for twenty years. Well, if you've been doing something that long and it still sucks, then stop!" There he was again, the Asshole of Magic, telling it like it is. Xavior has never been one to suppress his opinion, and that is one of the reasons why he has become so well respected. But, more than anything, it's because he's not just a shit talker, not just a troll dishing it out for kicks; he has built a reputation not only for pointing out the flaws of other magicians' methodologies but showing specifically how their approach could be better. If a move or type of presentation looks bad, he will develop a way to enhance it, and openly share his work. Many younger magicians—as well as some members of the older crowd—have come to accept Xavior's abrasive personality in exchange for his knowledge and willingness to make his ideas public.

As I watched other older magicians speak about the craft, and compared their ideas to those of Xavior and his peers, it was glaringly obvious to me how the two generations differed, clashed even. Those from the old guard still view magic as an insular passion with set rules and boundaries, as if the art already hit its peak with the likes of Dai Vernon and that new heights can never be reached. From what I could tell, older magicians refused to take their gaze away from past heroes; they didn't want to admit that the younger generation had developed better ideas than those that came before them. In a way, the young guns have decided to ignore all the old peaks and have chosen instead to look for different mountains.

While annual meet-ups and group lectures like the Buffalo gathering are staples on magic's yearly calendar for aspiring young magicians, some members of the52 have carved out a new line of work: headlining lecture tours stationed all over the world where they're the only teacher in the classroom. Some magicians are so sought after for closed sessions that they make their entire living just from touring the globe and sharing their knowledge.

Alex Pandrea (the Seven of Spades, one of the earliest members of the52), a thirty-year-old bearded and sharp-faced New Yorker, has given lectures in more than 130 cities around the world on sleight-of-hand maneuvers and the inner workings of his exclusive routines. Pandrea grew up in Forest Hills, Queens, not far from Xavior. His parents divorced when he was young, and his mother and grandmother split parenting duties. His grandmother would also babysit neighborhood kids after school, and one kid's father was a professional clown. When he'd pick up his son, he'd do some simple tricks for Pandrea, and volunteered to perform at his seventh birthday party. At age eleven, Pandrea started going to August Moon, a now-defunct magic shop in Queens, taking lessons from one of the shopkeepers. When he began learning more advanced material, his mother took him to Tannen's Magic in Manhattan, the oldest shop in the city, where he met Magick Balay. Magick, who had a long ponytail and wore a leather jacket, made magic cool for the young Pandrea. He'd take him to gigs and show him how to perform for real people, including good-looking women.

"I thought, *Wow! I can use magic to pick up girls!*" Pandrea told me once, laughing. "I never thought I was cool when I was younger, so I figured I could stand out if I showed people tricks. I was always super skinny and had braces, and girls never really liked me. I was never part of the popular clique." His mother and grandmother always supported his love for magic. "My grandmother would react the best out of anybody," Pandrea said. "She'd scream, run away, the whole thing." But then she was diagnosed with Alzheimer's and wouldn't remember that her grandson had already shown her the same tricks. Pandrea practiced on her constantly; him refining his moves, her laughing at the wonder of the moment, not knowing that she had seen it all before.

In college, Pandrea saw that the magic industry was growing rapidly. There were a lot of young entrepreneurs opening their own online stores, so he decided to open his own shop, too. He took out a $15,000 loan from his father, who was a wealthy dentist, taught himself how to build a website and film and edit videos, and, in March 2011, launched the Blue Crown. "I wrote myself a check for one million dollars when I started, to be cashed on December 20, 2012," Pandrea said, adding that he would look at the check every day as encouragement. When the date on the check came around, he looked at his finances; he had cleared $1 million in sales in just eighteen months. He framed the check and kept it above his desk as a reminder of what hard work can accomplish.

But in 2014, Pandrea—who had been married during this time, and whose wife was part of the business—got divorced, and he lost his fortune; he had to liquidate the company's earnings to pay his wife a settlement. But he didn't give up; he relaunched Blue Crown alongside NOC, his namesake card brand, and also began lecturing around the world. "I'm a gypsy. To this day, I have no physical home, no apartment. I live out of a suitcase," he told me with a nonchalant shrug. "But it's funny. What started as something selfish—learning magic so I wouldn't have to be the nerdy kid anymore—has turned into me inventing new magic and giving my perspective to others."

I first met Pandrea in Blackpool. Ramsay and I were wandering around the dealers' room, checking out some of the magic for sale, when he pointed to the far end of the room.

"Oh, shit, dude," he said. "You have to meet Pandrea."

"Who is that?" I asked, craning my neck to see where he was pointing. I saw a guy, probably in his late twenties, standing behind a table, a deck of cards in his hands. It looked like he was performing to a large crowd of people.

"He's a close friend," Ramsay said. "He knows Laura and Madison and everyone else, too."

"Is he . . . good?" I asked.

"Dude," Ramsay said, rolling his eyes at me. "He's one of the best. Don't worry, he'll do something for you."

We walked over. Pandrea had a dealer table and was selling effects from Blue Crown, as well as his NOC playing cards. We waited for him to finish and for the crowd to move on.

"Pandrea!" Ramsay shouted, raising his arms in the air. They embraced in a hug. "This is Ian," he said, introducing me. "This is his first convention—he's never really seen magic before. You should show him something."

"Yeah?" Pandrea responded, rubbing the scruff on his chin, clearly tickled that he had access to fresh meat. I was still so green back then—enthralled by every illusion performed for me. I was desperate for someone, anyone, to fry my brain.

Pandrea picked up his deck off the table and fanned it in front of me.

"I just want to do something simple, but I want you to make all the decisions," he said, "so pick a card."

I reached in and chose the ace of hearts.

"You like that one?" he asked.

"Yeah, sure," I said.

"Great, now put your card back into the deck, and take the deck and give it a good shuffle for me." I grabbed the cards, shuffled, and gave the deck back.

"So, what we are going to do is split the cards into piles," he said, placing them into two different stacks. "Now, choose one." I pointed to the one on the right. He picked up the pile I chose and began to shuffle. He split those cards into four small stacks and had me pick a pile again. I pointed to the one farthest to the right.

"Do you want to change your mind?" he said.

"You know what," I said, "I do." I was trying to psyche him out, to throw him off his game. I pointed to a different pile. He picked it up and discarded the rest. We repeated the exercise until one card remained. A crowd had formed, watching and waiting for the big reveal.

"There are a lot of people here, so I'll give you a choice," he said. "You can flip the card over and see if we narrowed it down to your card and show everyone if it's right or wrong, or you can peek and keep it only for yourself." He looked at me and waited for my response.

"I'll just look myself," I said, a guy in the crowd groaning audibly at my decision. I bent down, shielded the card from the other spectators, and peeked at its corner. It was the ace of hearts. Pandrea and I looked at each other. I tried not to smile, but his eyes told me that he knew what I had seen—he knew it was my card. I walked away from the table in silence. I didn't tell anyone the card that I saw.

Ramsay came up behind me and tossed his arm around my shoulder. "See? I told you I'd show you the real deal when it came to magic." He threw his eyebrows up, cocked his head, and laughed. Pandrea and I saw each other a few more times that weekend in Blackpool[*] and kept in touch after the trip was over. A few months later, he shot me a DM on Instagram: Would I want to tag along during his next lecture circuit—in Spain?

"Are you kidding? Yes!" I wrote back. I had already become familiar with how the industry worked, and I was eager to see this facet of the business, touring the world and lecturing to other magicians, firsthand. The trip was set. First stop: Barcelona.

Pandrea sauntered through the hotel lobby clad in a black tuxedo jacket, waxed jeans, and suede Chelsea boots. His girlfriend,

---

[*] At the club later that night, Pandrea slipped into a booth with three girls and offered to show them some magic. He began talking to one of them when, all of a sudden, she dropped her head and started puking, a fountain of pink slime crashing onto the seat. (Fruity drinks were two-for-one at the bar.) Her friends didn't seem to care much, and they didn't help her as she heaved. As the girl continued to vomit on the floor, Pandrea looked up at me, shrugged, and started performing for the two other girls. They squealed at the illusions and completely forget about their sick friend, who was now fully passed out at the other end of the booth.

Kristina, petite and blond, wrapped in a tight black dress, walked behind him. On a fourteen-city, eighteen-event jaunt, they had driven north to Barcelona from Madrid earlier that day. I myself had just landed in the city and was staying in an Airbnb down the street. Although he sells custom decks and effects through his online store, Pandrea makes a good chunk of his income from these lecture tours: at least $50,000 per trip, sometimes reaching closer to six figures.

Spain loves magic, with a specific style of performance that lends itself more to narrative storytelling mixed with illusion rather than stand-alone tricks that have no connecting threads. After leaving the hotel, we visited a private museum of magical memorabilia in the city center. The small building housed a slew of books, props, and other artifacts dating back to the eighteenth century, including a room devoted entirely to cards, with an archive of 1,400 decks. At the end of the venue stood a small stage that hosts private performances.

That night's event was not a lecture hosted by a local magic club, or a private performance. It wasn't even in the museum itself, but rather a private dinner at the upscale restaurant Aire. A dozen local magicians, ranging in age, had offered to combine a lecture by the esteemed young American with a fine-dining meal. They positioned Pandrea, Kristina, and me at the head of the table. I realized after we sat down that the entire restaurant had been rented out for us. The chef came out and introduced himself and explained the details of the meal. We had an eight-course dinner of authentic Catalan cuisine: some sort of cold fish that reminded me of ceviche, grilled calamari served with bread smeared in tomato sauce and topped with serrano ham, bowls and bowls of green olives, sardine soup, credo with grapes, anchovies laid atop more bread, artichokes wrapped in strips of haddock, mussels in cream sauce, juicy steak cooked rare, and ice cream with espresso for dessert. It was a feast.

After dinner, the group eagerly waited for Pandrea to begin. One of the magicians most fluent in English translated, and Pandrea showed them card controls, exclusive routines, and gimmicks he had developed. He also did some iPhone magic, including a trick where a phone's battery instantly charges to 100 percent while in the spectator's pocket. He spoke with confidence and made clear points: More than anything, Pandrea said, he wanted to create easy-to-use effects that still produced a powerful experience for the audience. "Spectators do not care about the method because it is the only part of the trick that is purposefully hidden," he told the crowd. "It's irrelevant how it's done; what matters is what it *does.*" As Pandrea spoke, I realized that this is exactly what I would want in a routine of my own. If I was going to invent something, I needed to keep the method simple but still pack a punch. In magic, it's the ultimate conundrum.

The next day, we packed our bags into Pandrea's rental car, a candy-apple-red Mercedes B Class hatchback, and drove west through the countryside to Basque Country, which stretches along Spain's northern coast. We pulled into San Sebastián, a small waterfront city that hugs a gorgeous inlet of bright cerulean sea. Boats dotted the water and people lounged on the white-sand beach. A light breeze carried in from the ocean and the sky was clear and bright. We ate lunch at a café along the shore before heading to that evening's event.

This crowd was much younger than the one in Barcelona and, to me, more thrilled to take a selfie with Pandrea than hear him talk about magic. This lecture, held on the top floor of an old stone-faced home in the city's residential sector, carried on the same way as his other events: the same tricks explained the same way, with the same pitch at the end for attendees to purchase DVDs, download codes, handmade gimmicks, and playing cards. Night fell during the talk and we drove back to the hotel in silence. Kristina took the wheel as Pandrea nodded off in the front seat. Although these tours offer Pandrea a lot of travel experience, a good chunk of cash, and visual fodder for his Instagram, they are clearly draining. But, when compared to the lives of countless others who have to hustle to succeed in the world of magic, Pandrea had it made, and he knew he couldn't take it for granted.

In Buffalo, the real work begins after the afternoon lectures end. All the magicians grab drinks at the bar—mostly beer and whiskey—and get down to the nitty-gritty. Although the talks anchor the event, what people really came here for—same as in Blackpool or Vegas—was the close-knit camaraderie. They wanted to see what each other had been working on, share and receive tips on difficult sleights, chew on new plot twists spun into an existing routine, or spitball completely new effects altogether. The older guys mostly kept to themselves, rehashing experiences from memories past or immodestly showing each other moves that had been invented decades ago. The young guys gathered around and asked to see what the others had recently posted on Instagram.

Xavior held court at a corner table and showed a small crowd his work on Raise Rise, an effect invented and made famous back in the 1990s by legendary magician Ray Kosby. In this trick, the spectator's card is placed toward the bottom of the deck, protruding halfway (or out-jogged, in magic parlance). The card then magically rises up and up the deck—still sticking out of the pack—until, at the end, it's resting on top. For years it has been labeled one of the most technically difficult card tricks ever invented.[*] Xavior is

---

[*] It's so hard that there's even an alternative: Lazy Rise. "If you've ever wanted to perform Raise Rise but don't want to break your fingers," inventor Chris Mayhew boasts in the effect's advertisement, "this is the perfect trick for you!"

known to do it better—more seamlessly, more magically—than the trick's inventor. In fact, the trick became a pillar of his reputation. Xavior is obsessed with the minutiae of moves involved: certain types of grip, slight changes in finger placement, variations in spectator management for a more deceptive execution. He spoke on these elements to the small group that surrounded him that night in Buffalo.

"If you move your thumb up on the edge of the deck, here," he explained, showing the others, "you get less friction with the move, and it works better." He also talked specifically about how to better deceive the spectator. "When you do the move, come right up to their line of sight," he said, demonstrating with the deck. "It really helps the illusion. They can't see what is happening."

This is possible on a biological level because your eyes aren't built to accurately track movements of very thin objects, such as playing cards. The macula, which is at the very center of your retina, is packed with photoreceptors, and helps bring objects into high resolution. As Xavior gently brings the deck up, moving the protruding card just outside of your macula's range, your brain can't process that he's executing a sleight. It just looks like the card rises up the deck, unprovoked. Xavior did the move once, twice, three times, and everyone audibly gasped. It was so flawless—it was like art.

"Some people say the way I do things is impractical, but that's only because they aren't good at it," he said. "That's why people call me a move monkey!"

From across the room, I saw an older gentleman watching, arms folded, brow pinched. He was in his early sixties, with a lean frame and a full head of black hair. He wore a brown suit jacket and relaxed-fit blue jeans. He looked confused, nearly transfixed, as if he couldn't believe what he was seeing. He obviously knew what was being done with the cards, but he was shocked at

Xavior's skill. It was as if the card just *floated* to the top of the deck.

"Say, uh—" the man started, easing his way closer to Xavior. "Can you do that again?"

"Sure," Xavior responded matter-of-factly. He did the move again.

"I've been doing magic for over forty years and . . . wow. That's . . . that's amazing," the man told him, mouth agape, hands on his hips. "You young bloods are really taking things to another level, aren't you?"

Xavier smiled and said, "Something like that, yeah."

The amount of respect being paid to Xavior during this exchange was clear. Magicians are evaluated by what they contribute to the craft. Being able to invent compelling magic, or improve upon effects already in existence, is what separates everyday enthusiasts from truly influential creators, no matter how old they are. I had seen the connection formed between magicians—in Buffalo with Xavior or in Spain with Pandrea—because of what these guys had contributed to the community. And I knew that, if I wanted to make an impact on the world into which I had been accepted, I would need to do something similar. I would need to invent my own trick.

Xavior showed his move a few more times as he explained the finer mechanical details. The man stared down at Xavior's hands. Then he pointed at his finger, his eyes narrowing.

"What's that tattoo on your finger?" he asked. "The Three of Spades?"

Xavior didn't respond. He didn't even look up. He just shuffled his cards, a smile spreading across his face.

15

JUST A SIMPLE PLAN

Sports anchored my childhood. My father had always been a football fanatic, which was exacerbated by his time as a student at the University of Tennessee, a quintessential southern football school, during the years leading up to my birth. As I became older, however, secured by the goings-on of our small Massachusetts town, sports quickly built itself as a bridge between us. He coached my Pop Warner football team and eventually became president of the regional organization. We would drive to away games in his truck, me drinking chocolate milk and eating a cinnamon roll, him sipping coffee. He wore a navy-blue windbreaker with sunflower-yellow stripes, our team's colors, and kept a laminated playbook jutting out of his back pocket. Although he continued to work long hours to expand his business, and to save money to build the big house in the woods, he still always made time to be involved with—and champion my participation in—sports-related hobbies. To him, it formed a camaraderie with my peers, taught the value of teamwork and leadership, and could instill in me the characteristics of becoming a well-rounded teenager and adult: things he wasn't shown as a kid, but that he somehow knew to be important.

During this time, Shaquille O'Neal had become the nexus of children and sports. His boisterous personality and off-the-court endeavors appealed to young kids, and I was a poster boy of that influence. My father supported my fascination with Shaq. He played Shaq Fu, the video game, with me at night when he got home from work. He bought me Shaq's rap albums, his Reebok shoes (no doubt way above budget for our family at the time), and, most important, the kid-sized jersey that I wore when we drove to Boston that brisk morning in March 1996. I was eight years old, at the height of my fandom. He had gotten an inside scoop as to where Shaq and the rest of the Orlando Magic, his team at the time, were staying for their away game against the Boston Celtics, and surprised me the morning of the game.

"You're not going to school today," he said, popping his head into my bedroom.

"Why not?" I asked.

He smiled. "The Magic are playing the Celtics today," he said. "We're going to go meet Shaq."

I squealed in delight.

He was bringing me to meet my idol—the dream of any parent.

We parked across the street from the hotel's entrance in downtown Boston. My father had no idea what time the team was scheduled to leave for the stadium, so we stood out in the sharp, late-winter wind and waited. I wore my Shaq jersey over a T-shirt and my father draped his big coat over my shoulders to keep me warm. It smelled like him: dust and tile mortar and cigarettes. After a few members of the local press showed up with their cameras, we knew the time was getting close.

My father tapped me on the shoulder and handed me a marker. "I think he's coming," he said. I looked up at him. "It's all right," he said. "Don't be afraid." The press had a better line of sight into the hotel's lobby (we were slightly off to the right), but when they pointed their cameras toward the entrance, we knew he was coming. Shaq ducked under the doorway, sunglasses perched on his nose, wearing a sweatsuit of white and gold. My father grabbed his jacket off my shoulders, slung it over his arm, pushed some photographers out of the way, quickly shuffled me toward the front, and turned me around right in front of him, blocking his path.

"Shaq, please sign my son's jersey," my father asked him.

Shaq towered over me. He looked down, took the marker, latched his massive hand onto my shoulder, bent down, and wrote "SHAQ" in a modest cursive just above my shoulder blade, the marker's felt tip pushing gently into my skin. He handed the marker back to me and kept walking. Before I could turn to face him, my father had already lifted me off the ground and gripped me with his big arms, hugging me furiously, kissing my cheek, his thick mustache brushing against my skin. I could barely breathe. He then pulled away to look at my face. We both just smiled. We ran back over to his truck and made our way to the stadium. I was in such shock that I didn't realize that I was shivering.

After the game, my father immediately had the jersey and our tickets professionally framed. The jersey hung in the hallway of our home for four years until, in 2000, we moved into our new, much bigger house on the outskirts of town. The jersey came with us, too, and hung on the wall in his office next to the University of Tennessee memorabilia that he had collected over the years. The jersey was a memory for both of us, sitting in plain view, of his efforts to try to be a good father. Shaq's signature sat just above the jersey's number, where my tiny shoulder blade had been.

It rained the day he died. Twenty minutes into our drive home (a car pool of our relatives on my mother's side of the family), the rain stopped and the sky split open revealing a thick, pulsating rainbow. When my mother's brother Isoac passed away a few years earlier from a brain tumor (a slow, awful decline), a rainbow had also appeared in the hours just after his death. To my mother and her sisters, it represented the soul leaving his body—it was a way of him saying good-bye, and we kept a photograph of the rainbow in our house as a reminder of my uncle.

So, when, just after my father died, the sky opened up and the taut ribbon of color knifed through the clouds, everyone pulled over. The air on the highway, refracting off the hot black pavement and the gray dome of the sky, wrapped around us like a gaseous prism—an intangible cloud of greens and blues and purples and pinks, fractals of light embedding themselves into the tear-soaked whites of my mother's eyes. The skin on her hands glowed a strange mix of magenta and yellow as she used them to cover her face. I shoved my hands into my pockets, looked up at the sky, and thought, *This thing isn't my father.* He was still lying on that bed, bruised fruit, covered in a sheet that had touched perhaps dozens of other dead people as well. *This thing in the sky doesn't mean anything.* I walked back to the car and opened the door and sat down. Globs of rainwater coated the windshield. I waited for them to be done.

We came home from the hospital to find people waiting—family and friends who had gotten word that he was dead in the hour it took for us to get back to our house. I entered through the garage and into the basement and everyone's face was contorted in some strange, subversive way, like they felt guilty for not knowing what to do. And what *should* you do in that situation? How do you act around a boy who just lost his father?

How do you act when that boy is you?

So, I stood in the center of our half-finished basement, which had been turned into some semblance of a game room, and people came up and touched me in ways they hadn't before—a gentle hand on my forearm, an arm slung across my back—and I just nodded and said thank you and didn't cry. I said I wanted something to drink. And although there was a refrigerator right there, fully stocked with sodas and waters and the beers my father hadn't yet opened, I went upstairs to the kitchen. I opened the fridge but didn't take anything out. I walked to the small living room where he had the stroke, turned left, past the basement door, and peeked into his office. I knew he wasn't there, but I opened the door anyway. Papers sat strewn across his desk, invoices and scribbled notes and other random things. And above it, on the back wall, hung the framed and signed jersey of Shaquille O'Neal. I stared at the jersey for a short while, and then closed the door and walked away.

Time went on after his death. The house he built settled with age, and our lives carried on as best they could. I stopped playing football the year after he died, and my passion for team sports largely faded during my high school years. Whereas my mother had tried to recycle a past version of herself into her post-death identity, I did my best to start from scratch, to become someone new and entirely distant from what was originally planned for me: I decided to become a writer. I wanted to be in touch with the world, to try to understand it, to share stories of other people's lives, especially since I couldn't make sense of my own.

It was a life my father surely wouldn't have chosen for me. He was grooming me to become an engineer or an architect, always championing my analytical mind and intuitive people skills. They were the same characteristics that allowed him to escape Ohio and marry my mother and have a son and discover a better life. He must have been relieved that I could also rely on those traits to find my purpose as a man—to end up somewhere better than where I started. And, to him, pursuing an esteemed but still hands-on profession was the best way to apply those skills. He wore a Dartmouth cap while I was still in middle school, the plan already in place that that was where I would attend college.

Bits and pieces of him clung to our home over the years, my mother largely reluctant to wipe clean where memories of him still lingered. But, as time went on, many things were taken off the walls and put into storage, including the Shaq jersey that hung in his office. I remember rummaging through the attic while on a trip home during college. I don't remember exactly what I was looking for, but, through the course of my searching, I came across the jersey. Dust coated the frame's glass, but the memory was still vibrant. The two of us parking the truck across the street. Shaq's hand on my shoulder. Me jumping into my father's arms. Him doing his best to show his son how much he loved him, how much he wanted him to become a good person.

Ten years later, shortly after I arrived at the office building in New Hampshire, now a struggling writer, I was scrolling through Instagram and came across a post from Shaq. He boasted that he had secured a slot in the upcoming TomorrowWorld Festival in Georgia, a three-day electronic music event—the American off-shoot of the famed European circuit TomorrowLand—that every year boasts an attendance of nearly two hundred thousand. My eyes lit up. I knew how passionate Shaq had been about deejaying, especially as a teenager, and, four years into his retirement from professional basketball, it felt like he was trying to find himself again—to hark back to an old flame, a thing he has always adored. Shaq's turn to music felt ironically familiar; when I saw that post, I thought of my mother and her return to poker—an attempt to regain a piece of her identity that had been buried for a long time.

I immediately ran to my desk and emailed Jorge Arangure, my editor at *Vice Sports,* and told him about the announcement. I said I wanted to know what kind of man Shaq had become since leaving the NBA. I wanted to go to the festival with him. It was a long shot, though; the type of access I was looking for is rarely granted for such a prominent celebrity, but after I cold-called Shaq's management team and explained my intentions, they agreed, saying that they thought my take on the event was worthwhile. They'd let me tag along on the trip. I nailed down the logistics and, a month later, hopped on a plane to Atlanta.

Although I hadn't seen him in almost twenty years, Shaquille O'Neal was still a large man compared to me. He moved slower than his playing days, walking with a timid gait, favoring his left hip. Slivers of gray threaded the scruff on his chin and cheeks. His hands were soft and gentle, nails white and trim, with long fingers that found their way onto the wrists and shoulders of those around him. Deep brown eyes sat above his boyish smile, which he flashed often, tugging his lips slightly to the right. When we first met, he was a young man. When we met again, he was forty-three years old.

We took a limousine bus from downtown Atlanta to the festival grounds. Two of Shaq's sons, and a few other family members, joined for the festivities. It was dark now, the bus moving under the cover of trees lining the road off the highway. Signs started popping up for the festival entrance. The road turned to dirt as the bus went deeper into the woods. The bus rumbled down the dark path, careening through patches of mud, pushing through potholes and puddles. The road swung to the right, and the festival came into view. Neon lights—pink, blue, purple, green—shot into the sky like jagged streaks of lightning. Tents dotted the patch of grass between two clusters of trees, troves of oak knitted with pine, and, in the far distance, the main stage pulsed in front of a sea of a hundred thousand people—a glowing bubble of glitter, feathers, spandex, and lace.

We offloaded near the stage and piled into three golf carts. I rode in the front with Shaq, and his sons and the rest of the crew split up between the other two. When they arrived at the rear of the stage, he was swarmed by fans, other artists, and members of the media. Despite his lack of clout in the EDM world, everyone wanted a piece of Shaq. When he announced his performance at TomorrowWorld, reactions on social media were mixed. Some users thought it was a joke, a ploy for publicity not only for the festival but also for Shaq himself. Many were skeptical that his performance was just another shallow attempt to stay relevant—a way to not be just another retired athlete, forgotten and mused over as someone who once was.

Shaq stood behind a curtain at the rear of the stage. His sons had made their way to the front, to the left of the DJ booth and waited for their father to emerge. Shaq had taken off his sweatshirt, revealing his Lakers jersey, a team he played for later in his career, matching that of his son Myles. Underneath the jersey, a black shirt tucked into loose-fitting blue jeans. He wore neoprene and rubber rain boots, chunky and thick. They were ugly. He could have easily passed for someone's father—a very large dad.

He emerged from the rear of the stage and walked up to the turntables. He plugged in his headphones. His long fingers pushed buttons. He grabbed the microphone. "Let's go, TomorrowWorld!" he yelled, starting the music. He careened through the tracks, dabbling in some dubstep, his heavy frame shaking and bobbing behind the booth, steam rising off his shoulders and head, arms raised in the air. He came alive, looking younger and more mobile than his actual age. Toward the end of the set, Shaq's sons joined their father at the turntables. They danced and smiled. Fog spewed from the stage. Confetti shot from cannons. They were here and the crowd was cheering and everyone was together.

We made our way back to the golf carts after his set. "That was so amazing, Dad," his son Myles said as we got on the cart. We made our way to a VIP area for something to eat, and so Shaq could talk to the media. Between interviews, his sons headed back into the festival. Shaq told them to meet at midnight over at the main stage for Tiësto and reminded them to stick together. After we finished eating, a van brought us to the main stage and we walked to the VIP upper deck, overlooking the crowd.

Shaq mingled with fans, posed for pictures, and listened to the music. The main stage boomed in front of the massive crowd, live waterfalls gushing next to the DJ booth, fire blasting from large metal tubes into the air. Spectators hoisted their homeland's flags: South Korea, Brazil, Spain, Italy, Belgium. Lights funneled from the stage. It was loud. The boys came back and stood next to their father. They watched the crowd together, and Shaq draped his arms around their shoulders. As I stood next to Shaq and his family at the festival, I felt the most overwhelming sense of pride. He was a good father.

A few weeks before our trip to the festival, Shaq invited me over to his house in Orlando, Florida, for a meet-and-greet and a sit-down interview. As I drove onto the property, one of his assistants opened the gate and told me where to park. I waited in the guest living room for him and, a few minutes later, he entered and approached me. He reached out for a handshake. As we locked in greeting, I remembered those hands resting on my shoulder nearly two decades earlier.

Coming into the interview, I had been afraid of this. That, when Shaq and I were together, I would be thrown into a web of memories of my father. Us parking the car on the street adjacent to the hotel in Boston. The brisk wind on my neck as we stood outside waiting for Shaq's exit. The excitement in my chest as I approached him with a marker in my hand. Shaq bending down, resting that gentle hand on my shoulder, signing the back of my jersey. The smile on my father's face as I jumped into his arms. And now, twenty years later, I had the opportunity to talk to the man who was at the center of one of the most vivid memories I have of my dad. He led me into the central wing of the home and we sat down in his kitchen.

The two-decade span between our encounters snapped into

focus, a piercingly clear realization that I had become a thirty-year-old man who has continually tried to distance himself from the memory—the sheer existence—of his father. I've come to comprehend now, fifteen years after his death, that, even after accomplishing all that he did as an entrepreneur and a family man, my father knew deep down that he was still just a lost boy on the run, someone who has spent his whole life sprinting away from a painfully clear starting line but without a strong sense as to where he was actually running. People, I understood, are always trying to find a sense of purpose, or at least an element of control, in a life that has no obligation to take care of them, and I think, more than anything, my father just wanted to be normal, crushingly average—just a person, if nothing else, who had found true happiness. I have, ironically, become very much like him in this regard. But whereas he tried to shed the chains of his upbringing, I've struggled to not become just a kid with a dead dad, a tag that can haunt you for your entire life, an asterisk affixed to all that you do, a secret force that determines who you are and what you will become. But I wanted to know—needed to know—that the person I am didn't manifest because of his death, but rather in spite of it. And although I am someone he had not envisioned—would he be proud of who I've become?—he's still here with me, because the death of a father is not his alone. It transforms into a rock that must be carried in the pocket of his son, a ghastly thing that never seems to go away. And, despite being in my pocket for many years, I have never touched that rock. I do not know its grooves and crevices, its bumps and ridges. I know only its weight and its inability to be removed. To this day, despite this phantom weight constantly knocking at my leg, I rarely speak about him. I've come to realize I never knew my father as a man. That's hard for me. We never had the opportunity to become equals, to share a real and honest relationship. There just wasn't enough time.

Life does not cradle or catch. It only pushes and pulls—violent and unpredictable, like a storm at sea, the captain always looking over his shoulder, ready for the inevitable rogue wave to come crashing down, sinking the whole goddamn ship. To this day, my greatest fear in life is to never be able to truly understand his identity as a man—to fully grasp how much he sacrificed, how much he cared, how hard he tried—and how much we may share as adults. That I, perhaps, will understand we were both just two men who, at their core, were trying nothing more than to grasp the hard truth that sometimes finding purpose in life—truly finding yourself—is one thing you may never come to accomplish, that time is not a thing with which you can make a deal. The hard truth is that having a plan is worthless, because sometimes plans fall through. Sometimes having a plan is the worst fucking thing to ever have in your entire life. Because, when your life is cut short and your plan ruined, had you really even begun to exist at all?

After talking for more than an hour in his kitchen, going through what I needed for the article, Shaq said he wanted to show me the rest of his home. We checked out his movie theater and indoor basketball court. Then he took me down a hallway to his trophy room.

"This room is for my father," he said, referencing his step-father, Phillip Harrison, who passed away in 2013. Framed jerseys hung on the walls, photographs of Shaq playing on various teams perched on tabletops, trophies from high school and college lined display cases. A photograph of him and his father beamed from across the room. He stood there in silence for a moment and shifted his weight from left foot to right, hands on his hips.

"My father is the man that made me who I am today," he said.

I nodded. "I know what you mean." I took out my cell phone. "I wanted to show you something," I said. I held out my phone, showing him a photograph of the framed jersey, the two ticket stubs underneath. My mother had sent it to me just before I came.

"A long time ago—I was just a kid—my dad brought me to

meet you. I was a huge fan, and he surprised me with tickets for the game and we sat outside your hotel forever, waiting—it was freezing!—and then you walked out and signed my jersey. It was surreal." Shaq smiled and took the phone from me. "My dad died when I was thirteen," I continued, "and this is one of my best memories of him. It meant so much to me that he took me to meet you. I know this really isn't part of my job now, being here, writing about you. But the jersey—it's somewhere at my mother's house—is still framed, just like that."

"So, we have known each other for a long time, then," he said, putting his hand on my shoulder.

"Yes, I think we have," I replied. We stood next to each other in silence, his hand still resting on my shoulder.

He turned to leave the room. "It's strange, what a father will do for his son, and how that affects them later," he said.

"I've been thinking about that a lot recently," I said. "Even though he died, it's like I've been searching for something to show me that I'm still a part of him, in a way, that I'm still his son, even though so much has changed." Shaq nodded, a gentle tip of the head, and I knew he didn't have to say anything else. He understood what I meant.

I walked out to my car to leave and it started to rain. I turned on my rental car's windshield wipers. It was a twenty-minute drive to my hotel, in downtown Orlando. The air was dense, and steam oozed from the pavement. When I arrived, the rain had slowed, and I was hot, so I decided to go for a swim. I took off my shirt and dove into the empty pool. I thought about my conversation with Shaq and how, despite being one of the best athletes of all time, and a by-product of his father's influence, he was still searching for a true version of himself. Maybe that's why he dipped back into music, I thought to myself. And maybe that's why my mother went back to poker. But for me, I had, at that point—before I found the magic thing—likewise been on a quest to find my place. People spend their entire lives searching for the radical event, the epiphany, that finally reveals the truest version of themselves. Thomas Pynchon once wrote that everyone has an Antarctic. And I hoped, one day, that I would find mine.

I stood in the shallow end of the pool for a while. I swam from one end to the other and, after gasping for air, wiped the chlorine from my eyes. I rested my elbows on the pool's deck, my back resting against its lip. It had stopped raining. The clouds were gray along the horizon but, coming from the far side, a stream of color beamed out of the darkness. A rainbow carried itself across the sky.

I sat there in silence, looking up.

16

SPIES, SNITCHES, SKULLDUGGERY, AND SCHEMING

Inventing a magic trick is hard.

Your brain has to be wired a certain way to fully grasp illusion—not only in how to build an effect and choreograph all its moving parts but, even more important, to understand how a spectator will interpret it. Will it be magical or merely a clever trick? Like any muscle, it takes time to train your mind to think in terms of trickery and deceit. Even then, some magicians work on effects for years before performing them publicly.

In the weeks after the Buffalo meet-up, during the cold, dark approach to winter in Brooklyn, I spent many hours sitting at my desk thinking about what type of effect I wanted to create. I knew how powerful some tricks could be, and that my new crew of friends had themselves invented some real jaw-droppers. But how could someone like me, with no discernable history in magic, come up something from scratch? I felt like a high school band member trying to write a symphony. I had a sense of all the tools needed to create a song, the various sounds that when combined could create something beautiful, but it would take time—and no small amount of luck—to transform random squeaks and grunts into a cohesive tune.

I knew what types of effects I enjoyed the most. I loved tricks that include random information freely chosen by the spectator, or when the spectator themselves dictated the narrative of the effect. Pandrea's dazzling trick from the Blackpool convention, with the ace of hearts, came to mind, or when Ramsay later pulled me aside and performed in that barroom basement, the queen of hearts laid gently on my palm. I also enjoyed the ones that had a twist ending—being led down a road, thinking I knew what was going to happen, only to have the reveal be the exact opposite—that the entire premise of the trick was an illusion in itself. These routines left me with an experience completely different than what I envisioned and therefore transformed into something entirely more profound.

One trick that Ramsay had performed for me over dinner in Blackpool, a perfect example of a twist ending, instantly popped into my head. He had me pick a card and put it back into the deck. He shuffled and gave me the cards, instructing me to cup my hands around the stack so they were hidden from view. Then he reached in between my fingers and pulled out my chosen card. I was stunned. What a great trick! How did he know exactly where it was in the deck? He held my card in front of me and, with a wave of his hand, the card vanished. "What would you say if I made the entire deck disappear, too?" he said.

"Well," I responded, "I don't think you can do that because *I'm holding the damn thing in my hands!*" He just smiled and nodded. I opened my hands. I was no longer cupping a deck of cards. I was holding a block of glass.

Magicians have invented some truly incredible illusions. Back in magic's golden age, French magician Jean Eugéne Robert-

Houdin, who built ingenious mechanical props, became re-nowned for his exclusive effects, performed only by him. One of his most famous mechanical inventions was the Marvelous Orange Tree. The effect began with Robert-Houdin borrowing a handkerchief from an audience member and rubbing it in his hands, the crumpled fabric becoming smaller and smaller until it disappeared. Onstage sat a table adorned with an egg, a lemon, and an orange. He then told the audience that the handkerchief was now inside the egg, which he held up for all to see. Instead of cracking it open, he rolled the egg in his hands until it also disappeared. He then peered at the lemon. "The egg is now in the lemon," he explained, grabbing the yellow fruit. He also made it disappear, saying it was now inside the orange. He then grabbed the orange and rolled it between his hands. The fruit got smaller and smaller until it became powder cradled in his palm. An assistant brought out a small orange tree rooted in a wooden box. It was placed on the table. The magician poured the powder under the box and lit it on fire. When the flame's smoke hit the tree's foliage, the leaves fluttered and slowly re-vealed flowers. After a moment, the flowers disappeared and small oranges sprouted in their place, rapidly growing larger and larger while still attached to the tree's branches. Robert-Houdin invited two audience members onto the stage, who plucked the fruit, peeled it, took a bite, and confirmed that they were in fact real oranges.

The reveal, however, was a work of art. Jim Steinmeyer de-scribes it in *Hiding the Elephant*: "One orange remained at the top of the tree. Gesturing with his wand one final time, he com-manded this orange to open. It split into two sections, reveal-ing the borrowed handkerchief tucked inside. Two clockwork butterflies, flapping their tiny wings, appeared from behind the tree, lifted the corners of the handkerchief and spread it open in the air as the magician took his bow and the curtain closed." Routines like this set the standard for magic moving forward.[*]

Exclusive effects became a benchmark for all magicians, and everyone clamored to invent (or secure the exclusive right to perform) unshared material. Halfway through the Penn & Teller show I saw in Vegas, Teller took the stage by himself. A large red ball sat motionless on the floor next to a wooden bench. I craned forward in excitement. I had heard about the Red Ball act. It is one of Teller's most famous effects: a gorgeously simple routine where he tries to train the ball like a pet. The ball levitates and bounces around the stage—but Teller never touches it. It's as if the object has a mind of its own: fickle, disobedient, running amok as Teller desperately tries to keep it under control.

Penn & Teller have never shied away from revealing the secrets behind some of their tricks, especially if divulging the method will make the audience's experience more memorable. "If you understand a good magic trick, like if you really understand it down to the mechanics and the core of its psychology, the magic trick gets better—not worse," Teller once said. And so, in 2017, Teller went on *This American Life* and did just that: he told the story behind the Red Ball.

He sourced the idea from an old, out-of-print book written by Nebraska-based amateur magician David T. Abbott,[†] who only performed his effects for private audiences in his living room (Houdini was a regular patron). After reading the book, Teller became obsessed with an effect where Abbott floated a golden sphere around his parlor.

---

[*] Robert-Houdin's influence is still acknowledged: Ramsay has the orange tree tattooed on the backside of his left forearm.

[†] The sole copy of his book, written in the 1920s, was lost for more than forty years before being discovered and subsequently shared with a few hand-selected magicians.

"I like stripping things down to absolute simplicity," Teller told Ira Glass, host of *This American Life*, "and it seems like a ball and a hoop and a person is about as simple as you can get." Teller sought out Abbott's book and began learning the methodology and performance techniques of his predecessor, adjusting them as he saw fit for his own character and style. But one thing seemed fairly obvious in how the act came together: the ball was on a thread. To claim otherwise was almost an affront to the audience's intelligence. "We see that the ball is on a thread; we can see how it's done," Glass narrated on the show, "and at the same time it totally looks like he's this sorcerer who enchanted this inanimate object into obeying him."

Watching Teller perform onstage in Las Vegas, and knowing full well that an invisible thread was involved, I couldn't help but feel the same—not because I was being fooled, per se, but because after supplanting the feeling of being straight-up duped, I saw a principle of magic that is very hard to implant into an audience's mind but is something that, with the Red Ball, Teller seemed to transcend: The deception is no longer encased within the method, but in the transparency of the presentation. It's a way to break the fourth wall of magic—to boil down an effect to its utmost simplicity, almost to the point where how it's done is obvious—while still holding on to a core element of its intrigue and beauty, the almost undefinable characteristic that morphs a trick into a piece of performance art.

In true Penn & Teller fashion, the trick wouldn't be complete if they didn't somehow, at the end of the routine, punch you square in the jaw. When Teller was finally able to train the rogue ball, Penn stomped onstage holding a large pair of scissors. He grabbed the string by which the ball was affixed, raised it up into the air, and cut the thread. The ball fell to the stage, bounced a few times, and went still.

This level of transparency, however, is rare. A trick's secret is

normally vehemently guarded from the public—and other magicians. And it is here that we enter magic's dark side. Trick stealing
and blatant espionage have been rampant problems for more than
one hundred years. In the early twentieth century, Harry Kellar
went to great lengths to obtain the secret of John Nevil Maskelyne's Levitating Lady trick. Maskelyne was quickly becoming
one of the most lauded stage performers in the world, and Kellar,
who was still performing stale illusions from years past, saw that
his influence was on the decline. Kellar snuck backstage with the
hopes of eyeing a special apparatus or unique orientation of mirrors. He bought tickets to numerous shows and approached the
stage during the illusion, looking desperately for a clue. Maskelyne
knew Kellar would try to turn a stagehand into an informer,
so he hired an actor as a double agent, paying him to pass Kellar false information. Kellar never fell for the trap and eventually
bribed Maskelyne's real assistant for drawings of how the trick
worked. They met in the dark of the night and swapped secrets for
cash. This undercover operation, however, was only the tip of the
iceberg regarding the lengths to which people would go to steal
the methods behind famous illusions.

"A great trick, like a great song, should be an inspiration," Jim
Steinmeyer told *Esquire* in 2012. "It should lead you to other things
that are also wonderful. That's what happens in literature, and it
happens in music, and it happens in art. But in magic, they don't
do that. They just take it. You would hope that what you do inspires, but instead it just inspires theft." When I hung out with
Penn Jillette in Las Vegas, he described the matter in more blunt
terms. "In music, they cover songs, but in magic they steal," he
said, shrugging his shoulders, as if it were a fact of life. "And sometimes they change a trick just enough not to get busted."

Spies, snitches, skullduggery, and scheming still exist. In 2017,
during a performance of his incredibly popular off-Broadway show
In & Of Itself, Derek DelGaudio saw a cell phone propped up in an

audience member's jacket pocket, possibly filming the show. The man turned out to be another magician. Another magician was also caught filming the show and was asked to delete the footage. "I'm kind of living my childhood fantasy of creating a Willy Wonka factory," DelGaudio told the *New York Times* after the incident. "And now we have real-life Slugworths trying to steal our gobstoppers." Both magicians were told to leave the show and were blacklisted from future performances.

Sometimes, however, trick stealing escalates into a full-blown lawsuit. In 2012, Teller discovered that Belgian magician Gerard Dogge was performing Shadows, a signature effect where a rose is dismembered when Teller cuts its shadow with a knife. Dogge was also selling the trick's secret to other magicians for $3,000. Teller confronted Dogge, but the Belgian illusionist sensed an opportunity. He allegedly demanded over $100,000 to stop performing the trick. He had kidnapped Teller's secret and was demanding ransom. Teller didn't pay the cash and instead filed a lawsuit.

Journalists picked up on the drama and TMZ ran a story titled "ROGUE MAGICIAN IS EXPOSING OUR SECRETS!!!" Instead of accepting his position in the lawsuit, Dogge instead dodged authorities and bounced around Europe. He was eventually served, but it took two years for a judge to make a determination. "While Dogge is correct that magic tricks do not fall under copyright directly, this does not mean that *Shadows* is not subject to copyright protection," U.S. district judge James C. Mahan wrote in his ruling. "Indeed, federal law directly holds that 'dramatic works' as well as 'pantomimes' are subject to copyright protection, granting owners exclusive public performance rights. The mere fact that a dramatic work or pantomime includes a magic trick, or even that a particular illusion is its central feature does not render it devoid of copyright protection."

It's true that magic tricks can't be copyrighted. In 1983, Teller filed his effect as a piece of theater, which allowed him some semblance of legal protection. Most everyday magicians, however, do not have the funds to copyright their work under this interesting loophole or sue someone who may steal an idea from them. Magicians are also able to file a patent for a piece of equipment used during a routine, but that largely defeats the purpose of protecting a secret. In order to file a patent (which is a public document), the magician has to reveal how the apparatus, and therefore the trick, works. The secret therefore must be revealed for it to be protected.[*]

There is currently some hope for magicians wanting to protect their hard-earned ideas. Congress is debating whether magic is a "rare and valuable art form and national treasure," and is therefore eligible for copyright protection. The 2016 bill was spearheaded by Republican Congressman Pete Sessions of Texas, and David Copperfield is a supporter of the legislation. Since the election of Donald Trump as president, however, the bill has stalled. In January 2018, it was referred to the House Committee on Oversight and Government Reform, where it has since languished.

From my experience, however, the honor system largely prevails today among young magicians. The ethical standard is to hit up the originator for permission if you are going to build upon their effect in a definitive way and release it publicly. Normally, when a magician asks for permission to use a certain move or method, and credits the inventor properly, there's no issue. Creators and performers just want credit where credit is due. There's also an element of pride in the exchange; if you are the creator who gets recognition as an influential magician (Dai Vernon was *the* guy in the twentieth century in this space), your reputation

---

[*] Some magicians have filed fake patents in the hope of throwing off pirates, and David Copperfield has even planted fake explanations online.

is only enhanced. It's a strange caveat for an art defined by its requirement to deceive: be honest.

I knew I wanted to create a card trick. That much was certain. I didn't have the resources or experiences to build a complex gimmick or prop, like Robert-Houdin or Teller, but I had a personal history with cards, was becoming more capable, and had the time and dedication to work hard. I also had a secret talent not afforded to most magicians: I was a storyteller. My job as a journalist is to not only inform the public but also weave information into a captivating narrative. You need a compelling character, a dynamic plot, a jaw-dropping climax, a satisfying takeaway. I knew all these elements could be embedded into a magic trick. I just needed to craft my tale.

That November, my roommate Tom briefly dated a girl named Lauren. I had met her a few times in passing and, when Tom mentioned to her that I was learning magic and hanging out with magicians, she asked if I would show her something. I had been tinkering with a routine and I thought, *Well, I guess I have to perform it sooner or later.*

We sat down at the dining room table in our Brooklyn loft and I told Lauren to pick a card—not in the traditional way where you grabbed one randomly, but as I thumbed through the deck in her direction, showing her the faces of the cards. I turned my head away, closed my eyes, pointed the cards toward her, and started riffling the deck, flashing each card's face as we ran through the stack. "Tell me when to stop," I told her.

"Stop!" Lauren called out about halfway through.

"You happy with your choice?"

"Yup!" she said, excitedly.

"Okay, great," I said. I handed her the deck. "Now shuffle for me." She mixed up the cards and handed the deck back. I turned the cards faceup and spread them out onto the table, so each card was slightly visible, tucked underneath the one that preceded it.

"Now, magic is something that relies almost exclusively on the spectator," I told her. "It's kind of hard to do a magic trick without someone on which to perform it, right?" She nodded. "And, to me, the best magic tricks try to involve the spectator as much as possible. You've already shuffled the cards, but you're going to need to do a lot more in order for me to find your card. So," I continued, "let me see your hand." She held it out, palm down, and I gently grasped her wrist. "Let's see if I can get a read here—if I can find your card. It's not something you are aware of, but people give off subconscious clues all the time." I slowly began to move her hand over the outstretched cards.

"Um," I said, letting go of her hand, "I couldn't get an exact location, but I think your card is somewhere in this area." I separated a selection of cards, just under half the deck, and discarded the rest. "Now," I said, turning the cards facedown and spreading them out on the table, "we're really going to find your card. But, like I said before, I need *you* to help me find it. So, I want you to pick one end to start from—we're going to start from the edges and work our way inward to find your card."

"That one," she said, pointing to the far end.

"Okay, great. But we obviously need a way to count down, so we can find your card. We're going to need a set of numbers to help guide us—but it has to be something completely specific to you. It has to be something that only pertains to you and no one else. So, what could that be?" A calculated pause. "How about your birthday?"

"Okay, yeah, my birthday," she said. "August fifth."

"Perfect. So, August is the eighth month," I said, putting my finger on the card farthest to the left, the end she chose beforehand. "One, two, three," I counted, removing eight cards in total. "And the fifth day," I continued, removing, one at a time, five cards from the opposite end.

When I was done counting, only one card remained.

"And we have one card left," I said. "We've gotten this far all because of you—nothing else." A dramatic pause, letting the possibility of this being her card sink in. "So, for the first time, what was your card?"

A smile spread across her face. "The eight of hearts," she said.

I turned over the card. "As you said, the eight of hearts."

"Oh my God," she gasped, her mouth hanging open. "That was amazing."

The trick worked, sure. It served the basic purpose of fooling the spectator, but in the grander, more nuanced context of magic as an art form, it had some fundamental flaws. First was justification. A magician's behavior and an illusion's structure have to seem normal; for a trick to land well, like acting natural during sleight of hand, a magician's performative arrangement cannot raise suspicion. Their movements must be justified. Magicians spend hours debating over this foundational principle. *Why do you pick up the card like that? What's the point of saying that to the spectator? Why do you need to do all of that when you could just do this?*

In his book *Tricks of the Mind*, legendary British magician Derren Brown dissects a simple coin illusion based on the justification principle. The scene is set as such: A magician sits across the table from her spectator. She takes a coin out of her pocket, places it on the table, and says she will make the coin disappear. In one fell swoop, she slides the coin back toward the edge of the table, picks it up, and encloses it in her fist. She slowly opens her fingers to reveal the coin is gone. The method is simple (you can do this trick at home; seriously, try it): when she slides the coin toward the edge of the table, it falls into her lap before she "picks it up." But the method isn't the issue here; it's why the magician had to put the coin on the table after taking it out of her pocket. If it's already in your hand after taking it out of your pocket, why put it down only to pick it back up again? There's no justification in that behavior; the movement is dictated by the trick's method.

Brown's fix is so simple as to be overlooked but gives an element of profundity not seen in the first version. When you initially sit down (this could be, say, before an hourlong dinner), take a few coins out of your pocket and put them on the table. When you're ready to do the trick, the coins are already in position, ready to go. The move is justified, and the effect is better because picking up a coin that's already on the table is much more natural—more believable, more real—than taking a coin out of your pocket, placing it on the table, and picking it up again. If something seems like a trick, surely it will turn out to be one. But if something seems innocuous and turns out to be an entertaining piece of deception, that's where the magic moment is found. That's astonishment.

Max Malini, a stout Polish sleight-of-hand artist from New York City, operated with a sense that magic only existed as a moment—something that just *was*, with no explanation of why. He wanted his magic to blend seamlessly into everyday situations—bending, but not breaking, the objective reality so many people were quick to accept as fact.

Malini performed for some of the wealthiest people in New York City during the 1920s and was known for his bold and aggressive style. He would scurry up to a famous politician or businessman, bite off one of his jacket buttons, spit it back into place, and walk away without saying a word. In one of his finest and most famous moments, he sat down for dinner at a restaurant with a group of friends. They ate a large meal that lasted several hours, and not once did Malini leave the table. At the end of dinner, he asked to borrow a hat from one of the women in his party. He spun a coin on the table, covered it with the hat, and asked her to call for heads or tails. When he lifted the hat, the coin had toppled and showed what she called. He did it a second time and again the coin fell on the side of her choice. The third time that he lifted the hat, however, the coin was gone, and in its place sat a large block of ice. This reveal stood as a private moment between Malini and his guests, something designed specifically for them, an effect that required intense planning for it to seem impossible. This was a key facet of Malini's brand of magic.*

Legend has it that he did this trick only a handful of times during his life, and only a few other magicians were privy to the method. Ricky Jay, the magician and magic historian who studied under Dai Vernon, was one of those people. While filming a BBC documentary in 1995, the director pressured Jay to do the ice-block trick on camera. Jay refused. He engaged in a heated argument with the BBC staff and stormed off set. He had another interview lined up that same day with *Guardian* reporter Suzie Mackenzie. Jay met up with Mackenzie and while they drove more than an hour to a restaurant for lunch on the other side of Los Angeles, he told her the story of Malini and how these types of tricks—and the feeling of astonishment and wonder they create—cannot be forced. The most magical of moments come out of nowhere; they seemed entirely justified, and that's how they made such a memorable impact.

Jay and Mackenzie continued to drive, the summer heat baking her rental car. The restaurant was packed when they arrived, and they had to wait twenty minutes for a table. Jay continued to talk about the trick after they sat down, detailing how Malini used the

---

* At another infamous dinner party, Malini got into a long discussion with his guests about the supernatural and claimed he could bring beings back from the dead. Just as the entreé was served, a whole turkey on a bed of potatoes, Malini stood up, announced he'd prove it to them, and stabbed the turkey with a fork. The featherless bird sprang up, ran the length of the table, and scurried out of the room. The guests were in complete shock. It's unclear whether they still held an appetite after that, or what they ended up eating as a main course.

hat and the coin as a lead-up to the twist ending. He held the restaurant's menu in front of him as he spoke, blocking the reporter's
line of sight. He lifted the menu from the table. In the space between them sat a large block of ice.

Mackenzie began to cry.

"I deceived you," Jay responded while she sobbed. "It's what I
do for a living." Mackenzie later recalled the event: "It's a moment
I'll never have again. I'll never forget it. It was a kind of supreme
piece of artistry that I witnessed, that was done for *me*. He had
produced this extraordinary effect *for me*. It was in that moment
that I realized this is what we all wait for, in a sense."

My trick already had a fracture in these regions of its foundation.
Where was the justification in showing the cards faceup, other
than for me to know where her chosen card was within the deck?
Where is the magic in that? *I can see all the cards!* Moreover, the
trick, in its most basic form, was a run-of-the-mill, I-will-find-your-
card trick. Although I used information specific to Lauren (her
birthday), the narrative I created was nothing more than a convoluted, roundabout way to find a chosen card. There was no
twist ending like with Malini's ice-block trick. It was a decent try
and the concept was coming into focus, I'll give myself that, but
I would need to keep going if it was going to be worthy of being
released into the magic community—if, sometime down the line,
a big retailer like Ellusionist would agree to feature the product.

In magic, inventing and releasing your own effect is a rite of
passage. If I was going to hit that standard, I needed to keep refining the effect. But, more than anything, I wanted to prove to
myself that I could accomplish something completely outside the
purview of my normal life. If my journey through magic was to be
a defining moment of my adulthood, I needed to prove to myself
that I was actually dedicated to the progression of the craft, not

just someone who learns the latest trick and performs it—and that my contribution to the world of magic could influence others, as well. I was watching the torch being passed down to the new generation in real time—I wanted to have a grip on its handle.

After performing for Lauren, I reached out to Ramsay. He had invented so much great magic and had impeccable taste regarding what makes an effect remarkable. I trusted him more than anyone. "I have a decent idea for a card trick—using information freely chosen by the spectator, which in the end helps them find their card—but it seems so rudimentary right now," I told him over the phone. "It just doesn't feel magical."

"How a trick unfolds is the key to a memorable experience," he said. "Remember, you're taking them on a journey, you're telling them a story, you're sharing a piece of yourself with them."

"But how do you turn that into a trick?"

"Let me put it this way: What do you want them to feel? What do you want them to take away from their time with you?" he asked. "If you have an idea, and you need a method on how to do it, you'll find a way. But don't stop here. Think bigger."

17

BY ANY MEANS NECESSARY

Madison was gone—disappeared, hiding, I didn't know. All I knew was that he had been ignoring my phone calls, text messages, and DMs. And then he deleted all of his Instagram posts; before that, he hadn't posted anything in weeks. When I saw that he wiped his profile, I knew something was wrong. I called him, and it went straight to voice mail. I sent more texts that sat unanswered. I knew he and Laura were ready to add the next wave of members into the52. What the hell was going on?

It was common knowledge that Madison had a precarious mental state, that his moods swung between hot and cold, outspoken and reclusive. In early adulthood, Madison began experiencing symptoms of low latent inhibition, a neurological disorder categorized by an intense awareness of one's surroundings, especially as it relates to specific sensory stimuli. It's a type of hypervigilance. "Anything can spark off a bad feeling," Madison told me. "Everything is shouting at you. You can hear the fucking tap dripping in the bathroom, you can hear your neighbor's door closing, the traffic outside your house, everything." He also avoided crowds.

"I had to be aware of everything about the environment around me," he said. "I had to look at every single face in a crowd." This type of hyperawareness can become all-consuming and in some cases evolves into full-blown psychosis. It can make you crazy. A monster in your head.

The irony is that the more you try to correct an episode, the worse it becomes. "The shitty thing about it is, you think, *I'll close my eyes and it will help,* but it doesn't, because now you're listening more, and you can hear everything," Madison explained. "A quiet room is like hell because you are aware of the silence, but you can still hear those little things. It's almost like your mind is saying, *Where's the noise? Let's find the noise. Let's focus on the noise. All right, there's a tap dripping. Let's focus on that.*" In his early twenties, Madison was prescribed antianxiety medication, which he hated. It didn't fully stop the symptoms, just flattened his personality. One thing did help, though: magic.

Madison never really enjoyed magic's social side. He grew to dislike performing for people or hanging out with other magicians. But he practiced religiously, usually alone in his home office or living room. A deck of cards allowed him some semblance of control over his mind. Digging into sleight of hand was one of the only things that made him calm. "If I am focusing on a trick, that's good. All the attention is here, on this one thing, so I can constantly focus on it. Playing with cards became meditative for me. It made me calm up here," he told me, pointing to his temple.

Most of Madison's magical innovations were just a consequence of his need for obsessive practice. "People who suffer from depression or anything else, it's the way you deal with it that matters—to try your hardest to find your own solution." To Madison, magic was a way to escape his own head.[*]

---

[*] For Chris Stanislas, however, magic failed to quell his internal demons. In September 2015, the California-based member took his own life shortly

Madison continued to self-medicate with sleight of hand, but the episodes persisted. By the time he turned thirty, in 2010, he had begun to accept that he would always live with this bug in his brain—constantly burying, digging, and scraping for something it would never find. But then, one year, he received an unexpected gift for Christmas: a bottle of whiskey. Before this, Madison had never been a big drinker, and never really went for liquor. "After a couple of shots, everything toned down and I felt like a human again," he told me. "Fucking hell! I found a solution!" It was the best he felt in nearly a decade. He traded his over-the-counter pills for booze. The soothing effect, however, came with a consequence: when the alcohol wore off, his mind started racing again. After a while, he told his doctor that if he drank all the time, he felt in control of his condition. The doctor replied that if he kept drinking, he'd eventually kill himself. "Without alcohol, the way my mind works, I'd probably kill myself anyways," Madison told me. "I'd rather not live with it every day."

As the years went on, Madison buried himself in playing cards and liquor, trying to keep his internal demons at bay. This was when he created his public persona, the character that became a barrier between the public and Daniel Madison the real man. It's ironic that he fed so much of his energy, both personal and professional, into this alter ego, which seemed to embody the most fragile aspects of his real-life personality: tortured, hard drinking, searching for a cure, desperately trying to find a way out.

---

after releasing his first and only book, which Madison published. "He was like a brother to me," Madison said. They shared both passion and pain. Also a reformed card cheat, Stanislas developed a move where he could swap an entire deck during a poker game. Called T.U.T., it was the basis, and title, of his book. "He invented these moves to feed that beast," Jeremy Griffith told me. After Stanislas passed away, the52 initiated a fund-raiser to cover the cost of his funeral. Even in death, his card, the Four of Hearts, still belongs to him.

Unbeknownst to anyone except his closest friends, the alter ego was actually a lens into the deepest reaches of Madison's true self. Despite his efforts, however, he sometimes couldn't fully control what went on inside his head. That's when he withdrew completely. When the demon came back, when the bug started to dig and scrap again—dancing, dancing, saying that it would never die—that's when Madison disappeared.

I saw Madison a couple of weeks after my Buffalo trip. He and Ramsay came to Manhattan to film some projects for Ellusionist. They both love chess, playing each other regularly online, and so they decided to develop a chess-themed deck of cards and an accompanying trick.

The cards, called Knights, were stamped with miniature gold pieces and the face cards were those of famous chess players, including Bobby Fischer. They developed an effect called Chess Guess, which mimicked the start of a typical game. To see who gets first move, one of the players holds a pawn of each color in a closed fist. If their opponent guesses where the white pawn is located, they get to go first. The trick was that the magician could guess, with 100 percent accuracy, the location of the white pawn. To create the marketing video, we kicked around the chess hangouts in Union Square and Washington Square Park, and filmed Ramsay fooling hustlers over and over again. The grinders shook in their chairs, slammed their fists down on their dirty boards. They loved it.[*]

---

[*] I also got to meet David Blaine during this trip. Blaine invited Madison and Ramsay to his office, but said, because I was a journalist, I couldn't come up. He was editing his 2016 special, *Beyond Magic*, wanted to show Madison some footage, and was nervous that a reporter would leak the details. When they were done, however, we all met at a bar. Blaine, cap pulled low over his eyes, asked me which magazines I wrote for and how I came to

Madison seemed normal, if a little quiet, during that trip. I could tell he wasn't sleeping well—sunken eyes, slouched shoulders, his voice garbled and groggy—and he barely ate. But he did what he had to do to get the project filmed. When his Uber came to take him to the airport, he put his hand on my shoulder and said, "Let's talk soon." I called him a week later and I could tell he had gotten worse. His voice swam in a dejected, almost angry tone, and his thoughts ranged between cynicism and hopelessness.

"What the fuck is all of this for?" Madison said. "I don't know, Ian. I'm just so sick of magic. What am I getting from it, anyways? I'm not a magician—I hate magicians." He reflected on his accomplishments and seemed to become disgusted at how he chose to devote his time. "It's not satisfying, really, getting to the top, to where I am now. I've achieved everything that the industry has to offer. I don't know. Maybe I'm in the wrong game."

I listened intently and tried to be gentle in my responses. "That's the eternal struggle of ambitious people, of creative people," I said. "You achieve your goals and look back and say, *Eh, it's not that special.*"

"My end goal is to be seen more like a performance artist, not just a guy who invents magic tricks," he said. "I am thinking in terms of Marina Abramovíc. She's a full-blown performance artist. The art *is* her. She *is* the art, rather than what she is doing. And I want it to be the same with me. Although playing cards and magic and all that shit is kind of a big part of me, I feel like I've picked the wrong thing. I feel like I am kind of halfway there in becoming that kind of artist. I feel held back by magic."

---

know Ramsay and Madison. I told him I was writing a book about magic. He sipped his whiskey and said, "I look forward to reading it." He quickly put down his glass, turned, and walked out. It was very strange. Ramsay later told me that, up in the office, Blaine made them sit in silence and watch over and over again the scene in which he regurgitates a live frog for Dave Chappelle. "It was the most awkward hour of my life," Ramsay said.

"But I feel like you are at the perfect place in your trajectory as an artist to go on to this next section of your journey." I had to keep him on track, to make him realize that this wasn't all for nothing.

"It's like the motivation is gone," he said. "It makes me think that this has been the wrong choice. If there's another choice, it's sitting back and doing nothing. I can't do that. I'll end up killing myself. I have to find something to get on with."

"You have all the time in the world," I said.

"But, like, is the52 even worth it? I almost want to step down and let someone else take the reins." My heart jumped. He couldn't just drop the52. He couldn't let it dissolve into nothing, not when the task was nearly complete!

"It's taken so long to get this far," he continued. "I was sure we would find fifty-two people instantly and start thinking differently. When we met you, that was perfect, organic, and the reason you got invited in. But it is really difficult to manage such a large artistic movement. I started it and I have to finish it, but I have to detach myself from it for a while. Laura will take the reins for now. It's good to be part of the52, but I sometimes feel that I've gotten it all wrong."

"You have all these tools now, more of a platform than you ever did."

"All of this is just keeping me connected to the magic world and the industry and community. Is that what I really want?" I assured him that what he had created was something truly special—it was what had drawn me into this world in the first place. But he was overwhelmed. "I'll find a way to get back into it," he said. "I just need time."

That phone call was the last I heard from him.

His newfound apathy tore me up inside. I had learned so much about myself during this adventure, about how a journey through magic, and the people you meet along the way, could bring out the best in a person. And to see him sinking deeper and deeper into anger and frustration, to be searching for meaning in his own life without looking at what was right in front of him, made me upset. He was pulling away, and I didn't know how to help him. He had given me so much up until now, and I couldn't give anything back.

I sat at my desk and flipped through a book he sent me after we first met: *Magic Is Dead,* a fifty-two-page manifesto, each page a short declarative statement, almost like poetry. The book's introduction was short. I read the lines, "Everything I have learnt to be true, relevant and important about magic is written between the covers of this book. I am Daniel Madison. Magic is Dead."

PAGE 1: Magic is the lowest form of entertainment.

PAGE 4: Magic is when people think it's real, and in order for people to think it's real, it cannot be presented as magic.

PAGE 6: The magician hides the art of sleight of hand so he can showcase it as something that it's not. This is devastating for the art, yet essential for the magician.

PAGE 7: Deception is a beautiful art often devastated by the hands of a magician.

PAGE 8: Magic has the power to be an art. It's a shame it's wasted on magicians.

PAGE 11: The strongest magic does not lie. It invites the audience to lie to themselves.

PAGE 13: Magic tricks are a perfect distraction from a person's overwhelming insecurities.

PAGE 25: By any means necessary.

PAGE 31: The more I try to understand magicians the further away from them I want to be.

PAGE 33: If nobody hates you then you're doing it wrong.

PAGE 35: Exposure to the lies of magic distorts the perception of truth.

PAGE 38: Magic is a stepping stone away from reality. This is both good and bad.

PAGE 41: The hours, days, months, years will teach you things that you may not want to know.

PAGE 50: Every once in a while, the Lion has to show the Jackal who he is.

PAGE 52: Magic is Dead.

He inscribed the title page, "Ian, thanks for your support," with his signature underneath. As I sat there reading, trying to find clues to Madison's next move, I realized something. I smiled. It was funny, sly even, and it kind of shocked me when it first popped into my head: I had only ever seen Madison perform in person once.

It was during his trip to New York with Ramsay. We were at As Is, a watering hole in Hell's Kitchen that has become the go-to hangout for young magicians in the city. We met up with other members of the52, including Xavior Spade and Tony Chang (the Ten of Hearts). Many people who come to the bar are just having drinks after a regular workweek and probably don't realize that some of the world's best magicians and card junkies are hiding among them.

After we grabbed a round, Ramsay sidled up next to a girl at the bar and leaned in to spark a conversation. She brushed a ribbon of chestnut hair off her face, cheeks pinched as a grin crept up toward her ears. She was intrigued. Ramsay had drawn her in. He raised his hands, palms out, as if proving their innocence, and slowly brought them toward her cocktail. Six inches away from the glass, he slowly began to drift his hands back and forth. Her straw started to move. It whooshed left, and then right, thrashing more and more violently as Ramsay waved faster and faster. The girl brought her hands toward her face but stopped halfway, frozen in midair, fingers splayed. Her mouth hung open and her glasses slipped down her nose. Ramsay threw his arms upward and the straw launched out of the glass, landing on her lap, droplets of the drink leaving small spots on her jeans. She screamed and jumped out of her chair. "What!" she yelped. "How did you do that?!" Ramsay didn't say anything. He didn't even pick up the straw, which fell to the floor. He just sat back, smiled, and took another sip of his beer. He never touched the girl's drink, I swear it. I saw it with my own eyes.

Madison and I clutched our glasses and watched Ramsay perform from afar. Madison was decked out in his usual all-black attire, and he intermediately sipped his whiskey—a double Jack Daniel's on the rocks.

"Hey, I know you," a tall, gangly blond kid with glasses said, leaning toward Madison and me. His face was flushed, his expressions animated; he'd clearly already had a few drinks. "Daniel Madison, right?" Madison nodded in response. The kid introduced himself as Jeff, a local magician. He had just come from a gig, "some boring corporate thing," he explained, fanning and fiddling with the deck of cards he held in his hands, the muffled sound of shuffling cradled underneath the thump of hip-hop music. "So, what are you guys doing in New York City?" he asked.

"Just here to film a few things," Madison said in his growling British accent, all throat and sandpaper. "See some friends." Jeff nodded sarcastically, as if we were keeping something from him. Jeff threw a look at me. "Are you working with these guys, too?"

"Nah," I told him, taking a sip from my glass. "I'm just hanging around." That animated nod again—he was sure we were hiding something. The life of a magician is built around deceit, and we were certainly no different—the sentiment ingrained in Madison's blood, me guilty by association.

He continued to look at me as we stood in silence for a moment. "So . . ." the kid started, trying to lift the conversation out of its awkward lull, "which one of you is going to show me a magic trick?" Madison slowly sipped his drink.

"I don't even have a deck of cards on me," Madison told him. After a pause and another swig of whiskey, he said, "But how about you just name a card." Jeff rubbed his chin, as if deep in thought.

"The jack of hearts," he said, adjusting his glasses.

Two jokers sat atop a stack of napkins on the bar (from someone else's deck, removed from a fresh pack) and Madison reached out to grab them, putting down his drink in the process. "I guess we'll just have to use these," he said, picking them up. "Jack of hearts, right?"

Jeff nodded. Madison pinched the Jokers between his thumb and forefinger. He swayed the two cards gently from left to right, as if fanning a Polaroid, and held them for a moment, arm outstretched. He separated the cards and revealed, between the two jokers, a jack of hearts.

"Like you said," Madison started, handing him the three cards, "the jack of hearts."

Jeff stood there, frozen in place, speechless. He grabbed the cards from Madison and just looked at them. "But . . ." he started, unable to complete his sentence. He glanced up at me, as if looking for help—trying to find a clue, anything to make sense of what just happened. Madison, the king of the underground, had just lived up to the hype.

After a minute, the guy looked back over at Madison and said: "How?"

Madison, in a rare moment of genuine happiness, smiled.

18

ORIGINS

I was plopped down on my couch in my apartment in Brooklyn, reading a book, when my phone pinged. *Yo! I'm outside.* It
was a text message from Ramsay. I tossed the book onto my
coffee table and opened my front door. Ramsay had his camera
pointed at me. He was recording.

"Look who it is!" he said, shoving the lens into my face.

"Get that thing out of here! What are you, the paparazzi?!" I
said, laughing, covering the lens with my hand. He pulled away
and turned the camera onto himself.

"All right, guys, just got to Brooklyn!" He was narrating now,
vlog-style, for his YouTube channel. "I'll be hanging with Ian for a
few days. We have some fun stuff planned, but I'll be taking you
along for the ride. Let's go!" He turned the camera off and slung it
around his shoulder.

"It never stops, eh?" I said.

"Gotta do it for the channel, dude!" he said, laughing. He reached
in and gave me a hug. "So, what's been going on? Have you been
working on your trick?"

"Trying, but I've been busy," I admitted. Although magic had become a daily part of my life, I still had to eat and pay rent, so I had spent the past few months working more on magazine articles than card tricks.

"Don't worry, man. It takes time. Nothing great happens overnight." We walked down the hallway toward my apartment. We stepped in, and Ramsay took out his laptop. "I gotta edit some footage, for the video that I'm supposed to put up today," he said. "Then we can go hang, fuck around, meet up with Xavior. Cool?"

"Yeah, whatever you want."

"What time are we heading into the office tomorrow?" he asked. I had pulled some strings and lined up a collaboration for Ramsay with *Complex*, the music and fashion news outlet. They wanted him to come into the office, do a short interview, and perform some magic for the staff. It had been a fast-paced few months for him, especially on YouTube, where he was really starting to blow up.

"In the afternoon," I said. "We have plenty of time, so we can grab lunch first and head over."

"Perfect," he said, opening his laptop. "I'm really stoked. I've got some good stuff planned."

After Ramsay started regularly posting on YouTube, months back, he quickly broke 100,000 subscribers and was becoming much savvier with his videos: sleeker cinematography, a more fluid and pronounced on-camera presence, crisp studio lighting, seamless editing, and enticing graphics. His channel had for years acted as a digital portfolio, chock-full of promotional magic fodder, but it lacked a sense of character and narrative so common with influencers nowadays. Fans want to follow someone's life through social media and, for thematic channels, perhaps learn something in the process.

When Ramsay decided to give his channel a real shot, he set up a strict production schedule. He began posting weekly tutorials, walking viewers through basic effects and sleight-of-hand moves. He also started vlogging (short for video blogging) and took viewers on his adventures around the world: to conventions and meet-ups, work trips and vacations. He started *Reacting to Bad Magic*, a series that became much discussed if not altogether infamous in the community, which showcased, front and center, what Ramsay and so many other young magicians saw as wrong with their craft, and from which they wanted to distance themselves. He also spoke to the camera in his home office, a ring of light illuminating his face, about his viewpoints on magic as an art form. He showed viewers what the life of a magician was all about. He opened up about his past, telling stories of learning magic from his grandfather. He let people in.

As his notoriety grew, he also made friends with other YouTubers, including King Bach, a former Vine celebrity known for his comedic skits (he broke 16 million followers and 6 billion loops before the mobile platform tanked), who agreed to do a collaborative video with Ramsay in New York City and post it to his 1.5 million subscribers. Making YouTube videos is much more complicated than just turning on a camera, pressing record, and dumping the footage online. Situational, self-documentary videos with a clear narrative through-line always perform well, and the guys wanted to make sure their collaboration had some substance. They agreed to have Ramsay teach Bach some magic, and they put a little performative twist on the project: Ramsay would be doing tricks on the street and Bach would see him from afar and ask if he would teach him some tricks, as if their meeting happened organically. It would give the video some semblance of a plot. After it was posted, the video grabbed hundreds of thousands of views and sent a bunch of new followers Ramsay's way.

As the months went on, Ramsay also started landing high-profile

gigs, some of which fell right into his lap. While waiting for a
flight to Los Angeles for an Ellusionist trip, he saw that Patrick
Adams, a Hollywood actor best known for his role in the television
series *Suits,* was waiting to get on the same flight. Coincidentally,
they ended up sitting across from each other on the plane. Ramsay struck up a conversation with the television star and did some
magic, fooling Patrick with simple card tricks. The guys exchanged
numbers and ended up hanging out while they were both in LA.
Ramsay took him to the Magic Castle, they became buddies, and
at the end of his trip, Patrick asked Ramsay if he would perform at
his upcoming wedding with *Pretty Little Liars* actress Troian Bel-
lisario. Patrick flew him out to California for the three-day affair.
Ramsay performed every night, after dinner and during cocktail
hour, and enthralled Patrick and Troian's guests, including actors
Chris Pine and Zach Quinto. Zach loved Ramsay so much that, a
few weeks later, he asked him to perform at his fortieth birthday
party at the Standard Hotel in Manhattan. Ramsay designed two
tricks specifically for Zach and his boyfriend, Miles McMillan, a
famous male model who has worked with the biggest names in
fashion, including Tom Ford and the late Alexander McQueen.
Following the mind-set of Max Malini, Ramsay wanted to create a
moment specifically for his two hosts. He wanted to leave them
with something they'd never forget.

As the sun set behind the Manhattan skyline, guests mingling
around the chic rooftop bar, Ramsay brought Zach and Miles
aside. "Let's try something," he told them. Ramsay explained the
concept of six degrees of separation, a theory that everyone and
everything is somehow connected. He proposed that they introduce random information to see if it made a connection for them.
Ramsay asked Miles to think of an animal and told Zach to take
out his phone and multiply a series of freely chosen numbers in
the calculator. Ramsay then wrote the arithmetic's result, a random number, on a napkin.

"Does this number mean anything to either of you?" Ramsay asked. Both Zach and Miles shook their head. It did not.

"Okay. Well, Miles, what animal did you think of?"

"A skunk," he responded.

"Does that animal mean anything to you?"

"Well, it's the name of our dog, actually," Miles responded, smiling, looking over at Zach.

"Oh really? That's interesting," Ramsay said. He took the napkin, the random number scribbled on its face. He turned it upside down. The digits now read as a word: "SKUNK."

He handed them the napkin. "A little something to remember this evening by," he told them. They ran around the room, showed everyone the napkin, and explained what had happened, what Ramsay had just done for them. Ramsay watched and waited. He approached them again.

"Actually," Ramsay said, "one more thing." He paused. "You know, some people think, when they choose a playing card, it represents them, kind of like in tarot—"

"The king of hearts and the king of spades!" Miles blurted out. Ramsay smiled. He fanned out his deck and removed the two kings. "You know, I was thinking the same thing." He asked Zach to take out his phone and turn on the spotlight. He put the beam of light to the back of each card. As the cards illuminated, a silhouette emerged. Zach and Miles looked closer, nearly squinting. What they saw were their own faces staring back at them, hidden within the cards and only visible when held up to the light. "Keep these, to go with the napkin," Ramsay said. Zach and Miles stood there, mouths hung open, astonished.

Despite the uptick in gigs, Ramsay kept his focus on YouTube. His reach skyrocketed and, when he hit 250,000 subscribers a few months later, he was contacted by a few production companies asking if he was interesting in doing a television show, landed branding deals with Skype and Squarespace, partnered with the

SyFy television show *The Magicians* for some promotional posts and a live performance for the cast, and was even flown to Italy to speak about magic on YouTube at the Masters of Magic convention, the largest gathering of magicians in Italy. His channel was now earning him thousands of dollars every week.

He soon realized that his career would benefit more if he dedicated himself to YouTube full-time. He didn't need to work for Ellusionist anymore—his vision for his personal brand, and magic in general, extended beyond the confines of the ordinary magic community. He could be his own boss. He pondered it for a few weeks but eventually made his decision and uploaded a video to his channel with the title "I Quit My Job to Make YouTube Videos." He spoke simply about his decision—from the heart. "Today I am venturing off onto my own path, and it is with a heavy heart that I am leaving Ellusionist. I am very thankful for the opportunity they have given me. But today is the day that I work for myself. And what an incredible feeling. I am terrified, but at the same time I have never been happier."

He called me the same day. "I did it," he said. "I'm finally following my dreams, man. It's all happening!"

Ramsay always stayed at my loft in Brooklyn when he visited. It's a converted industrial space with concrete floors and high ceilings cross-hatched in exposed beams. Being a full-time YouTuber meant traveling on your own dime (no more magic corporate credit card), so my door was always open for him. He stayed in our "guest room," which is basically just a small nook above our bathroom, kind of like a tree house.* He'd set up his workstation—

---

* My friend Matty, who once crashed in the guest room for a few months, named the space "Shit Sandwich" because it's directly above our bathroom

laptop, card reader, camera, lenses—on my dining room table, and edit videos in the mornings before heading out to film more stuff in the afternoons. He'd grumble at the mandatory workload—having your own reality show on YouTube is a full-time job—but he always woke up early and, coffee mug in hand, opened his laptop, put his head down, and got to work.

We woke up early the day after he arrived, had a quick breakfast, and Ramsay edited some footage before we made our way to *Complex* for his performance. We were early, so we decided to have a coffee and kill some time. We bought our drinks and sat down at a table on the sidewalk, traffic whooshing by, the Big Apple in full swing.

"What have you been working on, story-wise?" he asked, taking a sip from his cappuccino.

"I've been working on this big story for *Playboy*," I started. This was a story that had me by the throat, to be honest. I'd been dying to talk about it. "It's about this guy from Louisiana—a black guy who lived in this shitty, racist little town—who joined the army. He went off to war, hoping to escape the realities of his hometown, only to come back with post-traumatic stress disorder. When he was out there, his team ran over a roadside bomb, an IED, and he pulled his best friend from the wreckage. He saved his life, but it really took a toll on him. All that shit he saw in the war really messed him up, and he ended up moving back to his hometown. He never reached out to anyone for his PTSD and, one night, he was having a breakdown, and he called the Veterans Crisis Line for help. Cops came to his house, and the guy had a gun, so the cops shot and killed him. Just a super tragic story, you know? Like, this guy thought he could get away from where

---

and directly below that of our upstairs neighbor. All these years later my roommates and I still refer to the nook this way.

he came from, and the route he chose ended with him dead on the street in front of his grandfather's house, right back where he started. Just sad, man. So sad."

Ramsay sat silent for a minute.

"You remember how I told you my father was in the military, right?" he said. "And that's why I had to move around so much as a kid?"

"I do, yeah," I said.

"He had PTSD, too. He was in really deep with the Canadian Army—special forces, psychological operations, all these crazy secret missions he could never talk about. He helped a bunch of our allies, as well, with the worst shit that they needed done in Afghanistan and all over. He's been a part of every major conflict for the past few decades. He'd go off, be gone for a few months, come home, and try to be Dad again. But I could always tell that he couldn't shake off the things he saw over there. It really made an impact on my childhood."

"What do you mean?"

"I mean, he tried, he definitely tried, but you have to realize that war and the military, once you've been there, is something you can't escape. It affects how you see the world, how you treat others around you. It was such a strict household, the way he ran it. Like, dinner was at seven o'clock sharp, and if you were late, even by one minute, or if you wore a hat to the dinner table, you weren't allowed to eat. He'd make you sit in the other room while everyone else ate, and you'd go to bed hungry. And, sometimes, he'd do random cleaning inspections of our bedrooms. He'd walk in, and make us stand there, while he inspected how we made our bed, if our stuff was put away properly, if the room was dirty at all. I hated him, sometimes, for being so hard and so rigid, you know? I just wanted him to be there as my dad. When I was a teenager, I actually signed up for the army, to follow in his footsteps.

But I dropped out at the last minute." He put his cup down onto the table. "I just couldn't do it. I'm not sure he ever forgave me for doing that."

"How did that affect your relationship?" I asked.

"Well, you know, I started becoming defiant to his authority. After a while, I wanted to be the complete opposite of him. I wanted to be creative, I wanted to do my own thing. I wanted to be a musician, or an athlete, or a magician. I didn't want to go through my life knowing that I didn't become a man of my own making, as if my life was dictated by him, you know? I wanted to become completely me, not a version of him. So that's the real reason why I started dedicating myself to magic. I saw it as a way to truly be me—to be free, in a way. Magic, that creative space, that new way of looking at things, getting lost in that world, was an escape for me."

"You know, ever since I started this whole journey into magic, I keep thinking about the same sort of thing. Like, you became your own man in spite of the person your father was, right? But lately I can't help but face the question of what type of man I would've become if my dad hadn't died. Like, what would've happened? And would I have been happier with that path than this one?"

"I think the hardest thing in life," Ramsay said, taking off his sunglasses, "is to be truly honest with yourself in terms of who you want to be. There are always people and forces out there that want to mold you in a certain way. I think that I, personally, have found happiness in knowing that I was the driving force in becoming who I am today, however strange and unorthodox the path I've chosen has been—magic, YouTube, this whole thing. It feels good, you know, to be at peace with that struggle, that I'll never be my father, and that's okay."

I turned to look at the street. A cab screeched to a halt, nearly hitting a pedestrian. The driver rolled down his window, honked his horn, and shouted at the man, who just scurried across the street, lifting his hand in an apologetic wave.

A few weeks before coming to Brooklyn, Ramsay released his first for-sale trick through his YouTube channel. It was a new version of the classic voodoo routine, where the spectator chooses a card, signs it, and then makes a voodoo card; whatever they do to the voodoo card (rip it up, burn it) magically happens to their signed card as well.

Effects had always been disseminated either at magic shops or through self-published books and lecture notes; or, if sold digitally, through big online retailers. These companies acted as a gateway for upstart magicians to have their tricks, gimmicks, or routines reach a wide audience.[*] This path could also act as a stepping-stone for bigger opportunities, like working in the industry as a full-time creator, or accumulating contacts and accolades to obtain higher-profile gigs. As the magic community became more savvy with the internet, however, the necessity of retailers-as-intermediaries began to decline. For a hypervisible, big-time figure like Ramsay, who had built an intensely loyal fan base, he no longer needed to rely on a magic company to release his products, hence why he quit working for Ellusionist. With YouTube, he could do it himself—and keep all the profits. He sold the voodoo effect for a relatively cheap ten bucks. It was very much like the in-

---

[*] Magicians normally make a 25–50 percent commission for a download, depending on the company. It is not uncommon, too, for a retail outlet to negotiate that the creator transfer the effect's intellectual copyright to the company in exchange for placement on their online store—no doubt a long-game strategy in case the trick goes viral and a famous magician offers to purchase the exclusive right in which to perform it. I have heard a few horror stories about naïve magicians getting screwed over by this stipulation.

fluencer model spearheaded by fashionistas, wellness gurus, and fitness heads, but instead of only promoting other brand's products, magicians like Ramsay were able to market and sell things they created themselves. And the effect's release proved his point: he sold thousands of downloads and raked in a boatload of cash.

After proving that this approach held sustainability and promise, Ramsay began coaching others to also become YouTubers, including Xavior Spade.* It was an open secret that Xavior was struggling with Lost Art Magic. He couldn't get the company to grow. People respected his online store, and him as the owner, but the process of developing, marketing, and selling tricks—not to mention juggling a host of social media handles exclusive to his business—was cumbersome and time consuming. Plus, his personal page on Instagram was vastly more popular than that of Lost Art. People were more interested in him as a community influencer than the business he owned.

Ramsay told Xavior that using YouTube as a business platform afforded advantages that owning a company did not. For one, it elevated the personal brand of the creator rather than a faceless company, for which people proved to be entirely more loyal. Second, it combined all of the necessities of running a successful business into a single platform. Your channel was your content, your advertising, your marketing, and your store all in one. It was a one-stop shop for anything someone could ever want from a personality they followed online, especially if that person was a magician. They could get free how-to videos, vlogs and other

---

* Ramsay likewise pressured Peter McKinnon, a photographer and cinematographer from Toronto who also worked for Ellusionist, to start a photo-and-video-themed channel. Peter, energetic and affable on camera, quickly rose to stardom and left the magic world behind. He currently has more than two million subscribers and regularly collaborates with Casey Neistat, one of the most iconic creators on the platform. Some of his most popular video ideas, however, are those in which he consults Ramsay for help.

adventurous content, as well as shouts and murmurs on inside-baseball topics that other magicians cared about. The platform afforded connectivity and expediency not seen in other models run on a work-from-home, shoestring-style budget.

Moreover, once trust and loyalty is built with an audience, once they feel invested in the creator and the content in which he or she produces, viewers are much more likely to buy a product created by the individual personally; not only do they trust that it would be worth their money (and, coming from guys as skilled as Ramsay and Xavior, it obviously would), but they also feel an emotional attachment to this person, and want to support them in their hard-earned endeavors.* They want to see people like Ramsay and Xavior—people they look up to—succeed. With social media, fans feel wholly invested in the personalities whom they follow, and they're always ready to click, like, share, and drop money on their favorite creator's products.

It took Xavior a few months to get a handle on YouTube's ins and outs—playing to its algorithm, the need for a catchy title and enticing thumbnail, the little editing nuances that kept people watching—but over time he built a stable following of 20,000 subscribers. He then followed Ramsay's lead and released a how-to project through his channel. It was on the pass, a widely used sleight where a selection of cards are moved within the deck, and for which he was famously known. He did it better than almost

---

* This sociological phenomenon is called parasocial relationships. "We can feel a strong relationship, and *feel* like it's a two-way relationship, with a brand or a celebrity or an influencer, when really it's a one-way relationship," Ben Parr, author of *Captivology: The Science of Capturing People's Attention*, told *New York* magazine. "Social media specifically has increased the parasocial relationships we have with people, by making us feel like we're seeing the personal lives of our favorite people. And so we feel like we actually know them when we actually don't."

anyone out there. He filmed an enticing trailer and offered the project for $15. In just ten days (with a shout-out from Ramsay), he sold 1,400 downloads and netted nearly $30,000. It was the largest payday of his entrepreneurial career.

But making magic so visible online has its drawbacks. It's true that some magicians have overlooked the delicate nature of promoting a secretive art form on an unruly thing like the internet— a place with loose morals, the Wild West of the twenty-first century, where any tidbit of information, no matter how revered, could be exposed. Sure, random snot-nosed kids will always give away secrets on YouTube for the fun of it, but a lot of magicians are more worried about performers with large followings who are giving magic a bad name.

Recently, a small crop of so-called viral magicians have popped up on the internet, armed with a base-level understanding of illusion and a penchant for catchy (but equally mindless) content. Most of these magicians operate on Facebook, where quick-hit videos can spread like wildfire. They largely post clickbait meant to get likes and shares rather than something that will enlighten the viewer. Some of these magicians, like Jibrizy, a Chicagoan who sports colored contact lenses and operates under the tagline "Swag Magic," however, take it a step further. He actually coaches spectators on how to react—scream, run around in circles, the whole bit—before the trick is performed. After a hidden-camera video of Jibrizy stooging spectators surfaced, the entire magic community jumped on him, including Ramsay, who posted a video denouncing his immoral tactics.

Ramsay and many other well-known magicians have not only fought hard against these types of egregious trends, but they have also tried to make sure that, as their own followings grow, they understand the responsibility that comes with being the face of magic online. It's a strange set of circumstances that may only be specific to this esoteric art form: the inherent secrecy of magic's complex norms has created a system where spectators aren't able to differentiate good magic from bad magic, or which tactics for disseminating magic online are detrimental rather than beneficial to the longevity and widespread understanding of the art form itself. It's up to each individual artist to be not only a performer but also a gatekeeper of secrets and a critic of their own policies. It's an ever-evolving enigma: once you think you've found the solution, the puzzle transforms into something else entirely. Ramsay has taken it upon himself to present magic on YouTube in a way that allows his viewers to learn more about the craft and respect its artistic foundations, with the hope that they, moving forward, can themselves distinguish between right and wrong when thinking about how the craft can progress or be innovated.

People will always be able to find a clickbait magic video on their Facebook feed, or secrets behind tricks on YouTube, but if guys like Ramsay can instill an element of integrity into how they showcase magic online—by recommending books, crediting creators, giving history lessons, asking for permission to use certain material, consulting with other magicians on what should and should not be included in a video, and giving sound advice on how moves or tricks should be performed—they may be able to control magic's future and instill some semblance of respect that the art form has for decades so desperately tried to hold on to. And, after spending so much time with Ramsay, I could see how much he wanted, more than anything else, to establish a *community* based on his content. I could see how deeply he cared about creating sustainability through YouTube, not just for his professional career and personal ambitions but for the art form to which he has dedicated his entire life.

Ramsay didn't talk much about it, but fans sent him emails and letters all the time, some of which were incredibly personal.

"I mean, look at this," he said once, scrolling through the inbox associated with his channel. He thumbed through hundreds of unread emails. Dozens had come in that day alone. He kept swiping, picked a random message, and opened it. The subject line: *You saved my life.* He read it aloud:*

I may be one of thousands, tens of thousands who email you daily. When I say you saved my life I don't mean that lightly. I was a soldier in the army for 4 years and got severely injured, during my service I got married to who i thought was the person who i was supposed to spend my life with. In my accident I herniated 4 discs one bulging on the nerve sustaining paralysis in my right arm/fingers. Continuing to serve my condition got worse developing severe arthritis and scoliosis in my cervical spine. I was medically discharged and due to the amount of physical and emotional repercussion I developed severe anxiety ptsd and depression. My wife found it was too hard to bare so she wound up dippin back home to California. Within a month she had a new boyfriend and a baby on the way. I fell deeper and darker into depression and started to take pain medication. It wound up consuming me and leading me to heroin. I would pray at night I wouldn't wake up. Everyone told me to find a hobby but everything I pursued I quickly lost interest in. Until one day I went on YouTube and typed in magic. And there you were, Chris Ramsey. Needless to say I binge watched all of your videos some of them multiple times. I then went to Wal-Mart and bought a deck of cards and then went to my local magic shop. There I asked if anything magic related was available and believe it or not there was a magicians society here in myrtle beach south Carolina where I live. I went nervous and introverted. Because of you Chris I was able to reach out developing a major passion for magic and

---

* I have concealed the sender's identity for privacy reasons but I have not altered the message, for spelling, grammar or clarity, in any way.

gaining new friends. After a couple lectures and meetings, the
owner of the magic shop offered me a job . . . i almost cried after
everything I had went through. My first day is tomorrow. Wish
me luck. I don't even know you but I love you for legitimately
saving my life. Continue to do you, continue to inspire and
I already know through your videos you will always remain
humble. I will never be able to thank you enough for rekindling me
and my family and the new friends I've gained through branching
out all starting with magic. Again thank you Chris.

Ramsay looked up from the screen. "You see what I mean?" he said, his face pained. He must've been thinking of his father, I thought. "This all can't just be for nothing."

Ramsay and I came from very different worlds and experiences. But we have one very fundamental thing in common: both of our fathers wanted to watch their sons grow up, become men, and hopefully be like them in all the best ways and not like them in all the worst.

19

NOT JUST
A FEMALE MAGICIAN

I hadn't spoken to Laura in months. We sent each other the occasional DM on Instagram, or dropped a comment on each other's posts, but nothing really of substance. And then one day, out of the blue, she sent me a message: "Hey love," she began, "what are your plans coming up? Would love to have you over here in London. I see Ramsay has been taking you around, showing you the ropes . . . thought it'd be great to have you over here, too."

"Of course, would love to come," I typed back. Laura had always been the worker of the bunch, gigging relentlessly, someone who truly loves to perform. I wanted to see her in her element. "What are you thinking?"

"Well, I've been helping Daniel recently, you know, with his issues, and we have to figure out the next members of the52, so there's a lot going on. But I would love to have you along to one of my shows, to show you what I really do."

"I'd love that!" I told her. I felt a sense of maternal obligation coming from Laura, like she was holding all of this together, and

I held a sense of pride that she wanted to keep me around as the52 progressed.

She reached out again a few days before I left. "Let's meet up on Monday, the day after you get here," she said. "I am going to be bringing someone, but you can't tell anyone. It has to stay between us. Can you keep a secret?"

"Of course," I said.

"Perfect. I will see you soon."

During his months-long absence, Madison worked on a project related to *The Expert at the Card Table*, the 1902 sleight-of-hand classic by S. W. Erdnase. Despite his admiration for the text and all that it taught him about cards, Madison wanted to question people's devotion to the book. He was, after all, never one to pray to false idols. The ethos of the52 had always been to shake things up—to propel magic forward—and he wanted to shoot an arrow through the heart of the industry. And so Madison filmed an eight-hour-long video detailing his thoughts on the moves depicted in the legendary book, and how he had improved on them over the years. It also came with an exclusive deck of playing cards and an annotated book delivered in a high-quality custom box that mimicked the original text: gold lettering stamped onto a forest-green case.

The project dropped a couple of weeks before I went to London to see Laura. On the launch date, he promoted it with a simple tagline: *I am Daniel Madison. And I am better than Erdnase.* That's when the death threats started. "You'll be sorry you acted like an arrogant prick mate. Too big for your boots. Something is coming for you, I swear. TWAT!" one text message read, coming from an unknown number. "You got a death wish bro? People down here talking about having you killed, no joke watch your back bro," another anonymous magic vigilante wrote. The backlash—even apart from the physical threats—was swift and fierce. Card-handling legends like Jason England and Derek DelGaudio lambasted Madison on Facebook, with DelGaudio calling him "the Milo Yiannopoulos of magic." Memes were created, jokes were made, and Madison loved every second of it. He used it as fuel for his fire.

As the old saying goes, however, any press is good press. The hundred-dollar project sold out in two days. And people raved about it. They loved Madison's take on the historic book, and Ellusionist raked in tens of thousands of dollars from the stunt. Even David Blaine sent his praise. I called Madison the day the project came out and, to my surprise, he picked up.

"So that's what you've been up to!" I said. "But, man, people are really hating on you for this one."

He laughed. "It's better to be loved or hated than anything in the middle. I was in a lull for a while, and I needed to put some fire under my ass. I needed to get back into my character and really push the envelope. What better way to do that than attack magic's bible?"

Page 33: If nobody hates you then you're doing it wrong.

Madison also had a mission for me: induct the52's next two members. He and Laura had spent months debating. They decided on Nicolas Nargeot, a young sleight-of-hand aficionado and photographer from France, and Larry Fong, a highly respected director of photography and cinematographer in Hollywood. Larry literally makes blockbuster movies for a living. Both guys had plans to be in New York City soon. "Take them to get their tattoos," Madison told me.

Nicolas came first. I called Xavior and the three of us went to a small shop in Manhattan for the ink. Nicolas, square-jawed and well dressed, beamed at the opportunity. "This is the best day of my life," he told us in his lilting French accent, holding up his freshly inked finger: the Ten of Clubs.

Larry came a few weeks later. A longtime magic hobbyist, Larry has an intense Rolodex of films. He has manned the camera for big-shot movies like *300, Watchmen, Super 8, Now You See Me, Batman v Superman: Dawn of Justice,* and *Kong: Skull Island.* Larry always performs a little for the cast while they're lounging around on set, and while filming *Kong,* he posted a photo of him performing to Brie Larson. Over the years, he also made it a point to hide a three of clubs in all his movies—his secret signature, hidden in plain sight, known only to him and a few friends. In *Batman v Superman,* the card is tacked up on the wall in Wallace Keefe's apartment among a collage of newspaper clippings. In *Kong: Skull Island,* it's laid atop a table in a Vietnamese bar, seen during an overhead shot. The list goes on.

He actually got the call while filming *The Predator,* a reboot of the famed horror-monster flick directed by Shane Black, which hit the big screen in September 2018. When he saw the incoming FaceTime call, he scurried across set—smack dab in the wilderness of British Columbia—and locked himself in the crew's blacked-out Suburban. He answered and saw Madison and Laura sitting together. "What do you think?" they asked after offering him membership. Larry giddily accepted, hung up, and ran back over to the cast and crew, who were waiting for him to begin the next take. He became the Seven of Clubs.[*]

Larry had just finished filming *The Predator* when he came to New York for his ceremonial ink. Xavior came along again to film the induction. Eric Hu, another friend and local magician who owns Baby Grand, a karaoke bar in Brooklyn, also joined. We stopped at a bar across the street before going into the tattoo parlor. Larry threw down a shot of tequila. "It's an honor," he told me, clutching his empty glass. "I know what this group is all about."

We went over to the shop and Larry sat down. He grimaced in

---

[*] Larry will be hiding his new card in all his future films, starting with *The Predator.* Go watch the movie. Can you find it?

pain as the tattoo artist went to work. It was his first tattoo. A few minutes later, it was official. He held up his finger to the camera. "Welcome, Larry!" Xavior shouted, and we all gave a little round of applause. Everyone in the shop joined in and a chant rang out: *"Larr-y! Larr-y! Larr-y!"*

It's not surprising, although not well known, that many in entertainment are magic geeks. "I have no idea what gave me the confidence to start performing magic shows, for money, when I was twelve," said Ira Glass on the radio program *This American Life*, opening an episode dedicated entirely to magic. The segment came to be when Glass and his coworker David Kestenbaum realized they were both childhood magicians. They reminisced about hosting their own shows, compared techniques with cards and props, and talked method and sleight of hand. They also realized that they both were, as grown men, still captivated by magic. "Even as we have been writing and editing this story, like over and over, I've gotten that feeling of excitement about it that I used to get [as a kid] when I handled props or practiced the Cups and Balls," Glass said. "I still regularly have dreams that I am supposed to do my act—I just had one two weeks ago." Ira Glass is over sixty years old. He hasn't officially performed magic in almost forty-five years.

Academy Award–winning actor Adrien Brody also fell in love with magic as a youngster. "I was more than a fan," he told *Deadline* in 2015, an interview given to promote his role as Houdini in the History Channel series of the same name. "Not only did I have a fascination with magic, but I had aspirations of becoming a magician when I was a boy." During the interview, he also drew parallels between acting and magic: "You understand the workings of a trick and you make it your own, you develop a patter and you tell that story uniquely, and that's what makes a great show and a great magician." He ended up getting nominated for an Emmy for his role as the great escapist, which made him nostalgic for his childhood ambition. "Receiving recognition for a heroic figure in my life and for something as meaningful as magic . . . for it to have led me into acting and then led me to ultimately play the key figure in that world is pretty remarkable," he said. The actor Neil Patrick Harris is still a practicing magician. He has performed magic on daytime talk shows, including for Ellen DeGeneres and Kelly Ripa, and many of the characters he portrays on television have some loose connection to magic. He was also executive producer for Derek DelGaudio's show *In & Of Itself.*

Weirdly enough, a few days after taking Larry for his ink, I popped into Tannen's, the magic shop in Manhattan, to buy a few decks of cards. When I walked in, I found the director J. J. Abrams, a good friend of Larry (they worked together on *Lost* and *Super 8*), standing at the counter with his adolescent son. Abrams is also a big fan of magic, and even gave a TED Talk in 2007 about the Mystery Box, a cardboard box with a question mark stamped on its front that is sold at Tannen's. It costs $15 but is filled with $50 worth of magic. The catch is, obviously, that its contents are a mystery.

In his much-watched speech, Abrams explained that secrecy is a constant theme in his films, and his obsession with mystery stemmed from the power of this box. His own box was a gift from his grandfather, the same man who bought him his first video camera. Onstage, he reached inside his bag and pulled out the same box he received as a kid. It still hadn't been opened. "I realized I haven't opened it because it represents something important to me," he told the crowd. "It represents my grandfather. It represents infinite possibility. It represents hope. It represents potential." To Abrams, mystery is sometimes more important than knowledge. He explained that the building blocks of magic can shape our understanding of the world and help influence other forms of art, like film. To him, mystery is the catalyst for imagination. "I realized, wow, mystery boxes are everywhere in what I do [as a filmmaker]."

Hollywood directors and producers, when crewing up for a big-budget film, have likewise employed many of the community's most savvy magicians. These experts in illusion worked behind the scenes for the *Now You See Me* franchise and consulted for the Tom Cruise–led action film *Mission Impossible: Rogue Nation*. Directors understand that magicians have unique minds and can come up with clever ways for heroes to escape certain situations or save the day. "It really gets me excited to work on things that people would not associate with magic," Blake Vogt told me; Vogt lent his expertise to *Ant-Man* and *Now You See Me 2*. "The true identity of Ant-Man was a con artist," he said. "He was a deceiver. We can't go out and hire a professional con artist, so what's the next-best thing? A magician!"

Ocean's 8, the newest, all-female installment of the famed heist series, released in 2018, also employed a magician: the Portuguese sleight-of-hand artist Helder Guimarães. The film's production team saw his off-Broadway show *Verso*, later approached him to consult for the movie, and sent him a copy of the script for input. Then they had him on set for more hands-on involvement. "I spent hours training both Cate Blanchett and Sandra Bullock, explaining all the details about the con, the psychology of con artists, other related scams and tricks used by hustlers as well as some card handling," Guimarães told me over email. "They were both fantastic, hardworking, and wonderful to work with. It was very collaborative. They were always very receptive to my ideas and my comments throughout all the process. When I am consulting, my job is to help someone else with their vision. Producers, directors, actors: they all have their specific ideas and I am merely helping with them, using my knowledge."

The *Now You See Me* franchise is gearing up to release its third installment in 2019. During preproduction, Madison got a call. Would he want to come on board and consult for the film? In classic Madison fashion, he turned the offer down.

I got to Bike Shed, a motorcycle bar in Shoreditch, London, and ordered a coffee while I waited for Laura. My body was still on New York time and I was exhausted. Tucked underneath a brick-arched traffic overpass, the joint boasted a brushed steel bar, polished concrete floors, and a pair of bloodred leather couches smashed against the back wall. Stylish patrons in skinny jeans and knit sweaters clutched pints of beer and ate burgers. It was a hipster hangout not unlike most of the bars near my apartment in Brooklyn. A light rain fell outside, typical for London in springtime.

Laura trotted in. She wore a see-through black top and skintight black jeans tucked into knee-high leather boots. She beamed that wide grin at me and her crimson-red bangs swung over her eyes. Behind her, clad in a loose-collared T-shirt that flashed tattoos running under his collarbones, with a shearling jacket wrapped around his shoulders, stood Daniel Madison. They both gave me a hug, sniggering at Madison's surprise appearance. He had taken the train from Leeds that morning. "I couldn't pass it up, coming down to see you," he said as we took a seat on a couch. He looked much better than the last time I saw him, in New York. They both ordered a beer; I asked for another coffee.

I had just put in the two newest members, so we talked about the next wave of inductees for the52. "We need to find undiscovered talent, people that are doing great things," Laura said. "That's the whole point. We'll get there. We're going to get the next round going over the summer." Laura signaled over the waitress.

"Hey, love," she said, "could we be moved over to a booth? We have a few more friends coming and, ah, well, we might need a bit of privacy, yeah?" Laura told her that Dynamo, their longtime friend who is also one of the most famous magicians in England, was popping in to have lunch with us.

The waitress arched her eyebrow. "Oh, yeah. Yeah, sure, let me open one up for ya." A minute later, Dynamo walked in with his longtime manager, Dan Albion. Everyone in the bar shot glances as we walked to our booth. A father and daughter approached Dynamo for a photograph. Our waitress took our order and brought over a round of burgers.

Over the past decade, Dynamo has become *the* face of magic in England. From 2011 to 2014, he starred in his own television show, *Dynamo: Magician Impossible*, which racked up more than 20 million viewers. His subsequent British show tour sold half-a-million tickets, and his Australian leg sold another 100,000. Although they had taken wildly divergent paths as magicians, Madison and Dynamo were still two kids from Bradford who loved to geek out over moves and new tricks. They sat across from one another and tinkered with a deck of cards. Dynamo showed Madison a few new routines (which will remain secret), and he listened intently as Madison gave his opinion, embracing the rare one-on-one with his old friend.

Dan Albion and I talked about Dynamo's career trajectory, including how, before Dynamo was famous, the BBC rejected their show idea. "We were in the room, showing them the reel, and the executives weren't really even paying attention," Albion told me, adding that it took more than a year to successfully sell their vision for the show. They wanted to embody the raw, unscripted nature of a traditional street magic show, but also have Dynamo embody someone with otherworldly powers, who could perform impossible large-scale stunts in public. They also wanted to humanize Dynamo by digging into his hardscrabble past and his chronic health problems—to show how he overcame all the odds to become a famous magician. It was eventually picked up by Channel 4, who took a risk on the unknown talent, and became an overnight success.

"I'd like to see more women on television doing magic," Laura interjected, adding that misogynistic stereotypes—the busty assistant, the cutesy add-on—remain a plague in the industry. Laura had recently made some headway on the small screen, starring in the British show *The Next Great Magician*. She admitted there was still a long way to go. Laura had always championed her female counterparts in the community and at that point had already inducted some of the best female performers around into the52: Cat Boult (the Queen of Diamonds), a blond, high-cheekboned close-up magician from Los Angeles,* and Billy Kidd (the Three of Clubs), a Canadian stage performer known for her Prohibition-era tomboy style, all newsboy caps and tweed blazers. Billy has a range of skills, from cards to escapes to comedy, and has seen substantial screen time on television shows in the United Kingdom, where she lives full-time.

Laura idolizes Mercedes Talma, a British magician who rose to prominence in the early twentieth century and performed in the world-famous act *Le Roy, Talma & Bosco*, a troupe that included the famed Belgian conjurer Servais Le Roy, who also happened to be her husband. Although her career began as an assistant to her spouse, over time she herself became extremely accomplished. She eventually started performing alone as "the Queen of Coins."†

---

* Cat also consulted on fellow the52 member Shin Lim's winning performance for the finals of *America's Got Talent*.

† Legend has it that Talma, after being cornered by muggers and told to hand over all her money, made dozens of coins appear out of thin air. The robbers freaked out and ran away.

Houdini called her "the greatest female sleight of hand performer that ever lived."

Journalists covering her performances, however, still labeled her an ancillary figure, secondary to her male counterparts. "Leroy had very capable support from [Mercedes] Talma and his large colleague Bosco," a reporter for *Evening Post*, a New Zealand newspaper, wrote in 1914. "The lady showed herself a very capable conjurer and a sprightly comedian." Other magicians were similarly conditional in their praise. In a 1902 letter to Houdini, George Little, editor of *Mahatma Magazine*, wrote, "Servais Leroy opened here at the Orpheum (Brooklyn) with his triple alliance (Leroy, Talma, Bosco) and they scored pretty well. I would much rather see Leroy all alone in his own act—I feel certain he would be better appreciated, and you could see something of him, as I have always considered him a very exceptionally clever performer. I may say, that Talma received the biggest share of applause and for a woman, she deserved it."

Laura wishes that women who dedicated themselves to magic weren't still viewed this way. "The term 'female magician' is a problem in and of itself," Laura said at lunch between bites of french fries. "It's bullshit, really, being caught up in the simplification of labels and whatnot, trying to make it easier to mass market us just because we are women. I want to be known as a sleight-of-hand artist," she said, taking a deck of cards from her purse and slamming it down on the table, "not a *female magician*."

Laura holds a weekly residency at Café de Paris in West London's Piccadilly neighborhood. First opened in 1924, the two-tiered space is modeled after the *Titanic*'s extravagant ballroom and was a mainstay for London's elite during the city's jazz age. The space was destroyed by falling bombs during World War II but was subsequently rebuilt, reclaiming all of its former splendor. It's become quite a celebrity hangout and has hosted the likes of Harry Styles, Rita Ora, Hugh Grant, and Simon Cowell.[*]

Clusters of round tables wrapped in white tablecloths fill the main floor, flanked on one side by a long bar and, on the other, leather booths. The waitstaff wears black tie and the hostesses, glittery gowns. A massive chandelier bursts from the ceiling in a sea of pleated red cloth. A navy curtain, crusted in gold-tinted gems, anchors the rear of the stage and two curved staircases fall down its sides from the balcony and into the main dining area. French music filled the room as I entered, all walking bass lines and female vocals. The entire space was awash in a blue-and-red glow, with candles centered on each table. The well-dressed crowd filed in and took their seats.

Laura scurried into the back room to change into her performance attire. Patrons eat dinner before the stage show begins, and Laura performs tableside magic between courses, her aim to get guests warmed up for the evening's main attraction. She emerged in a low-cut, floor-length black dress with rhinestones running along the bustline. She walked around, greeted the waitstaff, sat down at a nearby table, and pulled a deck of cards from her purse. Patrons began to take their seats. She waited anxiously to begin.

Laura pounced after guests finished their first course. Her tableside routine is just under five minutes and fits snugly within the window between salad and entrée. Some of the waiters came by and shared insights about the types of guests at their tables. Acting like her sociological spies, the waiters know Laura tries to hit the liveliest tables first to incite a large reaction that can be seen by the whole room. If Laura's performance is a big hit, it makes the entire dining experience more memorable, and the waitstaff was there to help create that magical aura. I followed her as she

---

[*] Simon Cowell was also, coincidentally, a regular at Laura's mother's club in the 1980s.

bounded from table to table, repeating her card-based routine. She stopped at a table of young women, probably in their early twenties, who were celebrating a birthday. They were high-energy, downing flutes of champagne, and were immediately intrigued by Laura's dress and off-kilter haircut.

She began with her version of Dai Vernon's Ambitious Card routine. A signed card, after being put in the middle numerous times, keeps magically appearing, with a snap of her fingers, back at the top of the deck. She spoke quickly as she performed, and her patter had a tinge of self-deprecating humor, which is a great screen for misdirection.* She also performed a two-card transposition, a trick that I can also do. Laura had one of the girls sign a card, cradle it in her palm, and press her free hand down on top of it. After it was secured, Laura signed a card of her own. She held it out in front of her, gave it a gentle wave, and turned it over. She now held the girl's card, scratched in her signature. "Wait, if I have the eight of spades—your card—where is mine?" The girl opened her hands and turned it over. It was Laura's card, her signature scrawled on its face. The girls didn't shout or scream. They just stared at one another. One girl mouthed the words *What the fuck* to her friend, followed by a long drink of champagne.

I recognized the third phase of Laura's routine. She took back the girl's signed card, put it into the deck, and began to shuffle. "But it doesn't really matter how much I shuffle, because your card has already disappeared," Laura said. Laura glanced over at me and winked. She knew I was following along. It was the same

---

* Magicians use words to create a captivating and congruent narrative for their performances, but they also employ dialogue to divert attention. "Magicians merrily exploit the fact that attention-grabbing information from one sensory system leads to enhancement of attention in another," write Stephen L. Macknik and Susana Martinez-Conde in *Sleights of Mind*. "Thus a magician's rapid-fire patter serves to increase how intently you stare at the actions he wants you to look at."

trick she performed to me in that dark alleyway outside of Black-pool. "That box has been sitting at the center of the table the entire time," Laura said, picking it up. She shook it. Something knocked around inside. Laura lifted the flap, pulled out a folded card, and handed it to the girl. She opened it and screamed. The entire table began clapping.

Guests finished their dinner and we sat down to watch the stage show. Laura's friends came and joined us, a crew of fellow performance artists: singers, actors, and dancers, most of whom were women. The stage show, titled *The Seven Deadly Sins*, was hosted by a foul-mouthed, crude-humored gay man who tortured members of the audience with his cutting wit and performed in a series of sin-themed musical skits full of acrobats, sword swallow-ers, and fire breathers. At the end of the show, the host announced that Laura would be performing more magic downstairs in the VIP bar.

As guests shuffled to the bar's entrance, Laura quickly changed into more casual attire, hooked me by the arm, and led me down-stairs. The room was cramped, warped by neon lights and thump-ing bass. Laura bounced from guest to guest, several of whom she had performed for upstairs during dinner. She adjusted her effects, focusing more on one-off visual tricks rather than tiered narrative routines—it was loud and crowded.

She approached a fashionable couple and signaled to the deck in her hands. They both nodded excitedly. She fanned the deck, the universal gesture to choose a card. The couple picked one, took a peek, and placed it back into the center of the deck. Laura removed a small piece of paper from her pocket. She placed it gently on top of the deck and then leaned into the couple and asked if they had a coin. The man pulled one from his pocket, and Laura gestured for him to place it on top the piece of paper, at the deck's center. She took a lighter from her pocket and flicked the flame to life. A grin spread across her face. She brought the flame closer and closer to the piece of paper, which ignited in a burst of light, engulfing the coin. When the smoke cleared, a hole appeared in the deck, running from the top to the middle. The coin sat at the bottom of the hole, as if melting a canal through the deck. It rested on a card midway down. Laura spread the cards and gestured for the couple to remove the card on which the coin stopped. The couple glanced at each other in disbelief and slowly went for the card. They flipped it over and screamed. The man threw up his arms and his drink spilled all over his date's dress. She didn't seem to notice.

Laura continued with the tricks in the basement. I stood by her side, waiting for the reveal, for the audience's reactions. The dim lighting made it hard to see, but if she held her hands still for a moment, you could make out a red tattoo on the inside of her finger—a clue of the life she leads outside of this place, in the shadows of magic, a life she has built for herself.

We took the train home together. It was late, and we sat in silence most of the way. When we came to my stop, Laura put her hand on top of mine and said, "I'm so glad you came, so glad, Ian. Let's get dinner tomorrow, yeah? I have some things to do during the day, but I'm free after that."

"I'll be there," I said, and stepped off the train.

The next day, I met Laura at a restaurant near her apartment. A little pub, with wooden booths and Union Jack flags hanging from the ceiling, it served typical English fare: Scotch eggs, chicken liver, fish and chips. A soccer match blasted from the TV hanging above the bar, and small pods of men clutched pints of beer and watched the game. We checked in with the hostess and made our way out to the rear patio, where it was quiet. The sun had just started to set, and lights strung overhead popped on. The waitress took our order and brought us a round of drinks.

"So, Ian, tell me, did you always want to be a writer?" Laura asked.

"No," I said, matter-of-factly. "Growing up, my dad was a tile man—houses, supermarkets. He was really talented. He always talked about blue-collar jobs: building things, and he wanted me to be an engineer, or something along those lines. When I was younger, I was always really good at math, so it was an easy path for me. I loved fixing things, solving problems. And then, two weeks before my fourteenth birthday, my dad died. He literally came home from work on a Saturday, had a stroke, and died a couple of days later."

"Fuck."

"Yeah, I was always really close with him, and I had always seen myself becoming a version of him. I looked up to him. But after he passed away, I didn't really have a tangible connection to that anymore. So, in high school, I kind of shifted my view on the world a little bit. When I was sixteen, I took a creative writing class, and that's when I realized I wanted to be a writer. In college, I worked for one of my school's professors, and, my first day, I walked in and he told me I had to start writing for the school's newspaper. So, I started writing articles, and I fell in love with it. The job of a journalist is to go out and experience things, however crazy or mundane they may be, and then translate those experiences to the reader. And that, to me, was the most fascinating job in the world."

"And your mom? How did she cope?"

"This was her soul mate, right? When she graduated high school, she got in an RV and toured the U.S. She played pool—and was a really good poker player. She met my father and they fell in love and got married and when she became a mother, she put that kind of life aside, to be the caretaker, a life that required self-sacrifice. They worked their way up, built their dream house, the whole thing. And then he passed away. My mom needed to find a way to find herself again, a way to feel like she was doing something solely for herself. So, she started playing poker again, and she's been playing continuously for fifteen years now. We play together a lot, actually. And, I've realized, my mother has kind of a similar life as you, in some ways—the caretaker, this maternity figure to all the other people, who is also still trying to achieve her dreams."

"Oh, wow—poker? That's amazing. And what a great story, for you to, almost unintentionally, fall into this journey with magic, where you were already fascinated with something similiar, sort of because of your mum. That's really great. I kind of see more now why you want to do this. It makes more sense. It's easy to say, *Oh, I met these guys and it was fucking great and I want to write about them*, but this, now, has a real nice poetry about it. It seems it has come full circle."

"The one thing that I have come to realize, as I've gotten to know everyone better," I said, "is that everyone carries a little bit of deception around with them their entire lives."

"Find me a man or a woman who has no secrets."

"Exactly."

"She could forget about everything else."

"Yes, exactly, just forget about all the shit."

"She sounds like an incredible woman. And she must be so proud of you."

20

FOOLING BOURDAIN

My trick was evolving, and fast. I worked on it nonstop. It became more refined in its concept, more stream-lined in its presentation, and more deceptive in its reveal. It was almost ready to pitch to a big retailer as a product that could be sold online and performed by other magicians. I was *so close*.

What had started as a basic find-your-card trick morphed into a multilayered, plot-driven routine. Throughout spring and sum-mer, I thought deeply about what I wanted the trick to do—what kind of experience I wanted to share with the spectator. I tinkered with structure and style, theme and topic, and finally came away with a more detailed sketch of what I wanted to create. For one, I wanted to move away from the rudimentary find-your-card principle. There were so many more rich and nuanced options out there that could elevate mine from a one-dimensional trick to a profound performance.

Magic tricks can be broken down into seven main themes: ap-pearance, where something is produced from nothing; vanishing, where something disappears; transposition, where something moves from one place to another; restoration, where an object is destroyed and subsequently brought back to its original state; transformation, where an object changes from one thing into another; telekinesis, where something floats or moves on its own; or stunts, like the bullet catch or a Houdini-style escape. Some of my favorite tricks fell under the transposition theme. I loved when an object instantly appeared somewhere in which it was not originally placed.

So, I started there, and included a facet that, at the onset, was mandatory: information, specific to the spectator, that is freely chosen. But, again, my effect's original version had a flaw. If I was going to, say, use someone's birthday or address or phone number to make the trick work, I would need to be able to research them before performing the effect. That heavily diminished its spontaneity. I wanted to be able to perform the trick to anyone, anytime, and in any situation. Moreover, I needed a specific piece of spectator information that could also create a plot line. This would give the effect a deeper sense of purpose to the person on which it was being performed.

A best-friend plot, I thought. *Combined with a transposition ending. That's perfect!*

The trick's theoretical foundation became this: A spectator writes the name of their best friend on a Joker or blank card without me seeing it, and places it in a safe location, like in the box or their wallet. They then choose a random card from the deck (let's say the jack of hearts), memorize it, and put it back into the stack. The cards are shuffled. Their chosen card is then found using their best friend's name, spelled out in some way, with each letter of the name represented by a single card—a nice little tension builder for the climax. But when the card is revealed, it's not their chosen card at all. It's the card with their best friend's name on it. Then they open the box. Tucked inside is the card they picked from the deck, in this case the jack of hearts.

I thought the concept was intriguing. I loved the fact that the spectator's friend became the key to me "finding" the card, and that there was also a twist at the ending. The spectator thinks the trick is centered on finding a chosen card using a bit of hidden information, but the opposite becomes true: it's a transposition. Moreover, it seemed original. I wouldn't be ripping anyone off. It looked like I had devised an effect that was completely fresh. It was all mine. So, I developed an idea that I knew, at least on its face, had some merit. Now, how the hell could I make the trick work? I wanted desperately to feel legitimate among the magicians who had let me into their world, that I wasn't taking their acceptance lightly, and the pressure was on to figure out this trick.

It goes without saying that one of the benefits of being in the52 is that I had access to the world's best minds in magic. My effect had a series of problems that needed to be engineered—a gauntlet of locked doors for which I needed to find a set of keys. First, I needed to figure out how to switch the best-friend card with the card that would subsequently be chosen.* So: what would be the most deceptive way to make the switch? I needed someone who knew moves. I called Daniel Madison.

We went through the trick's beginnings step by step. The small, in-between moments typically reveal opportunities in which to pull off a sleight, so it's crucial to intimately understand every step of the trick in order to dig in and insert a deceptive method. "So,

---

* You must be asking yourself: how can the spectator choose a specific card if you've already swapped it with the signed card and it's sitting in the box? Simple: you use a duplicate. Transposition effects almost always use a duplicate object to make it *seem* like it magically disappears from one location and appears in another, but there've been two the whole time and, at the end, one is merely hidden, in the deck or otherwise.

they sign the card," Madison said. "Is your back turned while they
do it? Do they hand it back to you? Where is the box during all of
this? Are you sitting down at a table? Standing up at a bar?" I hadn't
thought of all these contextual details. Even the smallest things,
it seemed, were crucial when it came to inventing a trick from
scratch. We settled on this: I would turn my back while the spectator wrote on the card, and then I would instruct them to place
it facedown on the table, or bar, or whatever surface was nearby,
when they were done.

I'd then turn around, pick it up, and explain that their best
friend could come into play later on, but for now we should put
them in a safe place—like in the box. As I reach for the box, I
would execute a top-change.* A top-change is a move where the
card in the hand is seamlessly swapped out with the card on top
of the deck. The duplicate of the card they will choose in phase
two of the effect would be on top—I'd figure out a way, in phase
two, to force them to choose this specific card—and, after the
move, it would now go into the box, with the signed card taking its
place on top of the deck. They would then think that the signed
card is in the box, but because of the top-change, it would be
the duplicate of the card they would then "freely choose." But,
despite the sleight, Madison told me, you want to make sure the
spectator still feels like they are in control. To accomplish this,
I'd grab the box, place it in front of the spectator, and ask them to
open it. They'd see it was empty and would be holding it while I
slowly place their "signed card" into the box. No funny business,

---

* Reaching for the box (the big move) covers the top-change (the small
 move). Misdirection is not necessarily forcing someone to look one way
 while something secretive happens elsewhere. Force-focusing, or directing
 your attention to a specific thing at a specific time, even if it's in the same
 location as the sleight (as we see here with my trick), is a more widely used
 and effective approach. Neurologically, this is called sensory capture, but
 magicians refer to it as passive misdirection.

right? They'd set it off to the side for the time being. Now phase two could begin.

Ramsay came to New York City over the summer to film a few YouTube videos. On this trip, he scheduled a public meet-up for fans at Tannen's, the magic shop in Manhattan. Dozens of kids packed into the little shop, eager to meet their idol, get a photograph, and maybe even show Ramsay a few tricks. I filmed the entire event for him, standing on my tiptoes, holding the camera above the crowd. After a while, I took a break, stood off to the side, and gave my arm a rest. A young kid, barely a teenager, came up to me, holding a playing card and a Sharpie. "Will you sign a card for me?" he asked. "Sure, man, of course," I replied, taking the marker. When he turned the card over and handed it to me I saw that it was the two of clubs.

Xavior came to Tannen's as well, and after the event we headed back to my apartment. I told the guys that Madison had helped me with the first phase of my trick, but now I was kind of stuck. A bigger problem presented itself: I found a way to secretly get the signed card on the top of the deck, and the duplicate in the box, but in order for the trick to continue I needed to figure out two things: a way to force the spectator to choose the duplicate card, and a way to see the name written by the spectator on the blank card. We sat around my place and brainstormed.

There are numerous ways to secretly catch a glimpse at a card, but I needed to see the whole thing in order to read the name written, not just an index tucked up in the corner. This made things much more difficult. We pondered the issue. Not only did we need to find a way to peek an entire card, but it also had to be a justified movement. Anything out of the ordinary would arouse suspicion.

"Wait," Xavior said. "What if you had a short card?"

"Yes!" Ramsay exclaimed, slapping his hands together. "You

could peek the signed card and force the other card on them *at the same time.*"

I sat there in silence. "What's a short card?" I asked. They both burst out laughing. Although I had come a long way in the past two years, there was still a lot I didn't know about magic, or what methods could make a trick work, but, despite their poking fun at me, I felt proud that they continued to share their expert advice.

A short card is exactly what it sounds like: it's a card that is slightly, almost indecipherably shorter than the others (you can make these at home, using a ruler and a razor blade). Using a short card can create a few different technical advantages, but in my case, it acted sort of like a marker: a way to see—and feel—where you are within the deck. At the start of the trick's second phase, after I've swapped the signed card for the top card—we'll again use the jack of hearts as an example—and placed it in the box, I am standing there, holding the deck, the signed card on top. The short card would be directly underneath it, in second position, a duplicate of what's now in the box, in this case the jack of hearts.

"So, you'd cut the cards," Xavior said, demonstrating with a deck, "and your short card, with the signed card above it, is now in the middle of the deck," he continued, pointing to the middle of the pack. The short card was visible, plain as day, but only from the performer's perspective. From the front, the deck looked clean. From here, I could dribble the cards down, which is basically allowing them to fall, in quick succession, one by one, from one hand into another, in a flourishing motion. Before you do that, you'd tell the spectator to say stop whenever they'd like, Xavior explained, and that the card where they choose to stop will be theirs. So, you start to dribble. But once your thumb, positioned alongside the deck's rear edge, comes in contact with the short card, it skips slightly. You can feel it on your skin. It's a signal to stop dribbling. It all happens so fast that the spectator thinks it's completely legit. They said stop, and you stopped, so it's entirely fair, right?

"And it's all there right there in front of you," Ramsay interjected. "Genius!" When you hit the short card, it's the last card to fall into the stack in your left hand, the other half of the deck still held in your right. From here, it's easy: you merely point down to the top card of the stack in your left hand with your right index finger. This does two things. First, it signals to the spectator that that is their card (which is the short card, the duplicate, the card you've forced onto them, the jack of hearts in this instance), and it does a second, much more important thing: the move allows you to see, in full view, the signed card. When you point down with your right index finger, your hand naturally tilts forward, revealing the bottom card of the stack in your right hand—the one with the signature. You can read the name and your spectator is none the wiser. You're way ahead now. The rest is easy.

Another famous underground magician was also in my apartment for this brainstorming session: Doug McKenzie. I had first met Doug when Madison and Ramsay came to New York City to film their chess-themed project for Ellusionist. For that trip, they had rented a giant Airbnb in Williamsburg, Brooklyn, not too far from where I lived, and we spent a lot of time there. Doug's apartment was right down the street, and one night he stopped by.

In jeans and a hoodie, Doug reminded me of an average tech guy. At that time, I didn't know much about him, aside from what Ramsay had told me: he was an incredibly skilled performer (he once managed to steal Rudy Giuliani's watch off his wrist), booked gigs with celebrity clientele (Paris Hilton, LeBron James, Harrison Ford, Johnny Depp, Woody Allen, Bryan Cranston, Lenny

Kravitz, Ellen DeGeneres—the list goes on), and had invented some of the most innovative magic in the twenty-first century.[*] It wasn't long after Doug showed up at the Airbnb that Ramsay piped in. "Hey, Doug, ah . . ." he said, rubbing his chin. "Would you show Ian something?"

"Yeah?" Doug said, looking at Ramsay and then at me, his eyes thinning to slits. He took a deck of cards from his pocket. He cycled through a series of card tricks, impeccably performed, with a finesse and air of confidence that I had not yet seen up close. He was so smooth, so well rehearsed. He roasted me over and over. I laughed and stomped in place like a little kid. I loved every minute.

"Okay, one more," he said, fanning out the deck. "Pick a card, but don't look at it. Just put it into your pocket." I followed his instructions.

"Now pull out your phone and open a new text message and put in this number." He rattled off the digits and my fingers punched them in. "Now text the number, asking what card you chose." I paused, looked over at Ramsay, and rolled my eyes. Madison stood to his right, a grin plastered on his face. I texted the number. A message popped up almost immediately: *King of spades*.

"Check your pocket," Doug said.

"Come *on*, man!" I said, pulling out the card. It was the king of spades.

Doug always made time to hang out whenever Ramsay was in town and, after we brainstormed methods for my trick, Doug suggested we head to Ludlow House, a members-only club in the Lower East Side. A man-about-town with a slew of social connections, I had become used to Doug's spontaneous invitations

---

[*] Madison had been for years trying to get Doug to accept an invitation into the 52, but Doug was wary about getting a tattoo on his finger. He performs regularly for the Saudi royal family (he speaks fluent Arabic) and worried about how they'd react—they are some of his best-paying clients.

to swanky places—rooftop bars, underground speakeasies, clubs like Ludlow House—and knew, whenever we went out, that he couldn't help but perform for the folks we met. We were in for a fun evening.

The place was packed. A triple-decker spot with a dark, nondescript front, the club is a catacomb of various bars, lounges, parlors, and restaurants. We followed Doug from floor to floor, trying to find a place to sit. There wasn't an open chair in the house. Clusters of women in leather pants and high heels noshed on appetizers, finance bros in expensive suits sipped on bourbon, and rocker cliques in skintight jeans lounged in suede armchairs and on leather couches. Music rumbled through the building and waiters scurried about. We finally spotted a small couch with two tables occupied only by two middle-aged women.

"We are waiting for a couple friends," the women told Doug when he asked if we could sit with them. They must've been in their early fifties, well dressed in a Madison Avenue type of way, oozing money and confidence.

"We're just going to sit on this side; we'll find another chair," Doug reassured them, waving for us to come sit down. We crowded around the small table, on the butt end of the couch, and ordered a round of drinks. We all took out a deck of cards, eager to fiddle a bit. A few minutes after our drinks came, two men walked over to our couch and the women stood up to greet them, a peck on each cheek, hands resting on their shoulders. Both men had a full head of silver-fox hair, short but swept back, with a glowing tan, as if they'd just gotten back from a far-flung tropical location. One man was shorter and more full in the face than his counterpart, who was tall, sinewy in frame, and dressed in black. The taller man took off his suit jacket, revealing a shallow, V-necked T-shirt underneath. Tattoos fell down his arms.

It was Anthony Bourdain.

He was with his best friend and fellow television personality

Eric Ripert. Ripert is the owner of Le Bernardin, one of the best restaurants in the world. Doug and Ramsay looked at each other and smiled.

It wasn't long before the women asked us about the cards.

"Are you guys playing a *game*?" one said, leaning over toward us, clearly intrigued.

"Actually, we're magicians," Doug replied.

"Magic! Ah! I *love* magic!" the woman squealed. "You've *got* to show us something!"

Doug and Ramsay took turns showing the women some simple card tricks, warming them up, waiting for Anthony and Eric to catch a glimpse of what was going on. Deep in conversation with each other, slurping down a shared pot of mussels, they weren't paying much attention to our side of the couch.

"Ah! Oh my *God*!" one woman yelped after a trick. "Eric! Tony! Look! You've *got* to see this! These guys are *magicians*!" It was all over after that.

I sat off to the side and watched Doug go to work. He ran through his repertoire, including a few tricks that involved feats of mentalism—basically reading Eric's and Anthony's minds—seemingly knowing every card they chose, every bit of information they were thinking. Ramsay jumped in with his own effects, including a trick where Eric picked a series of cards, laid them out on the table in random order, and chose one card to be turned facedown—"X'ed out," as Ramsay put it. Ramsay then rolled up his sleeve and revealed a tattoo of the exact numbers in the exact order Eric had chosen, an X scrawled over the number corresponding to the card in which he picked to turn facedown.

Anthony sat there, smirking and chuckling with every reveal. But as I kept watching him, I started to see it: He saw most of the sleight of hand. But he let us keep going; he understood, like a chef with food, that magic is a practitioner's art form. The experience is not contingent upon the degree of transparency of its ingredients or methods, but rather the dedication of the specialist, the presentation of hard work, and the experience given to the spectator.

I felt my heart begin to race as I watched the performance. I had a deck of cards in my hand and I was *right here*. We had this entire group in the palm of our hands, completely enraptured. I debated if I should jump in and do a trick myself. *It was Anthony Bourdain, for God's sake! How could I let this opportunity just pass me by?* I had always looked up to Anthony: his adventurous, no-holds-barred approach to life, his understanding that profound moments could be found just about anywhere, his endless quest for wonder in a world that sometimes can feel so unforgiving. I was torn. I didn't want to steal the spotlight away from Doug and Ramsay or crush the mood by performing a lackluster trick, but I also didn't want to regret throwing away such an incredible opportunity.

Anthony got up from his chair. He threw his blazer on and went to shake our hands.

"Thanks a lot, guys, that was really great. But I have to get going," he said. I gripped his hand, smiled, and, before I knew it, started talking.

"Before you go," I said, "can I show you something?"

"Sure," he said, sitting back down. I fanned out the deck and had him point to a card. I removed it and ripped off the corner. None of the guys had performed Angle Z, and I knew it would go over well—he'd never be able to figure this one out. I opened my hand slowly, finger by finger. The piece was gone.

"It doesn't just disappear, though," I said. "Check your pocket." He reached into his blazer, pulled out the corner, laughed, and tossed it down onto the table.

"Okay, I am *definitely* done here!" he said, rising from his chair, shaking his head. He looked me in the eye, said thank you, and walked out. I sat back down and smiled to myself. My friends looked at me, proud of the little moment I gave to Anthony. Performing to a stranger—and a celebrity, no less—was a huge milestone for me. But it was more than that. With magic, the ultimate goal is to give someone something they can carry around with them for a while and, at his core, Anthony Bourdain did that very same thing with food and travel.

When I heard the news of his death in June 2018, I walked over to my desk and pulled open the drawer. There, underneath a stack of papers, was the card he chose, its corner missing. I rifled around, trying to find the missing piece. I thought he left it on the table that night—but it was nowhere to be found. Maybe he brought it with him when he left the club. I sat on the edge of my bed and held the torn card in my hand and thought back to that night. Although I could sense he knew how some of my friend's tricks were done, he didn't show signs that he knew the secret behind my trick. Was he really fooled? Was he astounded? Or was he just being nice because he knew that I, the nervous guy on the corner of the couch, was on some sort of journey—that, if he let me down by making it obvious that he knew how the trick was done, that I'd be crushed? That, perhaps, he had been giving to others his entire life and couldn't stop now?

I tried to pinpoint how long that moment of awe my trick produced stayed with him. Maybe it lasted just until he reached the stairs and moved out of sight, but maybe it stayed in his gut until he reached the street and hailed a cab. Maybe, after he climbed into the taxi, he cradled the card's corner in his hand—maybe that piece of the unknown was still with him there, at least for another moment. Much like a magician, Anthony instilled a sense of adventure and wonder in people—an honest quest not only to experience humanity and all its complexities through food and culture, but, more than anything else, the determination to give that same sense of discovery to an audience. He once said that travel—much like magic—is about the gorgeous feeling of teetering on the unknown. Now that he has passed away, I feel that

Anthony truly understood the power of that sentiment and tried
his hardest to translate that same sense of astonishment with his
own exploration of the world. That, if he tried hard enough, he
too could create magic for others.

Angle Z is a simple but highly deceptive effect. You don't actually
tear the corner off the card; you're only pretending to do so. It's
been ripped the entire time, with the corner planted in the spectator's pocket—or in their wallet, or anywhere else you choose—
long before the trick begins. You can stash the corner hours before
the trick's performance, in fact, and wait for the perfect moment
to strike.

When I decided that I would perform Angle Z on Anthony
Bourdain, I knew had to find a way to get the corner into his
blazer pocket without him knowing. He had wrapped the jacket
over the back of his chair; it would be nearly impossible for me to
get close enough to stash the piece. Nothing would be worse than
getting caught pilfering through his jacket. I could see it now: me,
kicking and screaming—*It was just a magic trick, I swear!*—as security dragged me out of Ludlow House for trying to pickpocket
Anthony Bourdain, no doubt that evening's most high-profile guest.

So I sat and waited for him to go to the bathroom. Right on cue,
about halfway through his meal, he excused himself. As soon as
he left the room, I nonchalantly got up and stood next to his chair,
under the guise of wanting to get a better view of Doug's performance. Eric and the two women were hyperfixated on Doug and
Ramsay—a bit of misdirection in and of itself—and I simply leaned
forward, blocked the jacket from their sight-line, and slipped the
corner into his pocket. I sat back down, careful not to arouse suspicion. Anthony returned a minute later and plunked down in his
chair. After about twenty minutes, he got up, put on his blazer,
and prepared to head out. Everything went according to plan. The

fact that he was wearing the jacket when I did the trick made it all that more delicious. To him, what had happened was impossible. It was the perfect deception. Madison would've been proud.

Madison invented Angle Z almost by accident. "I was thinking, here's the card, here's the corner," he told me once. "How can I make this look real, when this goes somewhere else?" We were talking about the trick I was trying to invent, and I wanted to know how he came up with new ideas. I wanted to know how a trick's conceptualization fed into the creation of a method. I wanted to know how a magician's mind worked when it came to the ultimate problem: invention. "It just clicked," Madison said. "I thought, hold on, I can just put the corner somewhere, like in someone's pocket, and then it will look real. If I *pretend* to rip the corner, they I have no reason to believe that I am just faking it."

Angle Z is more a cognitive illusion than a visual one. When a magician holds a playing card by its corner, with the other three corners and most of its face entirely visible and unobstructed, the brain detects a pattern. It knows a playing card is a rectangle, with four corners; when it sees three of the corners, it automatically assumes the other one is there, too, even though your eyes can't see it. "You don't really 'see' anything," explains Stephen Macknik and Susana Martinez-Conde in *Sleights of Mind*, "rather, you process patterns related to objects, people, scenes, and events to build up representations of the world."

The brain investigates what the eye sees in a hierarchical fashion, the information spelunking deeper and deeper into your primary visual cortex until your brain is able to make sense of what's in front of you. But if a simple pattern can be detected early on in this process, with the rest of the information inferred or assumed, the brain is cool with that. It doesn't want to work too hard if it doesn't have to. It accepts what it sees as reality—as truth—even though, in this case, it's most definitely not. Moreover, holding a card by your fingertips at the corner is a completely natural action.

This added behavioral norm—harking back to what Dai Vernon called "naturalness of motion"—makes the trick that much more believable; the spectator has no reason to think that the only piece of card obstructed by the performer's fingers actually doesn't exist.

But still, developing something brand-new with playing cards is difficult—nearly impossible, to be honest. Most magic, especially with cards, is just innovating previously invented material. With hundreds of years of history behind us, it has become harder and harder to develop something truly unique. "There are only so many things you can do with a deck of playing cards," Madison told me. "We all have similar hands. A deck is always the same shape, feels the same way. It's just fifty-two pieces of paper." But Angle Z stood alone as something entirely new.

Hearing how my friends had come to invent their tricks fueled my ambition. My goal at the start of this entire adventure had been to understand the mind of a magician, someone who sees the world through the lens of deception—people who strive, as a career choice, to hack the concept of reality for the entertainment of others. I wanted to capture that viewpoint in an article that I was sure was going to elevate my career to the new heights. But the journalist part of me was pushed aside long ago. I was now in it for something else.

It was this ability that I loved most about my new gang of friends—to see the world differently. The fact that I could now perform magic fluidly, to simultaneously charm and fool someone—especially someone like Anthony Bourdain—helped cement my understanding of magic not only as an art form but a philosophical principle. And these two things had connected in one day. My trick was getting closer to being perfect, and I had just fooled one of the most famous television stars in the world.

A few days later, still riding the high from my night at Ludlow House, I called Adam Wilber, general manager of Ellusionist. We had become close in the two years since Blackpool. He had just filmed his spot for the new season of *Penn & Teller: Fool Us* and was waiting for it to air.* We chatted about his experience on the show and what Ellusionist had in the works for the rest of the year.

"We have a lot of great stuff coming out soon," he told me.

"Well, that's kind of why I am calling," I said. "I invented a trick."

"Your own trick? No way! That's awesome."

I could tell he was genuinely surprised but also trying to be polite. *There's no way the resident journalist could come up with anything worthwhile, could he?*

"It's actually kind of good," I told him, "and I was wondering if you'd like to release it through Ellusionist. I am still finalizing it, but, I mean, I think it may be good enough. I think people would want to perform it, you know, themselves."

"Well, Magic Live is in a few months. Are you going to Vegas? I'll be there. You should just show me then," he said. "If it's good enough, we'll film it, edit a trailer, and release it around Christmas."

I took a deep breath.

"Perfect."

---

* He fooled the famous duo. The routine is on YouTube—check it out.

21

BEHIND THE SCENES

I became good friends with Doug McKenzie. When he wasn't pond-hopping for high-paying gigs or skydiving on the weekends (one of his many extracurricular passions), we'd link up, cruise around the city in his tiny blue-and-white Smart car, grab lunch, and chat about magic.

Doug was born in Scotland, lived in Oman and Saudi Arabia as a child, went to boarding school in the States, and eventually studied finance at New York University. He was a computer nerd growing up, drawn to hacking by the incessant need to know how technology could be corrupted and controlled. He was an avid reader of *2600: The Hacker Quarterly*. And then, at age fifteen, he discovered magic. He was visiting Manhattan with his parents before heading off to boarding school in New Jersey, and walked by Magic Max, a now-defunct shop in Times Square, and saw a magician performing in the store for customers. He was hooked. It wasn't long before he married his two passions and become a pioneer in tech-related effects, a subset of illusion that has taken the community by storm.

"I see a lot of parallels between magic and hacking," Doug told me. "It's the same mind-set. You are looking for loopholes, for ways to push people's ideas of perception." Strangely enough, the first "hacker" defined by modern standards was a magician. In 1903, Italian radio pioneer Guglielmo Marconi traveled to London to demonstrate his latest breakthrough in wireless communication. Marconi wanted Europe's elite to use his service, which could instantly—and securely—send information from one city to another without the necessity of wires. Marconi wanted to show the audience how his technology worked in real time, so he set up the machine and sent a message to one of his assistants. But instead of receiving the message Marconi sent, the assistant received the word "rats" over and over again, dozens of times, followed by "There was a young fellow of Italy, who fiddled the public quite prettily." They had been hacked.

Nevil Maskelyne, a revolutionary nineteenth-century British stage magician, had himself used a homemade radiotelegraphy mechanism during his act. His assistants could wirelessly transmit information to him in Morse code and, via a small device in his pocket that vibrated the coded language against his leg, he could discern the message. He could use this device to effectively "read people's minds." After getting word of what Marconi had planned, and not wanting the public (or other magicians) to have an inkling as to how this new technology could be applied to conjuring, he promptly set up his radio tower nearby and hacked into Marconi's (supposedly secure) signal. If Maskelyne could hack into the system to make it seem like the technology didn't work, or wasn't reliable, people wouldn't make the connection that it could be used for magic tricks. His scheme worked.

By 2000, Doug was hacking into old-school Nokia 6700 cell phones and using them for magic tricks. In one early trick, he would make a coin vanish and reappear inside of his phone's screen (merely a photograph in which he made the coin appear by pushing a button), and then magically made the coin "fall out" of the phone's screen and back into his hand. He'd do the same with a fly, catching an imaginary insect inside his phone (with it buzzing around on the screen, audio and all), later revealing a real fly in his hand.

Doug continued developing phone-related magic tricks, but the 2007 release of the iPhone revolutionized his approach. Many magicians jumped on this new technology, developing apps that could assist in magic tricks. Doug, however, wanted to take the technology to another level; he didn't want an iPad or an iPhone to just be a gimmick used to create an effect. He wanted to utilize the functions for which these pieces of technology were created— calls, texts, voice mails—to display a truly impossible event for the spectator. With this approach in mind, Doug manipulated things that were inherently more real to the audience. Hacking the phone itself was Doug's goal, not utilizing what the touch-screen technology was capable of. "I think, if you imagine sending somebody a text and all of a sudden they get a text message, sent by your imagination, that's magic," Doug explained. *"How the fuck did you do that? You don't know my number or his number! You didn't know what I was thinking!* Now *that's* a story people tell their friends."

Doug taught himself how to code and discovered a customizable software system that allowed him to write his own programs to be used for magic tricks. The software company that hosted the code eventually discovered what Doug was doing and reached out.* They loved how he was utilizing their technology, and even

---

* Doug requested that I not reveal the company name for fear that other magicians will steal his exclusive effects. Truth be told, a few magicians have already tried to copy Doug's trick, and he has since set up a security system that alerts him whenever another user is trying to utilize his code for their own means. A word to the wise for magicians reading this: don't steal Doug's effect. You will get caught.

showcased them in their SEC documents after they went public (the company's valuation broke $1 billion in 2015). The document reads, "Doug McKenzie is making magic new again by using his audience's own phones to perform classic street illusions. Audience members select a card, put it in their pocket without looking at it, and then [the audience member texts Doug], which tells them their card correctly, every single time." The effect they described in these documents is the same trick Doug performed for me outside Madison and Ramsay's Airbnb.

Doug continued to develop new effects based on his exclusive code. One day, I was having lunch with two friends when Doug called me and asked what I was up to. We were near his house, I told him; maybe we could swing by. "Do you have any cards on you?" I asked over text. "Would you show them something?"

"Why do I need cards?" he responded flatly.

We met on the street. Right away, he asked my friends to take out their phones. He then grabbed each of their free hands by the wrist. "Put out your pointer fingers, both of you," he said, "and hold your phones out so we can see the screens." He slowly brought their fingers closer and closer together. When they touched, both phones started to ring. They were calling each other.[*]

It was Doug's early penchant for tech magic that formed one of his most important friendships. In 2003, while at a New York Fashion Week after party, his friend Jake (son of the musician Sting) introduced him to David Blaine. Blaine was on his way out but told Doug to meet him at Marquee, a nightclub in Chelsea, later that night. While at the club, Doug brought out his Nokia and showed Blaine his coin-in-phone routine. Blaine was shocked; he had never seen anything like it. They became close friends, taking bike rides around the city, going to clubs, and jamming on

---

[*] Doug performed this same effect for a six-minute CNN documentary about his tech-fueled magic. It's a great segment—check it out.

ideas for magic tricks. It wasn't long before Blaine asked Doug if he would help him invent new magic for his television specials. He wanted Doug to be a consultant.[*]

Famous magicians rarely operate autonomously. All big-time stage performers and TV personalities have a secret crew of illusion-savvy consultants helping them develop their routines. These creators are a crucial part of magic's ecosystem. Without them, it would take a magician years to develop an entire television special's worth of material. Moreover, because different magicians have different specialties, they bring new takes and insights into the mix. Every magician on television, even those at the level of David Blaine, need new ideas and fresh approaches to performance. These creators are the unsung heroes of magic, as many forgo on-camera fame for the satisfaction of delivering a memorable experience for an audience through another magician's performance. In the twenty-first century, being a consultant has become a coveted role in the magic industry; not only is there a fat paycheck attached, but, more important, a high degree of respect is instilled from fellow magicians.

But this is nothing new. World-famous magicians have been hiring inventors for decades. In the early twentieth century, Houdini's success was contingent upon the mechanic Jim Collins, his right-hand man, who was a master of wood and metal. He began working for Houdini in 1910 and helped build his most famous illusions, including Water Torture Cell, which took the pair three years to complete. "Collins was hugely important to Houdini," John Cox, a Houdini historian, told me. "Specifically, about his escapes: Houdini conceived the ideas, but Collins was really the man that made it work." Another assistant, Charles Morritt, who specialized in mirrors, created the infamous Vanishing Elephant

---

[*] Doug and Madison, two of Blaine's closest confidants, can also be seen in Blaine's custom decks, their faces replacing those of the court cards.

illusion that Houdini performed in 1918 and whose secret has yet to be conclusively revealed. During the effect, he marched a full-grown elephant onto the stage, walked it into a massive box, and closed it for a brief moment. When Houdini opened the box, the elephant was gone.

Around this time, the popular American magician Howard Thurston hired his own secret weapon: Guy Jarrett. Jarrett worked with a range of materials and engineered complex props like the Siamese Cabinet. During the trick, Thurston would wheel out the cabinet, open all its doors to show it was empty, and then close it back up. A second later, people would start coming out of the cabinet—it could hold nine in total. He could also have people enter the cabinet, close it up, open it again, and have them disappear. One 1914 newspaper article described Jarrett as "the man with the know-how . . . whose brain builds the show for the big magician." Jarrett, however, eventually took his skills to Broadway. He became cynical of magicians and their abilities, once writing that "not a single one has guts or ideas or imagination. They just got hold of a bunch of tricks and walked out on stage. So, they are only a bunch of 'drugstore magicians.'" This is a sentiment no doubt shared by some contemporary performers like Ramsay and Madison, who are frustrated when young magicians just buy the latest and flashiest gimmick and post a video of their performance online.

Doug worked as the lead magic consultant on Blaine's 2006 special *Drowned Alive* and helped conceptualize and build effects such as the Hundred-Dollar-Bill Face Switch, where Benjamin Franklin's face turns into that of the spectator.[*] In 2011, Doug

---

[*] In addition to being close friends, Madison worked with Blaine for years. He helped develop new routines, worked on-site for private performances, and spitballed ideas over the phone. During one memorable trip to Miami,

worked in the United Kingdom on the first season of *Dynamo: Magician Impossible* and, two years later, designed magic for Blaine's 2013 special *David Blaine: Real or Magic*. In these shows, Doug would sit down with Blaine or Dynamo and brainstorm what kind of tricks they wanted to incorporate into the show, or how they could use the overarching theme of the special to come up with appropriate effects. In one brainstorming session with Dynamo, who wanted to do a trick that involved dozens of people, Doug, utilizing his skills in technology, came up with (and subsequently designed) an effect where a sea of spectators' phones in Times Square would ring at the same time.

Inventing magic for television, however, is far different than doing so for live performance. "It's a challenge," Dynamo told me over lunch in London. "It's hard to make a show that's not boring television. On TV, you can't really do long, laborious routines that technically might be some of the most amazing things to experience, because for the person watching it at home, they want it to be direct: the phone penetrates inside the bottle, the card appears on the other side of the window, the butterfly comes alive. A television channel knows that they have thirty seconds to keep someone from clicking away. It puts an immense amount of pressure on us." Dynamo and his team (now led by two full-time consultants, young guns Harry De Cruz and Tom Elderfield) developed more than 500 pieces of magic for his show's four-season run, only 100 of which made it on-screen.

Some magicians have quickly forgone consulting to produce their own shows. Anthony Owen, head of magic at Objective Productions from 2002 to 2016, was a performing magician before getting into television, booking corporate gigs and designing

---

Madison told me, Blaine gave him a paper bag stuffed with $50,000 in cash as payment.

effects for other magicians. "I realized very quickly that just being a consultant was frustrating because I didn't have final creative control or decision-making powers," he told me. "If you're not David Blaine or the star who has control, often you are battling with so many other things with making good magic on the screen. It's hard if people you are working with don't share the vision, or don't have the understanding of what makes magic work, or don't have a deep-seated passion for magic in general."

In 2003—done with consulting, and now a part of Objective Productions—Owen teamed up with British magician and mentalist Derren Brown, one of the most famous performers in the United Kingdom. Anthony wanted to try something new for Derren, who isn't a street magician. "We weren't just going to copy the model of a Blaine special—we wanted to rip that up," he said. "We wanted to take the documentary feel and the vérité feel but move it onto a three-act structure and include forms that weren't just seen in magic shows." They pulled structural inspiration from old David Copperfield specials—building toward a large climatic event or effect—but gave the concepts a modern twist specific to Derren's unique performative skills. They also nodded at traditional film. For Derren's special *The Great Art Robbery*, in which he employs a small gang of senior citizens to steal an expensive painting from a gallery, Owen and Brown borrowed cinemagraphic touches from Hollywood heist classics like *Ocean's 11* and *The Thomas Crown Affair*. Derren's other specials pushed the boundaries of how the human mind could be manipulated. In *The Heist*, for example, he provokes, over the course of weeks, regular people to rob a bank under their own free will.

Consultants are being utilized more than ever before, budgets have grown exponentially ($50,000, or more, is a typical payday for working full-time on a show), and business models have adjusted accordingly. theory11, which launched in 2007 as a traditional online retail shop and playing card company, has morphed into a full-on magic consultancy. Led by the enterprising and business-savvy Jonathan Bayme, the company has worked behind the scenes of *Now You See Me* and *Now You See Me 2*, the popular blockbuster Hollywood franchise starring Jesse Eisenberg, Isla Fisher, Dave Franco, and Woody Harrelson as deceptive magicians; produced Dan White's popular parlor room show *The Magician* and Justin Willman's *The Magic Show*; and collaborated on a reinvigorated Mystery Box with J. J. Abrams's production company Bad Robot.* They also designed playing cards for *Saturday Night Live* and Jimmy Fallon.

Working behind the scenes, both for Hollywood productions and magic shows on television, however, has become especially cutthroat. The big-money, high-stakes nature of magic consulting has pushed Bayme to exaggerate his company's accolades when privately pitching new clients. As evidence of this, I obtained the marketing one-sheet that the company sends to prospective clients. In the document, Bayme claims that theory11 has engaged in "recent creative collaborations" with David Blaine and Dynamo and has "consulted on almost every major magic-related project on stage or on screen over the past 5 years." The two big-named examples, however, were not official collaborations, but rather current employees' gigs before joining the theory11 team, or jobs obtained independently while on staff at theory11. When I reached out to Bayme, he acknowledged as much, saying over email that "the intention . . . is to convey that our team worked on [David Blaine] projects for many years." Bayme also told me over email that, regarding Dynamo, team members' "engagements were negotiated / contracted by theory11 on their behalf," an assertion that was categorically denied by a business associate

---

* The first customer to solve all the puzzles in the box found, on his doorstep, a 1930s Underwood typewriter with a personalized note from J. J. Abrams challenging the winner to create more mystery and wonder in the world.

close to Dynamo who was involved in the hiring of consultants. Bayme's puffed-up branding, it seems, is a by-product of trying to be the biggest and the best as magic hits a new high in mainstream media—even if that means, ironically, using a bit of misdirection to accomplish that goal.

I parked my rental car, fed the meter, took out my phone, and typed out a text message: "I'm here."

I stood in front of a massive gray and black building in downtown Los Angeles that reminded me of one of those structures that could be, based on its overt blandness, a CIA bunker. I waited for a few more minutes in front of the main entrance, and then the man I came to see sauntered out of the elevator. He wore black-framed glasses and his head was shaved. He flashed a bright smile as he opened the door and led me through the lobby.

"We are all so stoked to have to you here, to show you how things work behind the scenes," he told me.

"Yeah, man. I'm really thrilled that you let me come hang out. I know all of this is pretty secret, especially for such a big project."

"It's all good, bro," he said, stepping into the elevator, "It's about time people get a glimpse at how all this comes together." The doors closed, and we went up.

The man I had come to see was Danny Garcia, one of the world's most prominent consultants for magic television shows. Danny, an incredibly innovative creator, has, like Doug McKenzie, been a mainstay in the consulting community for more than a decade. He worked behind the scenes on Dynamo's show in the United Kingdom and has been a go-to consultant for David Blaine since his 2008 stunt-based show *Dive of Death*. Danny even made a few cameos in Blaine's 2016 special *Beyond Magic*. One of the show's plots follows Blaine as he practices his death-defying bullet catch, a trick where he shoots himself in the mouth with a real

.22-caliber bullet. During a practice session, Danny guides Blaine as he lines up the shot and pulls the trigger. Blaine gives Danny a fist bump after the stunt's success.[*]

That was the first time a major magician revealed the team working behind the scenes, acknowledging on camera that famous performers have consultants helping them. This, in some ways, is taking a cue from what a modern audience seems to want to see out of a magic show. They no longer want the all-powerful wizard doing supernatural feats; they want a real person dedicated to an art form, their struggle to overcome obstacles laid out honestly and evolving in real time. They want the magician to be more human than ever before, and they want to see the people with whom the magician chooses to surround himself as he accomplishes the show's goals. In a word: authenticity.

But I wasn't here in Los Angeles to see the makings of another special featuring a magician, like David Blaine, who was already a household name. Magic's latest cultural renaissance has not gone unnoticed by mainstream entertainment companies, especially those with a large streaming platform, and these corporations have been digging for fresh talent for new magic shows. In 2017, boosted by a $6 billion original content budget, Netflix commissioned its first series of nonscripted magic shows, to be aired the following year, including a comedy production from Justin Willman titled *Magic for Humans*, a one-off show from Derren Brown and the rerelease of two previously-aired specials, and an eight-episode series from young British magician Drummond Money-Coutts, better known as DMC.

DMC, tall and svelte with an aristocratic swagger in Savile Row suits and polished Oxford wingtips, is the heir-apparent to the Baron Latimer, a British bloodline that stretches back to 1492. He comes from the Coutts banking dynasty, which manages the

---

[*] Asi Wind, another well-known consultant, was also featured on the show.

British royal family's money, and was obviously set up for a life of finance. But after interning at Goldman Sachs, DMC decided to become a magician instead, a passion he held since childhood. He's starred in a few television programs in the United Kingdom on the National Geographic Channel, but as Netflix's reach exploded (from 48 million subscribers in 2014 to over 100 million in 2017, half of whom live in the United States), DMC saw an opportunity to break into the American market.

DMC linked up with A. Smith Productions, which has created a variety of shows—from *American Ninja Warrior* to *Hell's Kitchen*—and is credited with launching the reality food competition genre in the United States. They locked in a deal with Netflix for an eight-episode series titled *Death by Magic*, which documents DMC as he travels to a series of cities, performing street magic related to that city's history. He also re-creates a stunt of some kind that has, in the past, killed someone in that place—utilizing magic, obviously, to escape the stunt unscathed—including going over Niagara Falls in a wooden barrel and participating in a game of Russian roulette in Las Vegas. So: They had a strong show concept, backing from a reputable production company, and a deal with the biggest content provider on the planet. Now they needed a team to create the magic. That's when they called Danny Garcia.

The elevator stopped, and I followed Danny down a nondescript corridor. He took out his keys to unlock the door at the end of the hall. "It's pretty tight-ass up here," he said. "We can't have people coming in or out; none of this stuff can leak before the show is announced." A. Smith's wing, a small, nooklike cluster of offices, was filled with various producers. Some were working out scheduling, some equipment rentals, and even more organizing permits and other necessary paperwork. We walked by the worker bees toward the end of the wing and entered the biggest room. Four large tables lined the walls, and shelves were stacked with foam core, boxes of magnets, double-sided tape, X-Acto knives, construction paper, hot glue, paint, and dozens of decks of playing cards. It was like a magical arts-and-crafts funhouse.[*]

Danny, the lead magic consultant, brought on a team of in-house creators for the show, including his longtime confidants Marcus Eddie (who also consulted on Justin Willman's 2018 Netflix special, *Magic for Humans*) and Alex Rangel (who has worked with Danny on David Blaine's shows), as well as Jesse Feinberg, who was recommended by a mutual friend. Danny also enlisted his girlfriend and famed stage magician Lisa de la Vega, who has consulted for years for Cyril, the most famous magicians in Japan, and worked alongside Danny for David Blaine's latest special. When I walked in, the team was already bent over their desks, hard at work on the next trick that needed to be invented and built.

"Ian!" Lisa called out, standing up from behind her desk. I had met both her and Danny during my last trip to Magic Live, which is when I got the invitation to come out to L.A. to watch them in action. She came over and gave me a hug.

"How are things going with the show?" I asked. Lisa was wearing many hats, including coordinating all the episodes' finales.

"Oh, good," she said. "Just fighting a damn cold and trying to line up everything for our next round of shoots." I looked behind her and saw the six-month production schedule hanging above her desk. Block letters, in bold type, covered the entire month after the show was set to wrap. It read: SLEEP.

"So, what is everyone working on?" I asked.

Lisa turned to Danny. "Danny, what's on deck for today again?"

"So, we have this master list of tricks that we need to film for each episode," Danny explained. "We have some stuff that is just sleight of hand, that DMC can do without us having to build anything, but a lot of the stuff needs gimmicks or props or other

---

[*] As you can see, most magical effects can be made from simple materials; it's showmanship and execution that bring the tricks to life.

apparatus, so that is what we are really trying to nail down today. Marcus is working on a menu that, when DMC opens it, will produce a full plate of hot food"—Marcus, hearing us, raised the menu and smiled—"Alex is making some molds for a wooden prop, and I think we're going to try and get Jesse to make this card-castle thing I have been thinking about the past few weeks."

Jesse, having just come back from the bathroom, walked into the room.

"You mind if I draw something out for you?" Danny asked Jesse. "Maybe it will help when you're trying to build it?"

"Of course. I've been kind of racking my brain in how to make it work," Jesse said.

Danny grabbed a whiteboard and a marker. He started sketching. "So, DMC is going to have this empty paper bag," he said, drawing, "and we want, like, a cascade of card boxes to fall out of the bag and form a castle on the ground, with loose cards raining down on top of it." He scribbled furiously at what he wanted the end product to look like. "I want a Willy Wonka–type look, where the amount of decks that fall out can't possibly fit into the bag."

Jesse nodded. "Okay," he said. "I have an idea. I think I can make it work."

I piped in. "I mean, how long do you guys have to finish all these tricks?" I pointed to the master list of effects, tacked on the wall. It was over ten pages long. "It seems like a lot of work just to figure out a method, not to mention having to build something that will be filmed and put on television."

"It's crazy," Danny said. "It really is. Okay, so, let's look at it this way: We have eight weeks to concept, design, and create dozens of pieces of magic, to be shot in eight cities around the world. We're already slightly behind schedule for our next stop, Detroit, and we're simultaneously trying to plan and finalize tricks for future cities like Miami and Las Vegas. And we have to keep everything at or preferably under budget."

"Yup! Under budget!" Lisa shouted, laughing. I looked at them bug-eyed.

"Yeah, man," Danny said, smiling. "Putting together a show like this is no joke."

"So, how do you know what tricks you want to include? There seems so much to choose from, you know?"

"Well, I always start with the character, the star of the show," he said. "So, to me, Drummond is the James Bond of magic, right? If James Bond did magic—the Daniel Craig version, a little rough but still composed—how would that look? How would he act? That starts painting a picture of how this character will evolve during the show. You have to manage both specific tricks and how they fit into the context of the character."

"So, you want stuff that is a little more serious, perhaps even dangerous?"

"Yeah, exactly. And the theme of the show revolves around each city, so we are trying to build some effects that relate to that city's history."

"Right, kind of like how a travel show works."

"Exactly. You have to make the place come alive a bit, too. Like, for Detroit, the theme is regeneration—kind of how this city is bouncing back after the collapse of the auto industry. So, to open the episode, we want to have DMC sitting at a table, toy car parts strewn in front of him. He'll deliver some sort of short monologue about Detroit's history as an automobile manufacturing hub that fell on hard economic times, with the broken and discarded car parts a visual representation of that struggle. He'll take a box and place it over the parts. And when he removes the box, less than a second later, a fully formed car will be where the parts had once been—no camera tricks involved. Marcus is inventing that one."

Again, Marcus raised his hand with an exaggeratedly comedic smile spread across his face.

"So, you're doing some tricks straight to camera, without spectators?" I asked.

"Yeah, man. We're definitely getting a lot of inspiration from the type of magic done on Instagram right now," he said. He was right: a lot of magic these days is designed to be performed for the camera—a by-product of magicians showing off their chops through social media. These are normally hypervisual illusions that don't need an audience, or don't rely on a complex plot. Social media has changed magic so dramatically; now it is altering how magic was portrayed on television. "And I think people at home will like it, because of the types of magic they are seeing on the internet these days, just scrolling through on their phone."

I spent a few hours just observing the team—a fly on the wall. They worked intently, nonstop, even eating lunch at their desks. I felt like I was watching a team of sleep-deprived engineers collaborate on a big-time skyscraper rather than a group of magic geeks designing tricks. I got a little restless, grabbed a cup of coffee, wandered down the hall, and found director Simon Dinsell, who had previously directed shows for Derren Brown and Dynamo, in his office. I popped my head in and introduced myself.

"So, how do you see this show coming together?" I asked. "Danny and the team seem to be working really hard."

"Well, with this type of show, we have to integrate amazing tricks into a solid structure. We are creating a multilayered show," Simon told me. "You've got a high trick-per-minute ratio, but what happens when you don't like magic? How can we still get you to watch the show? So, we've got this really nice narrative; we are basically making a magic show with the spine of a documentary. And I think that's the unique thing about this show."

"I feel like people are way more into that type of thing now, with the recent boom in character-driven documentaries."

"Exactly. People want to feel like they are on a journey, you know? That's the key to building a captivating show." He checked his watch. "We have an all-hands production meeting in a few minutes. I have to get ready for it, but we'll see you in there?"

"Definitely," I said. I walked back to Danny's bunker.

I followed Danny and Lisa down to the conference room, and more than a dozen members of the team filed in and took their seats. A large whiteboard anchored the far wall, and framed posters from other A. Smith shows, including *Hell's Kitchen*, hung on the walls.

"All right, so, first order of business: Detroit and Las Vegas," announced executive producer Martin Turner. "Those trips are coming up quick. What do we need to finish up? Let's start with the magic," he continued, turning to Danny. "What do we have listed for those episodes?" Danny and Lisa walked through every magic trick for the two episodes and discussed in detail all the elements needed to properly execute them. More broadly, the production team had to secure permits, licenses, rental equipment, lodging, food, and even a helicopter. Putting together a magic television show is a hectic, multipronged effort.

"So, just so we all know," Martin said, "how many tricks can we squeeze into one day of filming?"

"Well—and anyone else, correct me if I am wrong—" Danny said, doing some mental math, "but I think, with all the moving parts, it could take four to six hours to film one trick, depending on what it is."

"And what's the crew count for these trips?" Martin asked.

Another producer jumped in: "They'll be about thirty of us on set."

"That doesn't include actors or anything, right?" Danny said. "We should try and secure permits for locations where there's a lot of foot traffic. If we need to bring people out somewhere for a trick, we have to make sure they aren't actors of any kind. They just have to be regular people. An actor may try to put on a fake reaction, and that could be a problem. It all has to be genuine." The team nodded in agreement. "And if we have to film more than one take, we need to bring in a new audience. We shouldn't be using people who have already seen the trick."

"We also have to make sure that the locations we choose fit well with how we want to film the segment," Simon said. His job as director was to create a vision for how the show would look and feel when filmed. "The viewers at home also have to know what the hell is going on," he said, "but we also can't make it seem like we are using the camera to deceive them."

"Yeah, like with the helicopter appearance in the desert," Danny said.

Helicopter appearance? In the desert? Danny didn't mention this one to me in the office.

"We have to make sure it doesn't feel fake," he added.

"I think we can definitely do that," Simon said. "I agree that we can't use any postproduction tricks to enhance the illusion. That wouldn't be right."

Danny passed around a diagram of how the illusion could be pulled off. "So, yeah, since we don't have a helicopter on hand, there's no way to really test this unless we are on location out in the desert," Danny said.

Simon looked over the diagram and closed his eyes, visualizing where he'd set up the cameras. "So," Simon started, holding the diagram in his hand, "if it's a millimeter off, the whole thing is blown?"

Danny looked down at the paper and then back at Simon. "Yep. That's basically it. We have one shot at making it work."

The next day, Danny started working on a gimmick for a bill change, where a $1 bill instantly transforms into a $100 bill. It was an inconsequential trick, a filler moment between two larger skits, but he wanted to try something new in how it was to be filmed. He pitched Simon on having two cameras pointed at DMC, one from the front and another from the rear, over his shoulder. They could toggle back and forth and make the trick, or at least how it was presented on-screen, seem more impossible. A lot of bill-change tricks exist on the market now, which work perfectly fine but only when viewed from the front. If you're behind the performer, the method is obvious. Danny built a few variations, using already developed methods. I watched him intently, his brow furrowing under his glasses, lips curled in grimace. It wasn't working.

"I don't think that design is going to work," I said.

"Yeah, man, it's tough because we are trying to push how this stuff is filmed, you know? It completely changes how we design a trick."

"I have an idea," I said. "Give me a minute." I ran over to their rack of tools and materials, plunked down with a knife and some tape and a couple bills, and made a different version, one that worked from all different angles—and, with the wave of a hand, instantly changed the bill. It could be inspected by the audience, too. I finished my handiwork, stood in that little magical room, and pitched Danny my concept.

"Oh shit, bro!" Danny exclaimed, smiling. "That actually looks really good. Let me see it." I gave him what I had crafted and he tried it out a few times in the mirror. Then he showed his team. "This is Ian's idea. What do you guys think?" Marcus, Jesse, and Alex all nodded in approval. Lisa even called out, "Good one, Ian!" Danny held the prop in his hand, looked over at me, and said, "I'm gonna keep playing with this, dude. Let's see if your idea will turn into something."

After I left Los Angeles, Danny kept playing with the concept. At the last minute, my idea was scrapped—but to sit in that room with some of the best creators in the world, and to have a concept I created seriously considered for a Netflix show, proved one thing: my mind had become hardwired for deception; I was becoming one of them. And now I had to prove it where it really counted, where all the chips were on the table: in Vegas, in front of all my new friends.

22

FLIPSIDE

The gold lion stared down at me, mane tucked behind his ears, fangs nearly bared, as if ready to lunge and defend his kingdom—which, of course, was a casino.

The cab trickled past the statue and pulled under the awning that hung over the main entrance of the MGM Grand in Las Vegas. Bellboys scurried between cabs, corralled hotel guests, opened doors, and lugged suitcases. A woman handed off her purse to one boy, a skinny kid with a buzz cut, and shoved a pair of large Tom Ford sunglasses on her face, her skin glowing a deep bronze in the shard of light that ricocheted off the building's glass façade. There are a few entrances to the hotel-casino, each anchoring a corner of its massive six-acre plot, but I thought I had chosen the correct one. I tightened the straps on my backpack, the fleshy grooves along my spine already pooling with sweat, and headed for the door. Three decks of cards in my bag's main pouch jostled around like tiny paper bricks.

Ellusionist's Adam Wilber told me to wait in the lobby, a glitzy white and gold room that extended to the casino, where its marbled floors turned to carpet. A boxing ring sat in its center, advertising an upcoming fight. I leaned up against a slot machine, my body clicking and buzzing to its demented, money-fueled mating dance, and waited for Adam to find me. When we spoke on the phone a few weeks earlier, he admitted that he had a packed schedule in Vegas. The team was tying up loose ends for the Christmas season and they needed to nail down a few projects during the trip. It's smart for them to schedule filming and other back-end production duties around conventions; more than likely, any magician Ellusionist needs to meet will be there. If my trick was good enough, he told me—if he thought people would actually perform it—then they'd definitely squeeze me in. Film the whole project in Vegas. Done. No big deal.

I had been practicing my trick over and over again in preparation for Vegas. *Naturalness of motion*, I told myself. *Confidence. Timing. Pacing.* Ramsay and I talked about the trick on FaceTime, and he gave me a crucial piece of advice: don't telegraph your moves. This is a pervasive problem with newbie magicians and I was falling into the trap. Sometimes my nerves got the best of me. I knew when the sleight was a few seconds away and, as I mentally prepared to execute the move, my body language shifted, reflecting this internal planning. When this happens, the spectator can sense that something is afoot, that a dupe is on the horizon. Ramsay said to not think too much, to just act natural, to always remember that I am in control and that a trick is a journey on which I am taking the spectator. And now, standing in the MGM Grand and waiting for Adam, it was time to put up or shut up.

After a few minutes, Adam sauntered through the cluster of slot machines. Sleepy-eyed, in the hideous plaid cargo shorts that Ramsay and I always tried to convince him to stop wearing,* he

---

* His typical response: "Dude, I'm fucking married and I have two kids. I don't give a shit what my shorts look like."

greeted me with a lazy "Hey, dude" and a sly smile. Adam and I chat frequently, and I could tell he was overworked. Not only does he run the Ellusionist team, but he also performs regularly, had to put in months of preparation for his *Penn & Teller: Fool Us* appearance, and was finalizing his book about creativity, which he hoped would parlay into a lucrative keynote speaking career.[*]

But he always made time for me, and I felt a sense of pride knowing that he got out of bed a little earlier than needed to give me a shot at releasing a trick of my own making—of achieving my little dream. He came down from his room with Lloyd Barnes (the Six of Spades), an Ellusionist employee from the United Kingdom—equally sleep-deprived, with dark circles under his eyes, but nonetheless prone to a quick joke and a gut-shaking laugh—who had flown over the night before. Lloyd was acting as the company cameraman for this trip. We scuttled over to the nearest Starbucks for a much-needed pick-me-up.

"I'm really excited to see your trick, man," Lloyd said as we waited in line.

"Yeah," Adam chimed in, smiling. "It better be fucking good." We all laughed. Adam paid for our coffees and we headed for the elevator. We got off on the twelfth floor and walked to the end of the hallway. Adam slipped his key card into the slot and opened the door, revealing a massive two-bedroom, two-bathroom suite. The entrance led into a wide-set living room, a gray L-shaped couch in its center. The city's Strip beamed through the other side of floor-to-ceiling windows. A big, complicated-looking camera perched atop a tripod, and a large light cradled in a softbox

---

[*] Adam himself has a backstory equally interesting to that of Ramsay, Laura, or Madison: He was busted in a DEA sting for selling weed. "I can still see that fucking badge clear as day," Adam told me. The agency, however, chose not to charge him. Realizing life was precious, he quit his dead-end job and dedicated himself to magic. He never again heard from the agents, and the crime's statute of limitations recently lapsed.

stood off to the side, all ready to go. I tossed my backpack onto the couch, unzipped it, and took out my decks of cards, each one equipped with the gimmicked short card and a duplicate. It was go time.

"Well," Adam said, looking at my cards. "Let's see it!"

Adam and I sat at a small table next to the master bedroom. I took the cards from the box, riffled through to find the blank card, and placed it on the table. I took out my marker, handed it to him, and dove into the patter that I had been practicing. I was clear and crisp with my prose, enthusiastic in its delivery, smooth through sleight of hand, and determined in my acting as the trick geared up for its reveal. At the end, I acted as if I had messed up the trick—a last-minute ploy I threw in, recommended to me by my friend Franco Pascali just a few days earlier—that made the twist ending that much more delicious. When Adam finally opened the box, revealing that his chosen card had magically switched places with the one in which he signed—inscribed with "Carter," his son's name—a broad smile spread across his face. Lloyd, too, stood off to the side, his cheeks reddened in excitement and surprise.

"Dude, it's great! I love it!" Adam said, laughing to himself, almost in disbelief, tossing the card down onto the table. "Shit, I would perform this at a gig. Let's film it right now. I have to go make some phone calls, but can you and Lloyd get it in, say"—he checked his watch—"the next hour or so?"

I was elated. *Yes, yes,* I told him. *Of course.*

I looked over at Lloyd, who nodded in agreement. "We'll tackle it," he said. "No sweat." Adam left the room, and Lloyd and I brought my cards and the tools needed to make the gimmick— a razor blade and plastic ruler—over to the set, in front of the camera. I sat on the couch, cards in front of me, while Lloyd turned on the camera, adjusted the lighting, and focused the lens. He gave me a thumbs-up, signaling we were rolling, and I launched into the secrets behind the trick.

"What's going on, everyone!" I began, a bit overenthusiastic, my hands flailing like a deranged game-show host. "Ian Frisch here! This is Flipside. It's a highly deceptive, transposition effect with a best-friend plot, something that I have been working on for about a year. It's my first offering to the magic community, and I hope you enjoy it."

I explained how the effect worked, slowly going over every detail a magician would need to perform it himself or herself. It felt so natural to explain the trick, its narrative and framework, its nuances and light touches. I had lived this routine for almost a year, tinkering with it nearly every day. It had a set of fingerprints that only I knew, and I tried my best to translate all its nuances. After a while, I barely noticed that a massive camera was pointed in my face and bright lights surrounded me. Hell, it barely registered that I was on the top floor of the MGM Grand, in a massive two-bedroom suite, translating to the magic community an effect that I had invented. My notebook, which I had normally kept stuffed in the waist of my pants, ready to take notes at a moment's notice, lay unopened on the table behind me. It was just the cards and me now.

Lloyd and I filmed for about forty-five minutes and, after we wrapped up, he asked if I would stay on camera for an interview, part of a longer project for Ellusionist. They were creating a documentary of sorts, he explained, about how people first got into magic. It was strange: I had never really reflected on the absurdity of the past two years. We talked a bit about experiences that probably didn't overlap with that of other magicians: the fact that I had stumbled into this world as an adult, became a close confidant with the underground elite, and wholeheartedly fell in love with magic—enough of an obsessive reaction, obviously, to invent a trick of my own in just under a year. Adam came back into the room and interrupted us, a hurried look on his face. He told Lloyd that they had to film their next project in thirty minutes.

"You guys get everything you need up here?" he asked me.

"Yeah, Adam. Ian *killed* the explanation—really great," Lloyd said.

Adam nodded. "Great, awesome. Okay, so," he went on, turning his attention to me, "do you want to meet us at the Orleans tonight to film live performances of your trick?"

My heart jumped into my throat. "*Live performances?*" I asked.

"Yeah, dude," Adam said, rolling his eyes. "You gotta perform the trick for *real people*, in a live setting. We have to get some genuine reactions. You think you can handle that?"

"Uh, yeah, yeah, definitely," I said, shifting in my chair, trying to act confident. "Sure. No problem."

I spent the rest of the afternoon at the poker table. I needed to distract myself. Adam, Lloyd, and I planned to meet at the Mardi Gras Bar at 8 P.M. to film three live performances, and I knew the anticipation would drive me insane if I didn't stay busy. So I took out three hundred dollars from the ATM, exchanged the bills for chips, and plunked down in a chair.

There's something oddly calming about deception at the card table, a comfort that comes with hiding behind a stone-faced glare, trying to pretend you're someone you're not. I thought of my mother while I played, and even called her during a short break to update her on my progress (down $60, but hopeful!) while I woofed some food. When I returned to the table, I remembered a trip we had taken just recently to Foxwoods Resort Casino in Connecticut.

It was Mother's Day. We spent the night playing cards and we both lost money. Just after one in the morning, we decided to call it quits. We walked to the car to drive back to our hotel. She sparked a cigarette.

"I'll tell you what I thought right after I doubled my money," she said. "All right, *Mom*, you need to get up and walk away." She paused. "But then I thought, *fuck that*, I always have to do the right thing. I'm tired of being the mom. I don't want to be Mom."

"Why not?" I asked.

"Because I want to be Pam. I don't always want to do the right thing for other people. It's been my whole fucking life. I don't do anything for myself. It's always self-sacrifice." She took a long drag.

I knew what she was thinking. Poker was her escape from all that.

"Playing cards lets you be you, doesn't it, Mom?"

"One hundred percent. When I am playing, no one else is there, it's just me and my own decisions. It's my choices. I don't want to have to think about making the right choices for everybody else."

"Do you think life is a constant battle between those two things? Trying to be the most complete version of yourself while also trying to understand that other people rely on you, that you have expectations to live up to?"

"Only if other people rely on you," she said.

"But people have always relied on you."

"Then I have never been a complete version of myself. Ever. Because it's always been about somebody else. Always. I just get the tidbits if they fit the mold. It was the same way with your father. It was all about him and his vision. He would call me constantly, at any time during the day, and have these ideas. I was supposed to just jump and do all the research and find out everything about his ideas. And that was fine, and that's what I chose. I made that choice, right? It was fun and exciting, building a life with him—we had a real purpose."

"Do you regret that choice?"

"No. Never. I wouldn't have you guys, my kids. How could I regret that?"

"You told me once that dad haunted you."

"For a long time—thirteen fucking years. He wouldn't fucking leave me alone. He would just be there, or appear in my dreams, but he would never let me touch him. He was angry at me for what happened. Every time I would have a dream about him, or feel him in the room, all he wanted to know was: *I need to go to work. Where's my business?* I just wanted to kiss and hug him."

"What happened when it stopped?"

"It was like a weight was lifted off my shoulders. And I stopped crying. It took me thirteen fucking years to stop crying. I woke up one day and he was gone. He just wasn't there anymore. And, Ian, it was like someone took a building off my chest. I was glad for myself, but I was hopeful that he was also able to move on. So, in that sense, I was glad for him, too. You know, he wasn't ready to go. He was a young guy. He had so much happening. The business. The house. You guys. He just wanted answers."

"I sometimes wonder how our lives would be different . . ." I said.

"So do I."

"Different in good and bad ways. It's hard to explain this to people."

"You can't."

"I sometimes say, I am kind of glad it happened, in this strange, demented way, because I am happy with the man I've become."

"Ian, I am telling you, you would not be where you are today if your father was alive. He wouldn't have allowed you the space that you needed to thrive and become the person you are today. He wouldn't have done it. He couldn't have. He was very rigid in his thinking: *This is what you do to get ahead, and these are the rules.* I don't fault him for that—it's what he did to make it in life, to escape Ohio, to build a healthy family—but he would not have given you the freedom that I did."

"After he died, did your plan for my life change?"

"I was always fearful for you. I was very worried that you would not have him in your life. He was very smart. He was very much like you, very driven like you. I mean, you are his son. Hands down. But I believe that you flourished as the person you are without him. So, all things happen for a reason. Life is all 'what-ifs,' and you just can't let those control you."

"I guess I always just wonder if I would've been happy, or happier than I am now, if he didn't die. Would I be as fulfilled? I've had so many adventures, you know? I've realized I was able to become my own man without the necessity of his presence. And I feel really good about that."

"I know you do. He would not have understood, though. He wouldn't have given you the freedom to go on the adventures you had, because he wouldn't have understood their value. He just believed that his way, just like you do"—she laughed—"was the best way."

"I mean, what have these past two years really been about for me? Not really about magic, or magic tricks, or hanging out with these cool people. I have done something kind of remarkable and it's all because of me, trying to become a man that I've alone created."

She tossed her cigarette butt into the street and rolled up her window. She looked at me.

"Yes," she said. "I say this with my whole heart, Ian: you've turned into the man you were supposed to be."

Throughout our conversation, I didn't even realize that we had become lost. I pulled over, made a U-turn, and tried to find our way again.

That afternoon in the Orleans, I was full of thoughts about my mother, myself, and the members of the52. I had come to know the histories of my new group of friends so intimately, with such transparency and honesty, that I couldn't help but connect them with my own life. Magicians use magic, deception, and trickery as vehicles of escape, as a way not only to distance themselves from the hardships of their pasts—Ramsay's militaristic and ping-ponged upbringing, Madison's internal demons, Laura's tumultuous adolescence, Jeremy losing his father, Xavior with his mother's cancer and his life on the streets—but also as a means of reinvention. The same had been true for me. After my father died, I tried my hardest to distance myself from any sliver of his existence. I didn't want to work a blue-collar job. I didn't want to go to Dartmouth, like he planned. I didn't want to live in a small town. I moved to New York City, became a writer, and decided to tell stories for a living. Like poker with my mother, my own journey in life has been a way to try to heal the hardships of my past. Magic can also aid in that purpose because, at its core, magic has always been something with the ability to repair damage. It promises reinvention and hope—things I also longed for. It's not that I fell in love with magic itself during the past two years, but rather with what it represented: a tool to both better understand the world around you but also, when flipped around, to have a firmer grasp of yourself—your goals and your shortcomings. For an art form built upon deceit, you sure as hell had to be honest with yourself to be successful at it—for it to mean anything at all.

The bet came around the poker table. I peeked at my cards and stared at the man across from me. I paused. I peeked again, grabbed a stack of chips, slid them into the middle, and waited for the next card to be dealt—hiding, as best I could, behind the shimmer in my eyes.

Half an hour before I was supposed to meet Adam and Lloyd at the bar, I went upstairs to my room to get my cards. I sat down on the edge of the bed and rehearsed the moves and patter again. My hands shook. My mind raced. Night had fallen, and the cheap bedside lamp glowed a sickly yellow. I dissected my routine, scrutinized it, poked holes in it every possible way I could. Sure, I had performed it well enough to get Adam excited, but he's a friend. This was different. In less than an hour, I had to go downstairs, grab random people, and fool them—*on camera*. If I didn't nail it, the trick couldn't be released. We needed to finish the project tonight. The thought of having to be a *real* magician, for even ten minutes, made me sick.

I tossed the deck onto the bed and dropped my head into my hands. I thought back to the dark alleyway and the long nights in Blackpool; the thumping clubs in London; the crusty motel room in Buffalo; the look on Bourdain's face at the bar in Manhattan's Lower East Side. And then I realized that magic, either as a single trick or a lifelong dedication, is a journey. I realized that the sleight-of-hand moves done during my trick, my largest vulnerability, are only a small piece in the larger whole of sharing a magical moment with someone. Magic is about experience. It's an art form that pokes at the brain and tugs at the heart. The spectator isn't privy to the moves; they aren't looking for them. They have no preconceived notion as to what is about to happen. They are really here for *me*; the magic is just a vessel that allows me to share a story with them. That's what I needed to do, I realized: just be myself. It was who I had been trying to be all along.

I chucked the cards into my backpack, got into the elevator, and made my way down to the bar.

The casino was packed with magicians. Dozens of them milled about the Mardi Gras Bar, showing each other moves and new routines. Drinks were flowing too: whiskey, beer, tequila, vodka. It was the last night of the convention and everyone was looking to relax. Ramsay, Jeremy, Xavior, and Laura all were there, chatting with friends old and new, excited to be sharing time with each other. Adam and Lloyd came down, camera in hand.

"You ready, dude?" Adam asked.

"Let's do it," I responded. We cleared off a small table on the far side of the bar, and Lloyd set up the shot while I took out a deck of cards. Adam walked over to a cluster of people and asked if any of them would like to see a trick and be filmed for a project. A hippie-looking couple, here not for magic but on vacation, agreed to participate. Adam brought them over, and Lloyd gave me the thumbs-up. We were rolling.

"Hey, how are you both doing?" I asked, shaking their hands, introducing myself. "Thanks so much for agreeing to be a part of this. Okay, so I need one of you to be the main player. Who wants to take the reins?" They looked at each other, and the man stepped forward.

"Okay, great," I said, taking out my marker. The blank card was already removed from the deck and on the table in front of us. "So, everyone has a best friend, right? Someone they can count on, someone who will always be there for them, someone that, if needed, would always come to lend a hand, yeah?" They both nodded in agreement.

"Okay, so, what I want you to do is think of this person. Picture this person in your mind. And I want you to write down their first name, here, on this blank card. But I don't want you to tell me who it is, or show me the card, and I am going to turn around while you do it and when you're done just place the card facedown on the table. Got it?" The couple nodded, and I turned around.

"Okay, we're done!" the girl called out, excitedly.

"Done? You sure? I don't want to see," I said, turning back around with a dramatically slow twirl. The man stood with his arms folded, the girl fidgeted with the necklace slung around her neck, both of them eager to see what I had in store, at where this was going. The sea of people surrounding us, the entire casino, seemed to go fuzzy and quiet. Even the camera, pointed at us, faded off. It was just the three of us in this moment.

"Okay, great. So, we have your best friend, here, on this card," I said, looking up at the man while grabbing the card off the table, still facedown.

"And they may come back to help you a bit later, but for now we should put them in a safe place. So, can you . . ."

I reached over and grabbed the box, put it in front of them, and placed the deck down, now holding only their signed card.

"Open the box for me. Yup, make sure it's empty. Now, what we'll do . . ."

I slowly brought the card toward the box.

". . . is put your best friend in the box. Close it up for me and, ah, place it wherever you'd like." He went for the table's far end. "Yeah, over there is fine."

I grabbed the deck off the table.

"Now I'm going to ask you to pick a card. You're going to have to remember this card. You think you can handle that?"

The couple nodded.

"So just tell me to stop wherever you'd like," I said, dribbling the cards into my left hand.

"Stop!" they called out, nearly in unison.

"Right there?" I asked, eyebrow raised. They nodded.

"Okay, take your card," I continued, placing the deck on the table while they looked at the card.

"Now," I said, "put the card somewhere in the middle. Anywhere you'd like."

The guy gave his girlfriend the card and she placed it into the middle of the deck. Then she squared up the cards with her fingertips, its edges smooth.

"Perfect. Now," I said, grabbing the deck, "I'll let you in on a little secret. Magicians are really good at estimation, so when I saw you put your card into the deck . . ."

I lifted it up, gesturing to it.

". . . I guessed that your card was maybe halfway down, twenty-five or twenty-six from the top. So now, I really want to mix up the cards," I continued, beginning to shuffle.

"Your card is now somewhere in the deck," I said. "But, honestly—ah, man—I don't think I can find it. . . ."

I paused for dramatic effect.

"But I think *you* can."

Then I pinched the deck between thumb and forefinger, like a delicate stone, and handed it back to the man.

"And I think your best friend can help you," I added, gesturing to the box, which sat at the other end of the table.

"So, what I want you to do is think of your best friend, and I want you to spell his or her name, one card for each letter." He placed one card from the top of the deck on the table for each letter in the name. *One. Two. Three*—six in total.

"Okay, so your best friend," I said, resting my hand atop the cards on the table, "got you to this card," I continued, pointing to the top card of the deck, still resting in his hand. "I want you to place this card into my hand, facedown."

And he did. A single card rested in the palm of my left hand. I held it gently, like a baby bird. I looked over at Lloyd, who steadied the camera on me. Behind him, I saw that the entire room was now watching me perform. Everyone stood fixated on my hand, ready for the reveal. I looked back at my spectators. Their faces were nearly cast in stone, eagerly awaiting what I was going to do next.

I had so thoroughly layered the trick that, by now, it's likely they didn't even recall me putting their signed card into the box. It was so long ago: misdirection by time.[*]

---

[*] A memory is a flawed and fickle thing; it's only as good as your last retelling of it. You may recall bits and pieces of a trick's structure, or the magi-

"So, if your best friend helped you, if your best friend came to your aid, this should be your card." I paused, glanced down at the card, took a peek, and looked back up at the couple. "The queen of spades?" I asked. They gasped and looked at each other.

"Yes!" they said.

"Well," I started, leaning forward, hovering the card just over the box, "next time you see Robert"—a gentle shake of the card, turning it over—"you should say thank you."* When they saw that I was holding not the queen but the signed card, they gasped.

"What. The. *Fuck*," the girl said, slapping her hand to her forehead.

"Wait," I said, "if the signed card is here . . . what's in the box?" The guy grabbed the box, opened it, and pulled out the queen of spades. Applause floated over from the crowd, carrying through the room. Off in the distance, Ramsay smiled at me and raised his glass in the air.

We filmed two more performances, each of them equally flawless in their execution, the reactions enthusiastic and genuine. I even fooled a magician with the trick. After we finished, everyone took turns giving me hugs and hoots of congratulations. Ramsay wrapped his arms around me and said, "I am so proud of you, bud—from journalist to a real magician!"

---

cian's behavior during its performance, but it's unlikely you can construct an entirely accurate portrait of what really happened. Moreover, in great magic, a sleight does not exist in a vacuum; the moves compound onto one another throughout the routine. The effect does not live solely within a single switch or palm or cull, but rather the combination of a series of different moves that lead you toward the climax. The routine's process is itself a piece of misdirection, the hallmark of a successful effect.

* This little touch was given to me by Tony Chang (the Ten of Hearts), who was at the convention and also lives in New York City. Tony is a legend when it comes to magic theory and the nuances of routine, and taught me a lot about these small moments, and how they can elevate an entire performance.

We hung around the bar for a little while longer and then made our way to the house of Chris Kenner, David Copperfield's executive producer. He lives just outside of town and Chris and his wife, Nicole, have a blowout party every year during Magic Live. Everyone is invited.

Someone was handing out freshly grilled burgers and cold beers, and crowds of people took turns going through Kenner's movie memorabilia collection, chock-full of mementos from Hollywood classics like *Star Wars* and various Quentin Tarantino films. Magicians gathered around tables on the patio, jamming on tricks as usual. I bounced around and chatted with friends, reveling in the congratulations. Eventually I sat down at a picnic table with Ramsay, Xavior, and Jeremy. Doug McKenzie, Alex Pandrea, and Laura stood nearby. A cool breeze rustled through the leaves and music cranked from the speakers, the sound of shuffling cards breathing through the noise.

These are my people, I thought to myself. *I am one of them now.*

Only Daniel Madison was missing.

23

KILL THE ARCHITECT

Ramsay broke half a million subscribers on YouTube.

"*Crazy*, right?" he said, sauntering down Ninth Avenue in Manhattan. He made the trek to New York City three weeks before Christmas for YouTube's Next Up Conference, held at their headquarters in Manhattan. This event brought together some of the platform's up-and-coming content creators for a long weekend of collaboration. He had done smaller creator camps in Toronto, with other Canadian YouTubers, but this was his first time being flown to New York. People from all over the world made the trip. They included a climate scientist, a bodybuilder, a sketch comedian, an impressionist, a tech critic, and a transgender man who transitioned in real time on his channel. They all had free rein on the space and an unlimited supply of equipment—all the tools you'd ever need to film videos and post them online. Ramsay was also slated to speak to the YouTube staff during a party on the last day of the event. He planned to put on a little magic show in the process, of course.

Ramsay had run outside to grab me, and we went back upstairs to the studio, situated on the sixth floor of the Chelsea Market building in Manhattan, a few floors above a wing of Google offices. Ramsay had just finished the first of two videos with Mike Boyd, a Scottish YouTuber whose channel documents his adventures learning random things. One of Mike's most recent videos, which netted him more than three million views, documented him learning to stack dice by swirling the cubes in a cup. They decided to collaborate: Mike would show Ramsay how to stack dice and Ramsay would reciprocate by teaching Mike to spring a deck of cards like a magician.

They chatted about production style, shot sequence, and introduction format for their next video. They set up in a 1950s-style diner set, at the far end of the space, with three cameras homed in from different angles. Their conversation quickly diverted into comparing metrics, likes, clicks, reach, engagement, shares, and comments—picking each other's brains, trying to figure out how to hack into their viewers' watching habits for a more engaging (and lucrative) experience.

Mike took a walk around, quickly rehearsed his lines, and sat down in the booth to start filming. I stood behind the cameras and kept an eye on the lenses' focus for them, but I couldn't help but reach into my pocket to check my phone. My trick was slated to drop that day, four months after we filmed it in Las Vegas, and I eagerly awaited the notification.

I had called Adam Wilber two days earlier. His segment from *Penn & Teller: Fool Us* had just come out (to much fanfare and gossip among magicians online) and he was nearly done with the cover design for his book on creativity. I wanted to congratulate him on both.

"You're also up for some praise, dude," he said. "Your trick comes out on Friday."

"No way!" I shouted, running around my living room. "This is so weird," I added, plopping down onto my couch, laughing.

"You deserve it, man. Just check the site, and we'll be blasting it on Instagram and whatnot, too."

Just after Ramsay and Mike finished, my phone pinged. It was a notification from Ellusionist's Instagram account: "Ian Frisch, in his first offering to the magic community, debuts FLIPSIDE, a highly deceptive transposition effect. Watch it now!"[*] The caption sat below a photograph Doug McKenzie had taken of me the previous summer at the pier near my house. The Manhattan skyline blurred in the background and "FLIPSIDE," in bold white text, ran down the image's left side.

I quickly posted my trailer to Instagram, which was the introduction I filmed in the suite at the MGM Grand, with a monologue overlaid atop visuals of me performing the trick. I barely remembered filming it, but my excitement jumped off the screen (again, more like a deranged game show host). Within minutes, my phone buzzed like crazy, with everyone commenting on my trailer and shouting me out on their Instagram stories: *Big moves! Hell yes! BOOM! Fuck yeah, dude!*

Jeremy called me as I scrolled through all my notifications, his voice tinged with laughter and mock confusion. "Hello? Is this *Ian Frisch*, the famous magician?!" he said, me giggling on the other end. "I saw you on Ellusionist!"

"Thanks for calling," I said. "I couldn't have done it without all of you coaching me along."

"You did what some people have spent a decade working

---

[*] The trick is hosted on Magic Stream, Ellusionist's subscription-based streaming platform, which is like Netflix for magic tricks. You pay twelve dollars a month and get unlimited access to their library of tutorials. Even if you aren't a member you can watch my trick's trailer.

toward," he said. "Good for you, buddy, good for you. You've officially made it."

Ramsay was still chatting with Mike Boyd when I tapped him on the shoulder and showed him my phone.

"Ah! Shit! It's up!" he exclaimed. I hadn't told him it was supposed to drop today. "Oh, shit dude, this is dope." A sarcastic grin stretched across his face. "Looks like they didn't drop your trick after all." He turned back to Mike. "Boyd, I am gonna head down for a smoke." I went with him. As we stepped out onto the sidewalk, tourists buzzed around us. A blade of cold air cut down the street. Ramsay pulled out his phone.

"Come here. Let's blast your shit," he said, tossing his butt onto the ground. He opened Instagram and centered the camera on his face. "What's going on, guys?!" he started. "Outside the YouTube space with my homie Ian Frisch." He panned the camera to me. "Follow him on Instagram but also check out his latest post. He just released his first contribution to the magic industry—*really* cool trick, lots of really nice card magic going on so, go support him. Peace!" He clicked the camera off and shoved the phone back into his pocket. He threw his arm around me, just as he had our first night in Blackpool, and said, "Well, I guess you're a *real* magician now."

As the days went on, I started getting DMs and emails from strangers. One guy sent me a fairly lengthy email that read, in part: "It's a really good and clean effect. I love the efficiency of the moves. The part of the video that most impressed me is when you mentioned you've only been dabbling for two years. That's fantastic!"

Comments on the trick's page were equally positive. One magician wrote: "I have been a huge fan of Chris Ramsay for a couple years now and I have always loved Ian. It's awesome to see him contributing!" The fans, however, did not exist without detractors. Someone composed a long tirade on Instagram against the trick, which read, in part: "It's unoriginal. It's not magical. There is no clear effect. Technically, it's a piece of garbage."*

I ran high on pride and adrenaline for days. But there was one person who never called—didn't text or reach out with a DM on Instagram: Daniel Madison. I hadn't heard from him in months. He'd gone dark again: unwilling to speak to anyone, closed off from the world, stuck in his own head. He ignored every text I sent, every call I made. But he had been posting on Instagram—cryptic messages that I puzzled over for days. One read: *We don't exist. I tried to own my body. So that it would no longer cage me. Inadvertently creating cages. That would torment. And enrage me. And now I am nothing more than an effigy of an ego. That I used to be. So, fuck it. I am no longer me.*

He also posted voraciously on YouTube. One video depicted him trashing his office—shredding pages of self-published books, ripping apart self-branded merchandise, massacring decks of his namesake playing cards, tattooing himself in ink mixed with whiskey. A cover of Johnny Cash's "Hurt" played in the background. The title of the video, "NOCERE," is Latin for "to harm, or hurt."

Madison also quit Ellusionist, a move that I had known he wanted to make for some time. Like Ramsay, he felt trapped by the confines of the industry, and he wanted to be his own man, not a product monkey for an online retail outlet. He posted a video announcing his decision. He also talked about how the "architect was dead." He looked off camera, to the side, while he spoke, as if being interviewed by someone—perhaps another version of himself. "If I am in a position where I can't be me, whatever 'me' is— 'me' doesn't have to fucking exist to begin with—but whatever this is that I am following, if that can't be allowed to grow and develop in its own directions, then obviously I've got to move on." He explained that the architect was a metaphor for the character

---

* Another magician said over Twitter that he liked the trick but couldn't handle how tight my shorts were in the video.

he had created, and how, after all these years, it had come to rule him. But now that person, that stage of himself, was dead. It was no longer in control.

Most of these videos and posts centered on distancing himself from the magic industry, but I couldn't help but see them as a larger metaphor for Madison as a man and as an artist. To me, his alter ego, and all it represented, became a cave in which he had fallen and could not escape. He had gone so deep, wrapped himself in the shadow of his alter ego so tightly, that he could hardly break free.

I had so many questions about Daniel Madison, questions I worried I'd never have answered. What if I have inadvertently become a sleight in Madison's years-long magic trick? What if, with me, he saw an opportunity to fully divulge everything about himself—a way, perhaps, for a sliver of truth to leak out into the public, a kind of transparency he so deliriously wanted but for which he didn't have the right tools? What if I was the one really being deceived? What if I was simply part of an elaborate plan: the record keeper for the52, brought in to help show the world the truth about deception—the perfect opportunity to prove how the art form has changed? And what if everything I write is a bullet that will enter into Madison's chest on the stage that he alone sees, finally dropping the curtain—vanishing once more, this time for good? What if this was his plan all along? Suddenly everything that had happened felt steeped in deeper meaning.

The last time we spoke, just after I returned from Vegas in August, Madison said he and Laura were trying to fill the remaining spots of the52. There were only a few cards left. We were nearly done. It was almost over. But to me he was still a shadow, an enigma. And I had no idea what would happen next.

My trick debuted on Ellusionist just before Christmas and, for the first half of 2018, I still hadn't heard from Madison directly.

He posted on social media with a high degree of regularity, led primarily by a marketing campaign for a new deck of namesake cards, his first off Ellusionist's payroll and under his own name. But then, in May, he wiped all of his social media. His Instagram profile went blank, his YouTube channel scrubbed clean. Shortly after, he posted an out-of-focus photograph on Instagram holding his passport. "One-way ticket to who gives a fuck," the caption read. He broke down. He hit rock bottom.

A few days later, I received a text: "I'm in rehab. Come see me in Leeds?"

I booked a flight immediately.

A lot had happened in the last six months. Ramsay's reach on YouTube skyrocketed: He hit 100 million total views and broke 1 million subscribers, nabbing the infamous gold-plated plaque that is sent to creators who break the million-follower mark. Laura secured a months-long, multi-city lecture tour in the United States— her first big jaunt overseas, no doubt spurred by her successful run of *CHEAT* in Britain, the premiere of which would land her on the stage at Magic Live in Las Vegas later that year (she also gave a speech about her idol, Mercedes Talma, at the Magic Circle's Historical Conference). Xavior, still plugging away at his apartment in Queens, celebrated his one-year anniversary of YouTube as a new business model. When he started, he was over $20,000 in debt. In his first twelve months on the platform, he netted a healthy six-figure profit for himself and Lost Art Magic. I, too, had landed a slew of stories in high-profile outlets, not to mention my life-changing journey through the underground world of magic, underscored by releasing my own trick. Everything was happening the way it was supposed to.

Our crew also launched a new magician-only meet-up. Ramsay dropped the idea in the first few months of 2018. He said he wanted to plan a different, more modern type of convention for magicians: a four-day, invite-only affair in Los Angeles specifically for those with a high output of magic videos on their social media. He called it the YouTube Magic Summit, and sent me links to a few Airbnbs in the Hollywood Hills and bordering neighborhoods— all mansions, extravagantly designed, beyond luxurious, and ca- pable of housing at least a dozen people.

He sent out the invitations via Instagram and, in March, I hopped on a plane to sunny Southern California for what would be the first event of its kind in the magic community. I picked up Ramsay at the airport and we cruised in my rental car through downtown Los Angeles—windows down, music blasting. Ram- say was anxious to get to the mansion, not only because the fun- filled weekend was about to begin, but because he had a package waiting for him. It was the first fully printed deck he designed completely under his own name. The line, 1st Playing Cards, in homage to his break from the traditionalisms of the industry— the first deck as his own man—had been launched a few months earlier. He spent weeks designing the deck, highlighted in gold foil and stamped in his custom logo, and released the product for presale before Christmas. Fans went nuts.

"I'm hoping to sell ten thousand decks," he told me the day be- fore presale started. He surpassed that number in two days. By week's end, he had hit 20,000 decks. And now, three months later, it was finally ready. We parked in front of the property, an old converted theater in Chinatown, and found the package in the mailroom. We were given the keys to the space. The garage door opened up to a long outdoor patio and parking area, flanked in palm trees and vine-covered brick walls, with lights strung over- head. Inside, twenty-five-foot ceilings etched in raw-wood beams hung over the living room, a broad space with a bloodred car- pet and matching conversation pit that could hold at least fifteen people. A projector screen covered the near wall and, moving to- ward the back, the space opened into a massive kitchen with teal and gray cabinets. A loft anchored the rear of the space, with an igloo-style dome housing dozens of pillows. The master bedroom sat opposite, which featured an adjoining stone bathtub, an open shower, and a small terrace that overlooked the patio. The space was gorgeous, absolutely massive, and perfect for the weekend we had in mind.

The rest of the invitees showed up as we entered: Xavior Spade and Alex Pandrea, my boys from back East; Wes Barker, a Canadian comedic stage magician; Chris "Orbit" Brown, a sleight-of-hand magician from the Bay Area who also owns the Orbit Deck, his namesake playing card company; and Nic Suriano, a master card thrower. Shin Lim, the world-champion close-up magician and *America's Got Talent* winner, and Spidey, a renowned mentalist, were also slated to join. Jeremy Griffith, who lived just an hour away, planned to visit the next day.

Everyone immediately took out their cameras and started filming the space, and I helped Ramsay with his introductory vlog. "Hey, guys!" Ramsay said into the camera. "Just checked into the mansion. It is absolutely baller!" After a quick tour, Ramsay gave his fans what they had been waiting for: a look at his new deck of cards. We then filmed a little mock trailer, full of slow-motion b-roll, of everyone handling the deck: card springs, huge fans, flourishes, some intensely visual sleight-of-hand moves. The deck looked perfect, and Ramsay was thrilled.

At sunset, we all walked downtown to take some photographs. A golden blanket of light fell between the sharp bends of the Walt Disney Theater's roofline. We all took turns standing in for portraits, and Ramsay took a few of me with a deck of cards in my hands. I sprung them from one hand to another, the ribbon of cards caught midflight by the snap of the shutter.[*]

---

[*] We also went to a swanky cocktail bar where Jason Sudeikis saw us playing with cards, approached us, and said he was also a practicing magician. He was with his girlfriend, Olivia Wilde, and of course we all traded tricks.

Jeremy showed up the following morning. He told us he could only stay for a few hours. He had a lot on his plate now: he was a father. The previous month, he and his wife, Kari, had their first child—a boy. They named him Oliver. As soon as they brought the baby home from the hospital, Jeremy snapped a photo of him holding a deck of playing cards and posted it on social media. He seemed to already be grooming him for a life of magic—and for himself, too, to be a great father. To try to give his own son what his father had given to him. I knew Jeremy's main goal in life was not necessarily related to magic, but rather to family. He had always wanted to be a dad.

Jeremy and I walked out onto the patio. Orbit was filming Xavior performing Raise Rise, but for a specific reason. Just before we came out to Los Angeles, Xavior had called Ray Kosby, the old-timer who had invented the trick. He had a request: could he republish Raise Rise under his own name, with all the advancements he had added to the effect? Ray agreed. Xavior would soon release his version of the trick, calling it Xavior's Rise. A legend had passed the torch to a member of the new generation. It seemed a fitting milestone, especially for how much work Xavior had put into making old effects better, and for openly sharing his knowledge with others.

The trip, more than anything, was about collaboration—how magicians could come together for a weekend under the common goal of pushing magic forward. Those few days in the mansion were, to me, the start of something new and exciting, the rolling of the snowball down the hill, growing and growing over time, picking up speed. Everyone had come so far over the past few years—me included—and it felt like we weren't even close to slowing down.

Later that evening, I stepped outside onto the patio. We floated high over the hills, looking down at the broad stretch that was Los Angeles. The Magic Castle, that bastion of old magic, was somewhere down there, nestled among the streetlamps and whooshing cars. I looked back into the house. Ramsay was still standing in the kitchen—lights ablaze and cameras on, whiskey swimming in ice. I took a deck of cards out of my pocket and removed the fifty-two pieces of paper from the box. I raised my arm and threw the entire stack into the night sky. I watched them float down, like a sea of peaceful, quiet birds. One by one they fluttered and disappeared into the darkness below.

Laura called me a week before I went to Leeds to find Madison. "I've sent the invitations out to the last members of the52," she said. "It's finally done."

While we were in Las Vegas, she had invited Demian Aditya, the famous Indonesian magician; Trip, a Chicago-based graffiti artist, who is also a low-key magic geek and incorporates community figures, including Madison, into his murals; and Lisa de la Vega, who worked behind the scenes on *Death by Magic* for Netflix. "Lisa is an amazing stage magician and consultant," Laura said, "and, you know, I am always trying to get more women into the52." Now she had the final members ready to go: she chose Think Nguyen, a Belgian creator and performer; Fatty Dabs, a Jordanian cardist and magician from Los Angeles; and Rico de la Vega, Lisa's brother, who is also a magician, as well as an engineer of props and apparatus for stage shows and television programs (he has consulted for David Blaine, Dynamo, and, most recently, Justin Willman's Netflix special *Magic for Humans*). Nearly five years in the making, every card had been carefully handed out, every magician meticulously chosen. The deck was complete.[*]

I was thrilled for her, that she had been able to take hold of the

---

[*] Danny Garcia, the famed consultant, and Garrett Thomas, a master at sleight of hand, became the Jokers.

club and induct the remaining members alone. She was so happy to have built a family with the52. But I had more on my mind at that moment. I had to find Madison—to figure out what all this really meant to him and to me. I took a flight to Manchester, England, and made my way to Leeds, Madison's hometown. Traffic whooshed in its midday bustle through the city center. People scurried about, grabbing a quick lunch and heading back to work.

Madison told me to meet him that afternoon in Yeadon, a small farming town a few miles outside Leeds. I stepped out of the cab on the edge of the Tarn, a public park with a small pond in its center. A head-high stone wall surrounded the plot, and a thriving lawn dotted with oak trees ran to the water's edge. A family of geese lounged on a small outcropping of rocks. The mother cleaned her chicks by gently pecking them. The early morning fog had burned off, and the sky beamed a clear blue. A crisp breeze ran off the water and cut through the warm air. I looked around and saw Madison lumbering toward me with his typical sluggish gait. But as he approached, clad in his signature all-black uniform, his eyes were bright, and a smile crept across his face.

"It's good to see you, man," he said as we embraced. The smile held even after he let go. He seemed genuinely happy—at peace.

We walked along the pond's edge, cut through the lawn to an empty picnic table, and sat down. Madison wanted to talk.

"About a year ago, I stopped drinking. It just didn't work anymore. It didn't get rid of the problem," he said, pointing to his head.

The drinking wasn't all, though. And it wasn't just the low latent inhibition that he had been diagnosed with. He had met with his sister, a psychologist, who had suggested it was likely that he had been living with undiagnosed autism his entire life.

"That makes sense," he said, "at least within the spectrum of the disorder. When I was diagnosed with this other thing, so long ago, it became such a distraction from what was really going on and the way that I was experiencing life. And I dealt with that by drinking. Drinking calmed everything down and made me feel normal."

I sat there, stunned into silence.

"It was expected that I was this hard-drinking guy," he went on. "It was all part of a character I created. And then the drinking stopped working. Alcohol was easy to quit, but then the problems in my head started getting really bad, and I found that cocaine really helped. It gave me this focus. It became a constant, everyday device to control what was happening inside my head. But then it went from self-medication to borderline addiction."

Everything was clicking into place. So much of what was driving Madison was, in fact, his altered way of looking at the world—altered by chemicals, but also altered by the makeup of his brain and the faulty wiring that he desperately tried to control.

"And then there was leaving Ellusionist and dealing with trying to free myself from this character and find my place in magic again. It all just came to a head."

He let out a sigh, dropped his head, and traced his finger over a fresh tattoo that covered the side of his opposing thumb.

"So, what did you do? What have you been doing these past few months?" I asked, quietly.

"I checked into a weeklong rehab program," he said. "I've been focusing on just taking care of myself: meditating, exercising, sleeping, and eating well. And I've never felt better. When you realize how easy it can be to fix something inside yourself, you start to hate that you didn't do it sooner, instead of skirting the issue for the past twenty years. I feel like a different person already." When Madison said the word "fix," I didn't see it as simply removing the conditions he has lived with his entire life—low latent inhibition, autism, or whatever was really going on inside his brain. To me, when he said he was able to fix himself, he meant that he was now able to accept the person he really was—faults and all—

and that he was ready to move forward and learn to love himself for who he is.

Madison changed his phone number, not to withdraw from the world, but to try to heal. He told me that he had only been in touch with a few people, David Blaine and me chief among them, as he tried to pull himself out of his character's shadow and stand up straight again.

"I spent twenty years being this character that has to do what the industry expects of me. I'm just tired of it. It became a mess. But I am past it now. I'm ready to become *me* again."

"You feel like you're going to get something out of magic again, right?" I had to ask.

"Now that the architect is dead, I've gone back to performing. I want to go back and find what made me fall in love with magic in the first place. I want to love it again, I really do. And I am proud of the52, what it means to everyone who's a part of it, what it's become."

"I think when people think of it, they think of you—something you created that is a shared identity with those who are a part of it."

"That's what it is supposed to be. And the amount of people who still reach out asking to be a part of the52, it shows you that it's still very much alive." He smiled and looked down at his hands again.

"You know, I've always questioned my own role in this," I said. "What does it all really mean, you know? Why am I here?"

"Your journey is the best story out of anyone. It's one of the best things about the52," he said. "You brought so much to it, and have taken so much out of it, and that's always been the point, you know what I mean? Magic can be a vessel to understand yourself in a different way, and you've been the most proactive in harnessing that power and taking advantage of the opportunity. With you, you're able to tell a story that no one else is able to tell. Not me, not any other member. The first rule of the52 is that you don't talk about the52, but you're the writer. It's the secrecy and the questions asked about the group that has kept it alive, but I always knew, with you, that you'd be able to breathe new life into what we represent by the way you describe us.

"I'll tell you that magic, in a lot of ways, is an obsession," he continued. "And without it, you're not really you. And that's been one of the hardest problems with this character, this whole persona I've created. When you take away the playing cards from Daniel Madison, it's just a character, someone with no purpose. And that's been the dilemma: How can I manipulate this character, this part of my identity, into someone who can exist without the necessity of magic? How can I make him *me*? I tried for years, but that didn't really work. I just got deeper into something I couldn't change. Is magic really dead? No, it's not, but while I was playing this character, this version of Daniel Madison, it kind of felt that way, you know what I mean? I was sacrificing so much to find my place in the world, as a man and as a magician, that the fact that magic is changing for the better, and that we've been a catalyst for that change, got away from me a bit.

"You know, I can turn a camera on and be the character for a few minutes and then turn it off and go back to reality, but I am looking forward to coming back and just being myself. There'll always be a bit of that character still with me, but now it'll be more me than him. I feel like people are always searching for the ideal version of themselves. I've come to terms with the fact that the ideal perhaps doesn't exist. I've become happy to just settle, and not really care too much about what happens, and just put magic first."

We sat on the bench in silence for what seemed like a long while. The breeze picked up and sang through the trees, their evening shadows stretching out across the lawn. An old married couple walked by with their dog. I breathed in a sharp draft of spring air—and felt, for the first time in a while, some understanding, that I had accomplished something not confined to a well-turned trick, but of being part of a larger whole, an ever-churning wave. The sea, it seemed, stretched out forever. The beauty of magic, I realized, was that while it also fought against the passage of time—always clinging to its past—time itself has become the art form's greatest asset. For secrets, too, can evolve, and the way we come to understand how deception is a part of us—and who we are, as a collective whole—can also become more clear and complete. For, when you talk about magic, you talk about a person's understanding of the world—and themselves. Magicians, at their core, are on a lifelong search for the intangible, a way to bend their own personal reality with sheer will, and to hopefully extend that self-grown olive branch to others. They inevitably find those who are on the same quest. And I have, unexpectedly, become one of those people. But, in the end, it's not really about card tricks or stage illusions, but about how the lens through which you view the world can be adjusted—for, like with any piece of glass, if you turn it just the right way, you realize that you're not only looking out at what's in front of you, but you're simultaneously seeing a reflection of yourself, too.

The day after our talk in the park, Madison came to Leeds and met me for dinner. It was my last night in town. I waited for him outside the train station. The clouds, so typical for northern England in the late spring, had held off, and it was warm. We made our way to a small restaurant and ordered sandwiches. We talked about the future—when he should come back into public view, and what sort of content or business opportunities he should line up during the months he planned to stay hidden.

"What do you think I should do—about my persona, about coming back?"

"Just be yourself," I told him. "Be honest about what happened this year, and about how the last twenty years of your career, anchored by this character, broke you. Now you need to be accepting of who you really are."

He nodded and agreed that it would be a relief, if a bit strange, for the man of mystery to be so transparent.

After eating, we took out our decks of cards and messed around with a new trick. For a moment, it was just us in the restaurant, playing with our cards, collaborating on something for the future. "We've got to do something with this trick," he said, adding that we should film a video together for his YouTube channel, "as something we created together."

After dinner, we went for a walk. The sun had not yet set, and the city still buzzed. As we made our way down the sidewalk, we heard a man from behind us call out in a thick British accent: "Oi! Hey! Hey! Oi! Can I show you something?!" He hobbled up to us, a single crutch stuffed under his right arm. An unlit cigarette butt perched between his lips. A grimy gray T-shirt hung off his rail-thin frame and his pants were caked in dirt. His eyes sank into his skull, and his skin was pale. He was obviously homeless.

He had a deck of cards in his hands.

"Can I show you a trick?" he said, showing us his cards. The deck was mangled, the cards frayed.

"Sure," Madison said.

"Okay," the guy started. "So, you have a six and a nine," he continued, showing us the six of hearts and the nine of diamonds. "And, if I put them back into the deck"—he went on, trying to shove the cards into the middle of his deck, his hands shaking—"I am going to try and have them jump out." He grasped the deck and tossed it into his left hand. Only two cards remained in his right: the six and nine. I knew this trick. It was the first magic trick I ever learned, taught to me by my mother when I was a child, between tips on how to cheat at poker.

"So, you've been practicing some magic tricks?" Madison said.

"Trying," the man replied.

"Do you mind if I show you something?" Madison asked. The man looked over at me and then back to Madison. "Um, okay, sure," he replied.

"Think of a playing card that best represents you," Madison said, "and tell me what that card is."

"The jack of hearts."

"Okay, the jack of hearts." Madison pulled a deck from his pocket. It was freshly opened. "As you can see, this deck is brand-new. The cards are still in order," he said, fanning it faceup. "But one card is missing." He slowed down as he spread through the cards. The jack of hearts was gone. "It's in your deck," Madison said.

The man looked confused. Madison motioned for him to spread through his own deck. Sitting right there in the middle was a beaming white card, sturdy and new, with Madison's logo stamped on the back. The man turned it over. It was the jack of hearts. He stood there for a moment in stunned silence.

"Wow," he said.

"You need a new deck," Madison said. "Here. Take this one." He handed him the cards. "Keep practicing. Don't give up."

The man smiled.

"Thank you. Thank you so much," the man said. Madison nodded, and we walked away. A half-block down, I turned to him and said, "Do you think he knows who you are?"

Madison slowed to a stop and looked at me. "Maybe," he said. "But does it really matter?"

ACKNOWLEDGMENTS

I have many people to thank.

This book wouldn't have been possible had it not been for the magicians who pulled back the curtain and accepted me as a member of this fascinating world: Daniel Madison, Laura London, Jeremy Griffith, Xavior Spade, Doug McKenzie, Alex Pandrea, Adam Wilber, Franco Pascali, Danny Garcia, Tony Chang, Eric Hu, Larry Fong, Dynamo, Penn Jillette, Eric Jones, Mark Calabrese, Shin Lim, Peter Turner, Demian Aditya, Dan and Dave Buck, Elliott Terral, Damien O'Brien, Dee Christopher, Alex Harris, Matt Whittaker, Garrett Thomas, Joel Greenwich, Wes Barker, Chris Brown, Nic Suriano, Ondřej Pšenička, Lisa de la Vega, Beau Cremer, Alex Rangel, Marcus Eddie, and Dennis Kim. I would also like to thank the countless others who agreed to speak with me for this project, and those who spent time documenting the history of magic, specifically Jim Steinmeyer and David Britland, whose work was instrumental during the researching process.

There is one person, however, to whom an acknowledgement in the back of this book does not suffice to encompass the generosity, patience, kindness, and trust bestowed upon me over the past three years: Chris Ramsay. Thank you, bud. I am eternally grateful for your friendship and guidance. It has been an absolute honor to watch you rise to new heights and achieve your dreams, and to have you be my partner in crime throughout this unbelievable adventure.

I am indebted to my sharp-eyed and supportive agents, Larry Weissman and Sascha Alper, who took a chance over breakfast on a young writer who spouted off crazy stories about a secret society, over-the-top deceptions, impossible illusions, and the art form's promising—but highly unorthodox—next generation of magicians. Thank you for always having my back, always pushing me to think critically, and for evangelizing my idea to the publishing world.

To my lovable and diligent editor, Carrie Thornton, who butcher-knifed and wood-shaved the manuscript into its final form, reminded me tirelessly that this book is really about me, and always championed my vision and voice as a storyteller. And to the entire staff at Dey Street Books and HarperCollins: Lynn Grady, Sean Newcott, Maria Silva, Ben Steinberg, and Kendra Newton, whose enthusiasm for the book really made it come to life.

To Warren Baker and Tim Brookes, my two earliest mentors; Warren Cohen and Michael Hirschorn, who guided my career in its earliest stages; all the members of Study Hall, specifically Kyle and Enav, whose passionate contribution to the freelance journalism community has blossomed into a family; and to all the editors who helped shape me into the writer I am today—especially Jon Eilenberg of *Wired*, who was my earliest champion when it came to diving deep into magic's vast underbelly, and Adam Ross of *The Sewanee Review*, who first encouraged me to write about my father.

To Aunt Shelly, Uncle Bill, and the rest of my family for supporting me in my ambitions; to my sister, Jillian, for always keeping me on my toes; and to Richard for being the rock when I wasn't around.

To Casey, Steven, and Brett at the Spruceton Inn, who graciously gifted me room #5, full of sunlight but without distraction, where much of the book came into focus.

To my best friend, Patrick, for growing up with me, always being by my side, and encouraging me to be the best possible version of myself. To Nick for letting me squat in that office building when I fell on hard times. To my roommates Tom, Mike, Curt, and Jose for enduring way too many magic tricks. To Meghan for always believing in me as a writer. To my girlfriend, Julia, for keeping me sane during the writing and editing process. To Jessica, Cole, Molly, Hogan, Brittnee, Fern, Ashley, Keegan, Jonno, Bill, Alix, Daniel, Lauren, Aaron, Eric, Sam, Kenny, Jimmy, Lucas, Pambo, Jamie Lee, Gabby, Greg, and countless other friends for their support over the years. The best parts of me are credited largely to those with whom I choose to surround myself; I couldn't have picked a better gang of misfits.

I wouldn't be the person I am today if not for my mother's love and kindness, her unwavering dedication to my passion for writing, and her slick and sneaky talents at the poker table. You not only taught me about cards, but also about the world—about being a man. And for that I owe you everything. I love you, Mom.

And lastly, I would like to thank my father, who gave me a life he never had, and whom I miss dearly. I wish you could read these words. I'm sorry we haven't spoken in a while. I'll visit you soon. I love you.

ABOUT THE AUTHOR

IAN FRISCH has written for *The New Yorker,* the *New York Times,* the *Washington Post Magazine, Bloomberg Businessweek, Playboy, Wired, Longreads,* and *Vice.* He has appeared on Bloomberg Television and was a finalist for the 2016 Associated Press Sports Editors Explanatory Award. He lives in Brooklyn, New York.